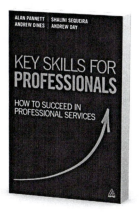

# Key Skills for Professionals

How to succeed
in professional
services

Alan Pannett,
Shalini Sequeira,
Andrew Dines,
Andrew Day

WITHI

KoganPage

LONDON  PHILADELPHIA  NEW DELHI

First published in Great Britain in 2013 by Kogan Page Limited

| | | |
|---|---|---|
| 120 Pentonville Road | 1518 Walnut Street, Suite 1100 | 4737/23 Ansari Road |
| London N1 9JN | Philadelphia PA 19102 | Daryaganj |
| United Kingdom | USA | New Delhi 110002 |
| www.koganpage.com | | India |

© Alan Pannett, Shalini Sequeira, Andrew Dines and Andrew Day 2013

The right of Alan Pannett, Shalini Sequeira, Andrew Dines and Andrew Day to be identified as the authors of this work has been asserted by them in accordance with the Copyright, Designs and Patents Act 1988.

ISBN       978 0 7494 6872 9
E-ISBN    978 0 7494 6877 4

**British Library Cataloguing-in-Publication Data**

A CIP record for this book is available from the British Library.

**Library of Congress Cataloging-in-Publication Data**

Pannett, Alan.
   Key skills for professionals : how to succeed in professional services / Alan Pannett, Shalini Sequeira, Andrew Dines, Andrew Day.
      pages cm
   Includes index.
   ISBN 978-0-7494-6872-9 – ISBN (invalid) 978-0-7494-6877-4 (ebk)   1. Professions–Marketing.
2. Service industries–Marketing.   3. Professional employees.   4. Career development.   I. Title.
   HD8038.A1 P36 2013
   650.1–dc23
                                                                                              2013003850

Typeset by Graphicraft Limited, Hong Kong
Printed and bound in India by Replika Press Pvt Ltd

# CONTENTS

*Acknowledgements*  vii

**Introduction:
acquiring the key skills of a professional**  1

**01    The professional services business**  5

Introduction  5
Management and economic performance  6
Business structures  7
Strategic planning and risk management  8
Effective financial management  13
Financial control  16
The engine of profitability  21
Getting profitable work  27
Conclusion  28

**02    Communicating with clients, professionals
and third parties**  29

Introduction  29
Differences in people  30
What is communication?  30
Verbal and non-verbal communication  31
A communication model – understanding the process of
    communication  33
Listening skills  36
Clarifying communication – asking questions  40
Emotional intelligence  42
Communicating with others in rapport  44
Communicating with clients  45
Conclusion  48

**03    Personal organization**  49

Introduction  49
The three circles of personal organization  50
Circle A: forward planning and priority setting  52
Circle B: self-organization  55

Further tools and ideas   62
Circle C: managing relationships and communication   68
Delegation   69
Conclusion   72

**04    Effective business writing**   73

Introduction   73
What we want to avoid   73
Your writing strategy   75
Action: making something happen   75
Structuring longer documents   81
Sitting down to write   83
Accuracy: spelling, grammar and punctuation   85
Conclusion   90

**05    Presentation skills**   91

Introduction   91
Do your homework   92
Choose your content   95
Structure your content   97
Prepare to present   98
Deliver your presentation   101
Dealing with the unexpected   102
Answer questions   103
Conclusion   104

**06    Meetings: making an effective contribution**   107

Introduction   107
Before the meeting   108
Effective preparation   110
At the meeting   112
Participating in meetings effectively   114
Dealing with difficult people in meetings   118
After the meeting   122
Video and telephone meetings   123
Conclusion   126

**07    Networking**   127

Introduction   127
What is networking?   128
What is a network?   128
Planning your networking strategy   132

Developing your network – places to meet   133
The networking event   135
What prevents us from networking?   138
Dealing with difficult people and situations   140
Managing your network and yourself   141
Measuring success – evaluation   143
Conclusion   144


**08   Negotiation skills**   145

Introduction   145
Styles of negotiation   145
Principled negotiation   149
Preparing for a negotiation   155
Your negotiation toolkit   160
Tactics in negotiation   163
Completing a negotiation   166
Telephone negotiations   166
Conclusion   168


**09   Team working**   169

Introduction   169
Individual performance and motivation   169
Roles, relationships and groups   172
Teams   177
The life cycle of a team   181
Effective team members   184
The team leader   185
Conclusion   186


**10   Managing performance, setting objectives, maintaining momentum and responding to feedback**   187

Introduction   187
The benchmark for good performance   188
Objectives   190
Maintaining momentum   192
Receiving feedback   195
Giving feedback   197
Performance reviews   199
Conclusion   203

**11   Financial and commercial awareness**  205

Introduction   205
Types of trading entities   205
The role of financial information within a business   207
Internal application of financial information: management
    accounts   210
External application of financial information: financial
    statements   211
The regulatory framework for statutory accounts   218
Interpreting the financial statements: assessing the financial health
    of a business   221
Conclusion   229

**12   Behaving professionally**  237

Introduction   237
Professional behaviour   238
Confidentiality   242
Conflicts of interest   243
Client care   245
Risk management   249
Conclusion   251

**13   Where do you go from here?**  253

*References*   257
*Index*   259

# ACKNOWLEDGEMENTS

The authors would like to thank our publisher Julia Swales for taking our idea forward to publication; Fiona Dempsey and Amanda Dackombe for their work editing the manuscript and producing the final copy. We are grateful to Rachel Berry, Claire Horney and Shirley Scott of **fresh** Professional Development who provided us with fantastic support by typing and formatting the final manuscript.

We would also like to extend our thanks to Dr Debra Davison for her insight into the key issues which guide the professional behaviour of GPs; Mr Gerry Crook, who provided examples of the many professional conduct issues which head teachers face and to Jenny Robertson whose overseeing of Chapter 11 was invaluable.

*Alan Pannett, Andrew Dines, Shalini Sequeira, Andrew Day*

# Introduction: acquiring the key skills of a professional

## The purpose of this book

This book is designed to help you acquire, develop and practise the skills needed for a successful career in one of the professions. This Introduction is intended to get you thinking about a number of things:

- What are the key skills of a professional?
- How will you acquire and develop these skills?
- How will you practise these skills and enhance your career?

## How to use this book

The decision to read this book was your key decision. You recognize that there are skills that a professional needs to acquire, develop and use in their day-to-day professional lives and you wish to gain further insight and review your existing skills.

How you use this book is up to you. The authors consider that we can contribute our knowledge, expertise and experience to assist you in two significant ways:

- to provide you with a theoretical foundation and framework on which to build your own ideas and thoughts, so that you may use this foundation to challenge assumptions that you may have made;
- to provide you with practical assistance, so that you can develop and implement the skills discussed in this book.

Rightly or wrongly, we believe that we have learned from our experiences and we are wiser as a result. We would like to share our insights with you.

Ideally we ask that you read this book as you would any other, with an open mind and from start to finish: from this Introduction to the final words of Chapter 13. We believe that by doing so you will gain a full understanding and insight into the theory, practice and implementation of the skills discussed.

Alternatively, you may use this book as a reference source, to enable you to consider a specific issue or the exercise and implementation of a skill in a particular context, eg the giving of constructive feedback to an underperforming colleague.

You may also choose to use this book to assist you in 'benchmarking' the skills that you have with the skills set out and discussed in this book. To help you in this process, you can take two online assessments, the first to test your written English and business-writing skills, the second to assess your financial interpretation skills. If you wish to take these assessments please go to **www.freshpd.com** and follow the links you will find there.

# The key skills of a professional

All professionals need to have a basic understanding of how a professional services business is structured, why it is profitable, and the factors that impact on profitability. In short, a clear understanding of what makes a professional services business 'tick' and the levers of profitability.

Good communication skills are crucial for all professionals. These skills include communicating with clients, professionals and colleagues using effective written, oral and presentation skills. Linked to oral communication is the skill of making an effective contribution in meetings: we will consider how you can do this. We will also look at networking skills and how to use your network of contacts to develop new business and manage client relationships to gain more work.

Personal effectiveness is very important for all professionals; we all need to be aware of the significance of personal organization and workload management. A strong combination of effective communication skills, personal organization and technical expertise is necessary for us to be able to deliver high-quality professional services; it is also a good starting point to define what it is to be a professional.

The ability to negotiate effectively is a key aspect of professional life. Negotiating on behalf of clients in a range of different contexts, with a number of different parties and agencies is a significant part of what many professionals do. We will look at the component elements of effective negotiation.

Professionals can no longer operate effectively as 'one-man bands' or 'sole practitioners'. We will look at the skills associated with effective team work and the leadership skills essential to lead teams.

Managing performance is an important skill; whether it is your own performance or the performance of team members for whom you are responsible. We will look at both.

Understanding financial information is another very important skill, which enables you to make decisions based on a clear understanding and an accurate interpretation of the financial information that is available.

Behaving professionally is fundamental to professional life. It is difficult to define exactly what this is – it is much easier to identify when someone has failed to behave professionally. We will explore the fundamental importance of behaving professionally, and the risk management aspects and commercial imperatives that may impact on this.

## Acquiring the skills

How can you acquire these professional skills?

Some skills are learned in the classroom. However, no amount of 'talk and chalk' can fully prepare you for exercising the professional skills that you are learning.

You will learn new skills by undertaking professional work – 'learning by doing': from the experience gained from your work and by exercising the skills that you have. It is not that long ago, that the essential learning experience was to get on with the job and learn by making mistakes. One would probably be 'told off' and given something else to do, with little or no explanation of how to do it, only to repeat the 'learning cycle' over again.

To develop your skills effectively you need coaching, guidance and support from those who have the relevant expertise. You can also benefit from their constructive feedback. To build your skills to a higher level of competence you need constructive feedback on your current level of performance. This is perhaps the most important aspect of how we all develop in our professional lives, since constructive feedback allows us to reflect on what we have achieved and how to further develop our skills.

## Taking responsibility for developing your skills and managing your career

We all need to take responsibility for our own development and for managing our careers. It may not seem easy at the start of a career, when the objective is to 'qualify'. From there, people's objectives may differ. Some will want to 'go for partnership' whilst others may want a long-term career but with a different 'work–life balance' and may look for a role that will enable them to have this. Others may use their professional qualification to enable them to move into commerce, industry or establish their own business.

This book is not about career management – it is about recognizing the need for 'life-long learning', or rather 'career-long learning and skills development'. As your career progresses, inevitably you will need to develop new skills and build on ones that you already have. It is important to maintain and develop your professional skills as well as your technical expertise. This book is about the challenges we face in doing that.

Later in this book we offer you guidance on proactively managing your career (see Chapter 10).

# Behaving professionally

In Chapter 12 we focus on the attributes of professional behaviour and invite you to think about what is, and what is not, professional behaviour. Maintaining client confidentiality and appropriately addressing issues where there is a conflict of interests are just two examples of what can be described as professional behaviour. Behaving professionally in *all* your dealings with clients is a further dimension – whether that relates to how you handle a particular client's money, their business or personal affairs, health or well-being. What defines being a 'professional' is how you behave.

In this book we will reveal all of the attributes of professional behaviour and its importance to you and to your clients.

# The professional services business

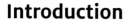

## Introduction

This chapter is designed to introduce you to some basic realities of managing a professional services business. We will consider *the structures through which a professional services business may operate*; the role that management plays in ensuring the economic performance of the business; the strategic planning process; effective financial management and the engine of profitability.

All of these issues are crucial. However, their relevance to your day-to-day work will depend on your role in the business. If you are embarking on a professional career and have little or no business experience it is really important that you seek to understand basic business principles, as they apply to your profession and the business in which you work. Everyone is affected by the profitability and long-term sustainability of the business in which they work – that includes you. If, later on in your career, you set up your own professional services business, or join an existing business as a co-owner or equity partner, the impact on you of the financial health of that business will be far greater, given the investment that you will be making in the business.

You will also need to be able to draft and implement a clear and effective business plan: to identify and assess potential risks to the business and, where possible, take steps to safeguard the business against adverse risks (including financial risks). In this chapter we look at these issues as well as the need to understand key techniques for managing the operating cycle of the business.

Acquiring technical skills and expertise is a first goal of any professional. You will also need to ensure that you convert your 'work in progress', once completed, into bills – get those bills drawn up and sent to clients, then get the bills paid and the money collected as soon as possible. This is of paramount importance to the business you work for and is a very good practice for you to adopt from the start of your career. Proactive cash flow management is crucial to the financial well-being of all professional services businesses.

You already understand the importance of keeping yourself busy with client work – the business term for this is 'utilization'. Your objective is to ensure that you are fully utilized and that you meet the targets set for you and the team in which you work. You need to understand the role that utilization plays in the financial health of a professional services business. Similarly, 'realization' (the amount of your time that is converted from 'work in progress' to 'bills' delivered to clients) is a key driver of profitability. Utilization and realization are explained in this chapter; a case study on individual and team financial effectiveness is also included.

# Management and economic performance

In *The Practice of Management*, Peter F Drucker writes:

> The first function of management is economic performance [...] management must always, in every decision and action, put economic performance first. It can easily justify its existence and its authority by the economic results which it produces [...] management has failed if it fails to produce economic results. It has failed if it does not supply the goods desired by the consumer at a price the consumer is willing to pay.[1]

Without economic stability, the professional services business cannot continue to provide the services that clients want and are willing to pay for, ie the ability to endure and survive difficult economic conditions.

So what are the key roles of management?

The first role of management must surely be to secure the future survival of the business. This will necessitate appropriate and timely innovation to ensure that the business moves forward and endures. Effective management will take proactive steps to secure the future of the business rather than always having to react to situations as they arise.

A further role of management is the process of getting the right things done by the appropriate people at the right time and to an acceptable standard of quality. Management is seen as a process, an ongoing continuum of change and development that does not stand still. This role introduces the ideas of delegation, supervision of tasks and team-working in order to achieve the objectives of the business. The ideal situation is that the services are performed by people who have the necessary level of skills, at the budgeted cost so that the business can profitably sell these services to clients. In this situation, management is acting as a catalyst, making things happen. It should ensure that the individuals who deliver the service have the resources to do so effectively in order to gain the best outcome for both the client and the business.

Management needs to be client-centred. This works to serve the needs of the clients of the business, and is driven by the need to maintain and strengthen relationships with existing clients, potential clients and key referral sources of new work.

An important distinction is drawn between: 1) delivery of professional services to the client; 2) management of the business. Client-centred management recognizes an overlap between the two. It is this area of overlap where management can have the greatest impact on clients. It is here that successful and unsuccessful management is most visible to clients, and where its breakdown can have the most adverse effect.

The culture of the business should play an important role in the organizational and management structures that are actually adopted by a professional services business. Whether that structure is successful will largely depend on how closely it is actually allied to the culture of the business!

# Business structures

The following are the structures that a professional services business may take:

- **Sole principal:** an individual practising their profession alone – the sole practitioner.

- **Partnership:** a partnership is an association of two or more persons to carry on as co-owners of a business for profit. Most business partnerships are based on a partnership agreement setting out the key terms agreed between the partners. Partners invest in the partnership and the level of their investment (equity) determines their share of the profits. A partnership is a legal entity in its own right and can enter agreements and bind the partnership as well as the partners as individuals. Individual partners can be held to account for the debts and liabilities of the partnership.

- **Limited liability partnership (LLP):** a limited liability partnership is a legal entity in its own right. The LLP structure also enables its partners (known as 'members') as well as the LLP itself, to limit their liabilities. This makes being a member significantly less risky than being a partner in a partnership.

- **Limited liability companies:** creating a company is often seen as the standard way to set up a business. A company is, of course, a legal entity in its own right, managed by its directors and owned by shareholders – in many cases these are one and the same individuals. There are significant duties placed on directors (by legislation) in terms of accountability for their actions. The creation and management of companies is highly regulated.

- **Franchises:** it is increasingly common for professionals to operate as a franchise of an entity with a strong 'brand value'. Franchise agreements have been a popular business model in retail and fast-food businesses. The brand of the franchiser provides underlying strength to the marketing of the business. A franchise agreement sets out the contractual obligations between the franchiser and the franchisee, who is bound by its terms.

### *Implementing an effective management structure*

Whichever structure is chosen by professionals establishing a new professional services business, an effective management structure needs to be set up. This should seek to eradicate status-driven hierarchies and provide an effective framework for communication, delegation of responsibility and team work. It should also recognize the need to manage risk effectively, through the introduction of processes that will need supervision and clear lines of responsibility and accountability. These management frameworks are essential in order to create a strong and profitable business.

If you are joining an established professional services business you should look for these frameworks in the management of the business you are joining. This applies whether you are joining as a co-owner or as an employee.

The culture of the business plays an important role in all of these decisions and in the establishment of appropriate frameworks. Thus, there will be many different structural variants, most of which will be effective management structures to a greater or lesser extent.

# Strategic planning and risk management

Strategic planning, including the development of a business plan, is vital to the long-term survival of any professional services business. As a preliminary to the strategic planning process, the leadership of the business must agree on the long-term vision and values for the business. Only when this has been clarified and agreed can the strategic planning process commence.

Most businesses measure their success through making a profit. For a professional services business to succeed in the long term, profitability must endure throughout long-term economic and political conditions.

Making a profit involves choices: about the services that are offered by the business; the markets in which the business operates; how the business will compete. These choices ultimately define the strategy for the business.

### *Competitive advantage*

There are three main options for gaining competitive advantage: cost, differentiation and focus.

### Cost

Price can be used to drive competitive advantage. By using cost to the client as the main attribute of your 'offer' to the marketplace you will inevitably be undercutting the competition's approach to pricing.

Price competitiveness can lead to 'low-balling', ie selling the service at a price below the cost of delivering that service. This may be used as a short-term approach to gain new work. However, such an approach can damage profitability in the short, medium and long term. It is also likely that the overall quality of the service offered will decrease in accordance with the price paid by clients.

## Differentiation

This can be achieved through the uniqueness of the 'offer'. It is an excellent way of demonstrating to the marketplace that you have something special to offer clients. Differentiation may be easier to achieve with products than with services (eg Dyson's bagless vacuum cleaner). However 'ethical' business models can be used as a differentiator in a number of ways: in terms of the business structure, how the business operates and the services that the business will/will not provide to clients. This can be seen as a key differentiator in banking and finance where, for example, the Co-operative Bank and mutual building societies (eg Nationwide) use their business structures (they are owned by their members) to differentiate themselves from other banks (owned by shareholders) – as well as the services they will and will not provide to clients.

## Focus

What you focus on depends on the market in which you operate. This may be influenced by the criteria used by existing and potential clients when deciding whether or not to purchase services, and what competitors are offering (ie the same/similar services).

## *Competitive forces*

When planning the strategy for the business you must always consider the competitive forces in the marketplace in which you operate. Here are some questions worth asking to help you identify the strength and direction of the competitive forces:

- How competitive is the marketplace in which you operate?
- How easy is it to find an alternative supplier of the same professional service?
- How strong is the bargaining power of existing and potential clients?
- How influential are intermediaries and referral sources?
- Are there other businesses that are entering the marketplace in which you operate or could enter that market and impact on the services that you offer?
- How strong is your bargaining power and position in the marketplace?
- How adaptable is your business to changes in the marketplace?

## *PESTL*

The PESTL mnemonic is a way to remember the key influences that affect the environment in which professional services businesses operate:

P = **Political** eg: a change of government in the UK

E = **Economic** eg: recession and government spending cuts

S = **Social** eg: use of social media

T = **Technological** eg: innovation in the use of IT to deliver services to clients

L = **Legislative** eg: legislative and regulatory changes

## *SWOT analysis*

SWOT stands for:

S = **Strengths**

W = **Weaknesses**

O = **Opportunities**

T = **Threats**

The use of SWOT analysis as a planning tool is long established. Start by analysing the strengths of your business – what are its key strengths? Then consider the weaknesses – what are the fundamental weaknesses of your business? Now consider the opportunities that are available based on both the strengths and the weaknesses (ie to build on the strengths and to minimize/ eradicate the weaknesses). Then consider threats. What are the major threats to the business and its strategy?

SWOT should be used as a tool for ongoing review of the business: where it is placed, the opportunities available to it, and the threats it might face in the short, medium and long term.

## *Alignment*

A strategy is most effective when all the resources of the business and the efforts and actions of its management are directed towards making the strategy work – this is known as alignment. It is easy to describe but much more difficult to achieve: people may be distracted by day-to-day operational issues and their focus on achieving the strategic objectives of the business become blurred or even lost.

Strategic direction is fundamental to a successful professional services business because it provides clarity of purpose (see Figure 1.1). It also sets out the roles that members of the business are to play in taking it forward.

**FIGURE 1.1** The strategic planning cycle

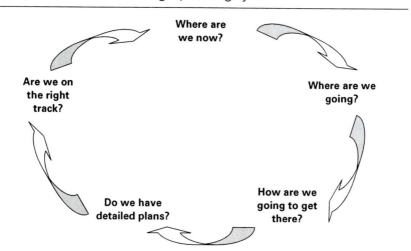

From the point of view of 'setting out the stall', a business plan outlines the range of services to be offered by the business and, perhaps as importantly, it makes clear what the business will not offer to clients. A business plan provides the framework for managing the resources needed – including money, people, equipment etc – in order to attain the goals that have been agreed during the strategic planning process.

## Putting the plan into action

Implementing the agreed plan requires cooperation at all levels of the business, particularly between the owners of the business. This cohesion is manifested in a number of human factors:

- shared values throughout the business (culture and ethos);
- commitment of the staff to the business, its culture and ethos;
- good communication at all levels within the business;
- simple and effective systems of work and organizational structure;
- compatible and complementary skills and know-how.

Management will have to devise an implementation plan for the whole business and then cascade that down through the business, so plans have to be realistic and achievable. Ideally, the implementation plans will address the needs of the partners, the employees and the clients. This can be a difficult balance to achieve, but bear in mind that plans aimed exclusively at achieving high levels of profit (ie ignoring issues such as salaries and welfare, and client retention) may prove impossible to fulfil.

An effective implementation plan is likely to be:

- simple to operate and understand;
- accurate;
- useful;
- followed through.

## Strategy and risk management

It is crucial to consider risk management as a key element of the strategic planning cycle. Consideration needs to be given to the 'what ifs?'. Risk management is relevant to every aspect of a professional services business.

An easily understood definition of risk is given by Joseph W Koletar in *Rethinking Risk* (2011), as follows:

> Risk management, which is closely interlinked with governance, is the process conducted by management to understand and deal with the uncertainties (ie risks and opportunities) that could affect the organisation's ability to achieve its objective.[2]

This means that professional services businesses should:

- minimize, monitor and control probability and/or impact of unfortunate events happening (downside risk);
- maximize the realization of opportunities (upside risk).

A professional services business needs to effectively manage strategic, operational and regulatory risk:

- **Strategic risk:** a clear risk management plan needs to be put in place for at least the next year (including measurable objectives) in order to manage those risks that may adversely impact on the chosen strategy for the business. For example, how will the business deal with one of the key members of the management team being unable to work for an extended period?
- **Operational risk:** every professional services business should carry out a thorough risk assessment of:
  - all the different work types undertaken by the business;
  - the causes of claims on the firm's professional indemnity insurance;
  - the procedures for supervising work delegated to advisers with limited or no experience;
  - the appropriateness of systems for reviewing and ensuring the quality of the services delivered by the business.
- **Regulatory risk:** every professional services business should make sure that it is complying with all the rules set out by their professional body, as well as the applicable legislative and regulatory requirements.

A member of the management team needs to take specific responsibility for risk management. That person will need adequate resources and expertise to tackle day-to-day risk management issues and to undertake a thorough annual review of the operation of the firm's risk management procedures.

Professional indemnity insurers look at risk from a different perspective; they consider a number of elements, which include:

- the sort of advice and services that the business is providing, because certain areas of professional practice give rise to a larger number of claims and to potentially high value claims against advisers;
- whether the business operates effective risk management procedures;
- the prior claims record of the business;
- the levels of supervision of the work of advisers;
- the quality of communications.

By way of example, an analysis of claims against solicitors has shown that there are certain common underlying causes of mistakes, irrespective of the work involved. These include:

- missed time limits;
- delay;
- ineffective communication;
- lack of supervision;
- poor delegation procedures;
- ineffective personal organization and work methods;
- lack of knowledge or relevant expertise.

This shows that a lack of effective communication and poor personal organization create more claims than are caused by a lack of technical knowledge or expertise. It is not what the solicitors involved 'know about the law' that is the main cause of claims, but how they manage their work and communicate with clients.

# Effective financial management

It is important to understand the key principles of financial management in a professional services business. These include: the sources of funds; budgets and cash flow management (the working capital cycle); average profits and revenue per partner; average profits and revenue per fee-earner. We will focus on strategies for managing the working capital cycle and, in particular, work in progress (WIP), utilization, billing clients, realization and the collection of fees.

It is important that those managing a professional services business run it effectively and in accordance with sound financial management principles. This will include systems and controls for maintaining the financial stability of the business and especially those for controlling budgets, expenditure and cash flows.

## *Funding the business*

There are various sources of funds for a professional services business. The first is capital introduced by partners (ie owners of the business) at 'Day One' – when joining the business as a partner or in response to a 'cash call' requiring partners to provide additional capital. The upside of this source is that the business is funded without resorting to loans or other finance from a bank or other lenders.

**Bank loans:** generally medium- to long-term loans are used to fund capital items and to ensure that there is sufficient working capital to sustain the business. Bank loans are appropriate where the need for funding remains at a constant level, but high interest rates can adversely affect profitability.

**Long-term overdrafts:** interest is charged on the overdrawn balance only and not on the borrowing limit. So, where cash flow fluctuates, an overdraft may be the preferred method. An overdraft is also used for meeting short-term financing needs. However, an overdraft is usually repayable on demand and so finding the funds to repay a high level of overdraft in the short term could be difficult, therefore a bank loan may be more appropriate. Long-term or consolidated overdrafts indicate that the business is undercapitalized or overtrading (so it is struggling to meet the demands of the operating cycle) or possibly undertrading (ie through a lack of work) and has insufficient revenue from client work to meet operating costs. Overdrafts are usually an expensive financing option, with higher interest rates applied and sometimes an arrangement fee.

**Profits retained:** only part of the profits of the business are paid to the owners. The balance is retained and used to meet the costs of running and developing the business. This is a cost-effective method of financing, as interest can be earned on the money whilst on deposit at the bank. It is, however, more likely that profits are retained because they have not yet been converted into cash – because they are caught in 'lock up' (see below).

### Using the funds

There are two main uses for the funds: 1) the provision of working capital; 2) investment in the future of the business. Working capital includes: operating costs (rent, utilities, rates etc), salaries, VAT and other liabilities, work in progress (WIP) and bills delivered as yet unpaid.

Investment in the future of the business means spending for the medium to long term on: premises, equipment and resources, IT and other information resources, learning and development of the people working in the business.

### Cash flow

Some of the funds will be locked into working capital, primarily as WIP and bills delivered.

This is caused by:

- delay between doing work (WIP) and delivering a bill;
- inappropriately high levels of unbilled work (WIP);
- slow payment of bills delivered (ie debtors).

These factors can adversely affect cash flow. This is because the business has to provide funds to enable it to carry out client work before bills are sent out and paid. Accordingly, each of these factors causes the business to use more of its own cash resources to pay salaries and other expenses.

Understanding the different periods is important:

- WX = the creditor payment period;
- WY = the work in progress period (WIP);
- YZ = the collection or accounts receivables period (also the length of time taken to collect the cash after the service has been provided);
- XZ = the cash cycle;
- WZ = the length of the operating cycle 'Lock Up'.

The aim in managing cash flow must be to complete the operating cycle as quickly as possible, ie to turn WIP into bills and bills into cash in as short a time frame as possible. The management of the cash flow of the business is vital for long-term success and profitability of the business. Funds tied

**FIGURE 1.2**   The operating cycle

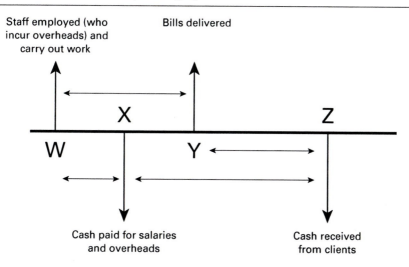

up in working capital would be better utilized for developing the business; developing partners, advisers and business support staff; or reducing borrowing costs.

# Financial control

## *Charge rates*

A primary decision for any professional services business is how the business will charge for the services it provides. Will the business charge clients a fixed fee for its services? Will the fee structure be based on time spent (ie an hourly rate for the work done)?

Many clients now demand fixed fees or will negotiate hard for discounts on standard hourly rates. It is important to get fee structures right as this will be essential for sustaining profitability. Some professional services businesses simply set their rates as a multiple of salary cost, or in line with market conditions, or to produce a budget. Others vary their rates according to the nature of the work and the experience of the adviser involved. Some use a wide range of rates to attract/'buy in' work and negotiate different rates with different clients.

The key factors that need to be considered when deciding on fee structures include:

- Different work types.
- Different levels of seniority and experience of the advisers delivering the services to clients.
- The cost to the business of individual advisers (ie salary and other direct costs). Fee rates should be set to recover these costs and produce a profit.
- The value of the service provided to the clients. If the client places a high value on the service a premium rate may be charged.
- The state of the marketplace for the services provided – eg there may be an oversupply, which will depress the rates that can be charged.
- The rates charged by the competitors – comparability is important to clients.
- The fact that follow-on instructions are often charged at more profitable rates because good client relationships have been built through prior instructions.

Where services are charged for at hourly rates, rather than a fixed fee or another fee structure, then accurately recording the time spent by advisers providing the service is extremely important.

> **Accuracy for billing:** most professional services businesses use time recording to measure the time taken by advisers on each client's work. For these measurements to be accurate (ie for bills to be

correct) it is essential that advisers record time accurately. Of course, a bill does not necessarily reflect all the time recorded. Some time may be written off for a variety of reasons.

**Accuracy for management:** a good policy is for all time to be recorded whether or not it is chargeable. This is because it provides an accurate profile of the time spent by advisers on all activities, eg client work, billing, training, administration, research etc.

**Accuracy for assessing cost:** if time records are accurate then management can make reliable calculations about the cost of each activity on which its advisers are engaged. These calculations can then assist with decisions on pricing the services that the business offers, especially fixed-fee work.

**Total time recording:** some advisers produce time sheets that add up to the required total for the day but fail to record **all** their time at work. The discipline of recording all of the time accurately can help management to make positive changes in working patterns in order to reduce wasted time and enable everyone to 'work smarter'.

## Gearing

Gearing, which is also known as 'leverage', means the ratio of partners (ie owners of the business) to other advisers. Typical gearing may be between 1 to 3 and 1 to 6.

It is a common belief that a high gearing is more profitable than a low one. The expectation is that employing more advisers will generate more profit. This may be true, but is not necessarily so. Higher profits also depend on other factors, one of which is ensuring that advisers are doing work that is appropriate to their skills, expertise and cost to the business.

Key factors that impact on gearing include:

**The total number of advisers:** too many and some advisers will be idle from time to time, ie they are underutilized. Too few and the business may fail to provide the level of service expected by clients.

**The availability of work:** can the business provide sufficient work to keep all of its advisers busy? It is the role of management to keep work flowing and keep all of its advisers fully busy, ie fully utilized and achieving budgeted hours.

Clients need to be prepared for work to be delegated to an appropriately experienced adviser. That person should be effectively supervised by a more experienced adviser or a partner. It may not always be possible to achieve this when managing day-to-day client matters.

Partners and experienced advisers must be willing and able to delegate: this is often easier to state than to do. Some advisers are guilty of hoarding work to maintain their utilization and an appearance of being busy at all times.

## Billing and recovering fees

It is crucial to manage clients' expectations about fee levels and payment of bills. Effective billing and recovery procedures will improve cash flow. It is important to ensure that the procedures used enable the business to manage the operating cycle effectively and maintain positive cash flow.

The business needs to manage clients' expectations regarding billing as well as encouraging them to pay promptly and without delay. Clients should be provided with accurate information (preferably in writing – either electronically by e-mail or in a letter of engagement or standard terms of business). This should include the basis on which fees will be charged to the client and the likely overall cost of the work to be undertaken. Any potential increases in the applicable hourly charge rates must be notified to the client. Expenses (sometimes described as 'disbursements') payable by the client (eg courier charges, photocopying) should be made clear to clients in a letter of engagement or standard terms of business. In addition, it is good practice to try to agree the final amount of any bill before issuing it, as well as providing sufficient information with the bill itself.

Bills should always be issued and sent to the client promptly when the work is completed. Where the client is being invoiced based on an hourly rate, all time recorded on the client's matter should be included, together with any applicable expenses or disbursements.

Clients should also be told what to do if they are dissatisfied with the service provided and they wish to complain. Complaints may well include concerns about fees.

Clients should also be informed about what will happen if they do not pay for the services provided and (where applicable) the availability of insurance to cover the cost of those services.

Payment on account is where the client pays for the service before it is provided, although most professional services are paid for at the time of delivery or after the service has been provided. Where payment on account is agreed with a client, this will have a positive impact on cash flow and will also ensure that work in progress (WIP) does not build up against a weak prospect of getting paid by the client.

Subject to agreement with the client, bills can be presented at regular intervals (eg monthly) as work progresses. This will limit work in progress to the period between interim bills (eg 30 days). It is also likely to encourage regular payment, which can iron out peaks and troughs in cash flow overall for the business. This will also assist the client in budgeting for the services that are being provided.

A professional services business may seek to impose a ceiling on work in progress. This encourages advisers to monitor the time they spend working on a client's matter, to review the work in progress that has accumulated and to bill the client regularly. It also limits the firm's exposure to clients in respect of work that they have not yet paid for; this is particularly important where clients are experiencing financial difficulties and may delay payment or ultimately be unable or unwilling to pay.

An accurate and up-to-date record of unpaid accounts should be maintained by the person responsible for financial management of the business. This will show how much clients owe the business and for how long they have owed it. It is an essential tool for controlling debtors. Prior to the current economic climate, many businesses delegated the monitoring of bills to a financial controller or to support staff. Over the past four years, however, the trend has been for the advisers to undertake a more proactive role in the recovery of unpaid bills.

What steps to take to recover outstanding fees, and when to take them, are questions that each professional services business must decide for itself. Many businesses are reluctant to apply pressure on 'good' clients for prompt payment. However, if clients are slow in paying, are they really good clients? Prompt recovery is best for managing cash flow.

Credit control is vital to successful financial management. Bills should be converted into cash as quickly as possible. There should be a process for chasing aged debtors for payment, otherwise delays in payment will increase and the working capital will be locked in. A business that is not adequately financed will run out of cash and may cease to operate as a result, despite trading profitably.

## Utilization and realization

### Utilization

This is the number of hours of chargeable time recorded by each adviser, measured against the number of hours budgeted, expressed as a percentage.

Ideally, each adviser should record all their budgeted hours each month and throughout the year (ie 100 per cent utilization), but often utilization levels are well below 100 per cent.

Utilization is essentially a measure of actual business activity set against budgeted business activity. It is an indication of how busy people are as compared with how busy you expected them to be.

Reasons for low levels of utilization include: a lack of work (eg insufficient work of the right quality); a failure to delegate work effectively; editing the time recorded and/or taking a decision not to bill all of the time spent; forgetting to record or bill time to the client's file.

### Realization

This is the number of hours recovered as fees (ie billed, collected and banked) expressed as a percentage of the total number of hours recorded. Again, this should be 100 per cent but often varies between 80 per cent to 90 per cent, even in the most efficient firms.

Poor levels of realization can be caused by any of the following: undercharging and discounting; ineffective project management (so the full cost of the work cannot be recovered); a lack of resources or effective support; negotiating a low fee that does not reflect the true value of the work done; poor quality work and/or client relationships.

## Controlling costs

Monitoring and limiting expenditure is essential to a successful business. When cost overruns occur, swift action is important. If costs exceed budget, it is vital to review the expenditure and the underlying reasons for it. This means making decisions and implementing changes to maintain budgetary control.

Expenditure that is directly referable to specific client work can properly be charged to the client as expenses/disbursements. To do this, the business must be able to trace specific items of expenditure to individual advisers and specific client matters. The cost can then be included in the next bill to the client, provided this has been agreed (or it has been set out in the terms of business or client engagement letter, which has been accepted by the client).

Staff and premises costs are very high in professional services businesses. They are often in the region of 40 per cent (of income) for staff costs and 15+ per cent for premises. These costs are not easy to reduce quickly and this can lead inexperienced managers to attack other overheads. Budget cuts that affect a business's ability to do its work efficiently, or to maintain its market position, are likely to do more harm than good.

The cost of professional indemnity insurance is now one of the five biggest overheads for professional services businesses. Ongoing effective risk management processes and procedures across all areas of the business are the key to keeping indemnity insurance premiums and excesses in check.

## Financial information

It is crucial that partners (ie those who own the business) and those with financial management responsibility have accurate and useful financial information with which to monitor and manage the finances of the business. The right information, in an accessible and clear format, will enable them to:

- monitor income/revenue;
- monitor expenditure;
- manage the operating cycle and cash flow;
- monitor profitability;
- take appropriate action as and when problems arise;
- compare actual performance with budget;
- make strategic decisions and change business plans;
- assess the strengths, weaknesses and overall performance of the firm;
- explain the firm's financial health as and when appropriate.

Those with ultimate responsibility for financial management need a wide range of information, but not everyone needs to see all the information available. What people need is sufficient information to enable them to contribute to the business more effectively. So the challenge is to get the right information in front of the right people at the right times.

The management information distributed to partners, managers and advisers should be appropriate to their work and to their management of client relationships.

# The engine of profitability

This section of the chapter is designed to enable you to apply the understanding that you have gained regarding financial performance and profitability in a professional services business.

---

**CASE STUDY**    Financial performance

---

Please read through the financial information set out below. You will be asked to analyse the financial performance of Teams A, B and C.

Please answer the following four questions:

1   Who is the most effective partner?

2   Who is the most effective senior adviser?

3   Who is the most effective adviser?

4   Which is the most effective team?

For each answer please give your reasons. (A model answer and analysis is to be found below.)

The budgets set out in Table 1.1 have been set for chargeable hours billed to clients and fees collected: partners – 1,100 hours is 100 per cent of budgeted chargeable time; senior advisers and advisers – 1,400 hours is 100 per cent of budgeted chargeable time.

Recorded hours is the total number of chargeable hours recorded by each person; billed hours is the total number of hours billed to clients by each person. Lost hours: the difference between the total number of recorded and billed hours, ie the hours that were recorded as chargeable but not billed to clients.

Per cent (%) of budgeted hours billed: this figure is the percentage of the budgeted hours, either 1,100 hours for partners or 1,400 hours for senior advisers and advisers, achieved by each person.

Rate £: hourly charge-out rate (in GB pounds sterling).

Recorded £: the value of the chargeable hours recorded (in GB pounds sterling).

Billed £: the value of billed hours (in GB pounds sterling).

**TABLE 1.1**    Data for last financial year (ended one month ago)

| Name | % Budgeted hours billed | Team | Billed hours | Recorded hours | Lost hours | Rate £ | Contribution Billed £ | Contribution Recorded £ |
|---|---|---|---|---|---|---|---|---|
| **Partners** | | | | | | | | |
| Nigel | 73% | A | 800 | 900 | 100 | 350 | 280,000 | 315,000 |
| Chris | 100% | B | 1,100 | 1,130 | 30 | 350 | 385,000 | 395,500 |
| Tina | 136% | C | 1,500 | 1,600 | 100 | 350 | 525,000 | 560,000 |
| **Associates** | | | | | | | | |
| Elaine | 114% | A | 1,600 | 2,000 | 400 | 250 | 400,000 | 500,000 |
| Satvinder | 100% | B | 1,400 | 1,500 | 100 | 250 | 350,000 | 375,000 |
| Michael | 129% | C | 1,800 | 1,850 | 50 | 250 | 450,000 | 462,500 |
| **Assistants** | | | | | | | | |
| Gillian | 90% | A | 1,260 | 1,700 | 450 | 200 | 252,000 | 340,000 |
| Gareth | 93% | A | 1,300 | 1,500 | 200 | 200 | 260,000 | 300,000 |
| David | 64% | A | 900 | 900 | – | 200 | 180,000 | 180,000 |
| Jane | 86% | B | 1,200 | 1,400 | 200 | 200 | 240,000 | 280,000 |
| Emily | 100% | B | 1,400 | 1,500 | 100 | 200 | 280,000 | 300,000 |
| Ranulph | 57% | B | 800 | 800 | – | 200 | 160,000 | 160,000 |
| James | 79% | C | 1,100 | 1,200 | 100 | 200 | 220,000 | 240,000 |
| Russell | 100% | C | 1,400 | 1,400 | – | 200 | 280,000 | 280,000 |
| Hannah | 114% | C | 1,600 | 1,600 | – | 200 | 320,000 | 320,000 |

**TABLE 1.2**   Team data for last financial year

| Team | Value of actual bills delivered | Value of bills at standard charge rate | Surplus/deficit on standard charge rate |
|---|---|---|---|
| Employment | £1,465,000 | £1,372,000 | £93,000 |
| Real Estate | £1,605,000 | £1,415,000 | £190,000 |
| Corporate | £1,670,000 | £1,795,000 | £(125,000) |
| | £4,740,000 B | £4,582,000 A | £158,000 C |

Additional notes, as per Table 1.2:

- A: this figure is the total **if** billed at the standard charge rates, ie before write-offs or premium.

- B: this figure is the actual amount billed to clients and takes account of both write-offs/discounts and premium rates (eg a higher agreed rate or success fee) charged on to clients.

- C: this figure is the difference (surplus or deficit) between B and A.

Commentary on each fee-earner's performance:

**Partners**

Nigel – Team A   The most senior person in the business; sits on the management board and spends a considerable amount of his time on client-relationship management.

Chris – Team B   Chris is a busy, effective and well-respected partner. He is ambitious and inspiring as well as strongly motivated and team-orientated. He is now the client-relationship partner for some major clients of the business.

Tina – Team C   Tina believes in 24/7/365 commitment to client work. She is a workaholic at heart and last year she was Team C's biggest biller.

### Senior advisers

Elaine – Team A    Elaine has extensive experience and has a number of important clients. She works all the hours available, including evenings and weekends. She likes to fill her timesheet.

Satvinder – Team B    Satvinder has an excellent reputation, he has worked for the business for 20 years primarily advising one key client.

Michael – Team C    Michael has built up a reputation as being extremely hard-working and ambitious, with very exacting standards. He puts in a lot of hours supporting the work of his team leader, Tina.

### Advisers

Gillian – Team A    Gillian works the hours. She likes to fill her time sheet and does a lot of non-chargeable business-development activity to support Nigel.

Gareth – Team A    Gareth is involved in knowledge management, training and client seminars for Team A.

David – Team A    David works part time (three days a week).

Jane – Team B    Jane is highly regarded by clients and colleagues.

Emily – Team B    Emily is a career-minded and hard-working young adviser. She was on maternity leave for three months in the last financial year.

Ranulph – Team B    Ranulph joined the business seven months ago. He worked for the firm for only six months in the last financial year.

James – Team C    James is hard-working but often finds himself out on a limb and scratching around for work to complete his budgeted hours.

Russell – Team C    Russell is a good 'team player' who makes sure that his work is always completed on time.

Hannah – Team C    Hannah is a rising star in Team C.

## CASE STUDY    Model answer

You were asked to read through the financial information set out in the case study and to analyse the financial performance of the partners, senior advisers and advisers and the three teams (A, B and C), then answer the following four questions:

1  Who is the most effective partner?

2  Who is the most effective senior adviser?

3  Who is the most effective adviser?

4  Which is the most effective team?

For each answer that you gave you were asked to provide the reasons for your answer.

### Q.1 Who is the most effective partner?

Here you need to look at the hours recorded and billed by each partner. On this basis Tina (the leader of Team C) has recorded 1,600 hours and billed 1,500. She has achieved billings of 136% of budget and to a value of £525,000.

Tina has out-performed Chris (Team B) and Nigel (Team A) in terms of her individual recorded and billed hours and also in terms of the value of actual bills delivered. However, Tina has 100 lost hours, which could be improved upon.

Chris has billed 100% of his budgeted hours – he has done what he was asked to do. He has only 30 lost hours, the lowest of all three partners.

Nigel has not billed 100% of budgeted hours – he has only billed 73%. Nigel has 100 lost hours. He is the least effective partner.

Some further thoughts:

- What are the legitimate expectations placed on partners?
- What does 'effective' mean in this context?
- Should partners be doing the work themselves or delegating it to advisers in their team?

The direct answer to Q.1 is Tina. Her individual performance is better than Chris or Nigel. However, this is not the whole story, as we shall see when we look at the answer to Q.4.

### Q.2 Who is the most effective senior adviser?

Elaine (Team A) has billed 114% of her budgeted hours. Elaine's lost hours are unacceptably high at 400 and this needs to be discussed to find out what the cause is. If the lost hours could be reduced then this would enable Elaine to be much more effective.

Satvinder (Team B) has billed 100% of his budgeted hours. He has lost 100 hours. He has billed £350,000, the least of the three senior advisers.

Michael (Team C) has billed £450,000, the most of all three senior advisers. He has billed 129% of his budgeted hours and has the lowest number of lost hours (50).

Michael is the most effective senior adviser.

### Q.3 Who is the most effective adviser?

The first point you need to consider here is 'full-time equivalents'. Three of the advisers have not worked full-time throughout the last financial year.

Ranulph (Team B) joined the firm and worked for only six months (0.5). He has billed 800 hours over half the year. Ranulph's full-time equivalent would be 1600 hours, £320,000 and 114%.

David (Team A) works three days a week – this is equivalent to 0.6. David's full-time equivalent would be 1500 hours, £300,000 and 106%.

Emily (Team B) was on maternity leave for three months during the last financial year – this is equivalent to 0.75. Emily's full-time equivalent would be 1866 hours, £373,000 and 133%.

Looking at the advisers who actually worked full-time, Hannah (Team C) was the most effective, billing 1600 hours (with no lost hours), producing £320,000 and achieving 114% of budgeted time.

In terms of: a) actual money billed and collected, b) the percentage of budgeted hours billed, and c) lost hours, Hannah is the most effective full-time adviser.

If all advisers are treated as 'full-time equivalents', the adviser with the highest actual money billed and collected, the highest percentage of budgeted hours billed, and least lost hours is Emily.

### Q.4 Which is the most effective team?

To answer this question, look at the second table of figures; at the column headed Value of Actual Bills Delivered. Look at the figure for each team and divide that figure by the number of full-time equivalents in each team:

Team A: £1,465,000 divided by 4.6 advisers = £318,000 revenue per adviser

Team B: £1,605,000 divided by 4.25 advisers = £377,000 revenue per adviser

Team C: £1,670,000 divided by 5.0 advisers = £334,000 revenue per adviser

On the basis of the revenue generated per adviser, Team B is the most effective team. This is so even though Team C generates the highest revenue figure overall – it is below the average revenue per adviser (£4,740,000 divided by 13.85 = £342,000 per advisor) and is therefore the least effective team of all three.

This question challenges the assumption that if a team bills the most it must be the most effective. This need not be the case.

# Getting profitable work

This is not always easy. It may not be difficult to obtain work though sometimes it is very difficult to get quality work at a fee that is profitable for the business.

Increasingly clients are inviting professional services businesses to tender for work. Tendering has 'hidden costs'. For example, in order to get new work through a competitive tendering process the firm will need to invest time and resources in order to prepare its response to the tender. Tendering is also used by some clients to get the work done at the cheapest possible fee, where price is the key purchasing criterion.

Getting new work from new clients will always necessitate spending time, resources and money to raise clients' awareness of the firm, the services that the firm has to offer and how these services can help potential new clients. Marketing and business development are key to success in securing work from new clients. Referral sources – such as people and organizations prepared to recommend and refer work to the business – can really help with this process. Having an active and effective network of referral sources will multiply the opportunities for new business. It takes time, hard work and a strong reputation for high-quality work in order to develop this kind of referral network.

If you are able to gain repeat instructions from existing clients, who have used your business before and trust you to provide a quality service, this is the easiest 'sell'; where you are able to negotiate rates, it is likely to be more profitable work.

In short, repeat business is likely to be more profitable than first instructions from a new client. This is most likely to be the case where you are able to work with the client in a way that enables you to delegate the work to be done to the most profitable level within your business. The strength of the relationship you have built with the client may also enable you to agree a fee for the work that is more profitable – because the client values the service you provide.

By cross-selling to an existing client, a business may obtain new work that will make use of different advisers and/or specialist skills not previously purchased by that client. Hopefully, this will be in addition to the existing types of work that the business undertakes for the client. It may be easier to achieve success through cross-selling to existing clients, who are already positively disposed to the business, than to get work from new clients who have not used the business before. Through cross-selling, the business may be able to achieve higher rates for the new work types than it might have been able to achieve with a new client.

The message is clear – strong relationships with clients usually enable you to do work more profitably than initial instructions from a new client. Hence, repeat business and work that is cross-sold are likely to be more profitable activities.

# Conclusion

In this chapter we have considered the structures through which a professional services business may operate; the role management plays in ensuring the economic performance of the business; the strategic planning process; effective financial management; and the engine of profitability. All of these issues are crucial to the business in which you work.

In times of economic uncertainty, the importance of a clear and flexible strategy and its effective implementation by means of a well-thought-out and budgeted business plan cannot be underestimated. You need to understand the key techniques for managing cash flow, ie the operating cycle. Converting work in progress to bills, getting those bills drawn up and sent to clients, then getting them paid and the fees collected as soon as possible is of paramount importance to you as a professional. It is the means by which the business ensures its survival and pays your salary. Proactive cash flow management is crucial to the financial well-being of every professional services business.

Utilization and realization are key drivers of profitability. Overall, management needs to monitor and review levels of business activity to ensure that the right work is done at the right level of adviser, so that it will be undertaken profitability. As a professional, you need to be aware of your own utilization and how this translates into bills delivered and paid by clients (realization).

Finally, it is worth pointing out that sound financial management depends on the relationships that the firm enjoys with its key clients. Effective communication must be made with clients to manage their expectations regarding the cost, and payment, of the services to be provided.

# Communicating with clients, professionals and third parties

## Introduction

Effective communication is the lifeblood of any professional organization and sits at the core of our professional lives and careers. Communication lies at the heart of all the skills we discuss in this book.

If your client does not understand what you have just been explaining to them or your secretary does not understand an instruction from you, then the client may misinterpret your advice and the secretary will not follow the instruction. In both instances, you will have to correct the miscommunication and any issues that may arise as a result. Situations like these are usually caused by either a lack of clear communication or a lack of openness and honesty.

Why do I need to read this chapter? After all, I have no problems with my communication skills. Consider the following quotes:

> The primary sources of quality failure in the professions are miscommunication and misunderstanding between the client and the professional.

> It is hard to convince a client that you care about his or her business when it is evident that you don't know what's going on in it.

> Professionals think they know what clients want of them, but frequently this differs from what the client truly wants (or at least expects).

These quotes are from David Maister, one of the leading advisers to professional firms, in his book *True Professionalism* (1996).[3] Our experience shows that over 80 per cent of professionals still think those quotes are as relevant now as they were in 1996.

In this chapter we will consider what communication actually is and how we can communicate more effectively. We will look at some of the basic communication skills and ask you to measure your current skills against the areas we have highlighted. We will then look at what effective communication means within the professional services environment.

# Differences in people

Communication can mean many different things to different people. Tony Robbins, a pre-eminent US self-help author and motivational speaker writes:

> To effectively communicate, we must realize that we are all different in the way we perceive the world and use this understanding as a guide to our communication with others.

The key factor in dealing – in whatever form or medium – with other people is that we are all unique and different. Our individual DNA, our parents, families and upbringing, our school and university training, and any travelling and work experiences we have undertaken will all affect our individual values, beliefs and attitudes. Philip Larkin sums this up well in a poem called 'This be the Verse':

> *They fuck you up, your mum and dad.*
> *They may not mean to, but they do.*
> *They fill you with the faults they had*
> *And add some extra, just for you.*[4]

Add to this basic mix, generational differences (baby boomers, X, Y and Z generations), different genders, religious and cultural differences, rationality and irrationality as well as different values and we can start to see further barriers to communication.

Our values, beliefs and attitudes may affect our relationships and may inhibit our ability to communicate. If we do not like somebody, or find them to be irritating or frustrating, we are likely to communicate differently with them, even though we may not be doing this consciously – the reason for this is that our emotions are triggered in a different way to our rational thought processes.

We must also be aware that one client will be different to another. The way in which a business has been created and developed results in it developing its own 'DNA' culture.

# What is communication?

Defining communication itself is very difficult as it will mean different things to different people. It could mean the transfer of information, the need for understanding or further clarification of a point in issue, the development of ideas, persuasion, or simply socializing and the ongoing development of relationships.

As a starting point we could say that communication is the sharing or transferring of information from one entity or person to another in an easily understandable way. *Effective communication* is when you get the result or response that you originally wanted from that communication.

To do this, we need to use the most appropriate medium, language, tone and behaviour in order to ensure that the message received is the one that we intended to send. Just as importantly (and this is often forgotten) we need to ensure that the message has been received and understood by the intended recipient of the message.

The role of communication within any organization, but especially a professional services organization, has often been described as its lifeblood. If all is working well, then the business will both work efficiently and effectively and there should be few problems. However, when communication breaks down, then problems start to appear.

# Verbal and non-verbal communication

## Verbal communication

This is a form of communication that uses words, either written or spoken, in order to convey thoughts, ideas and feelings. However, words in themselves do not always have clear meaning, as it is people and situations that give words their meaning.

Paralanguage is used to modify meaning and to convey attitude and emotion using such devices as pitch, volume, rhythm, intonation and emphasis and, by so doing, gives a particular piece of communication its personality.

All spoken communication has paralanguage properties that are affected by emotions and attitudes and so may be expressed either intentionally or unintentionally. For example, if you are frustrated or excited, your speech is likely to become faster and higher pitched; when you are feeling defensive your speech may be more abrupt; when you are feeling depressed your speech will probably slow down and become monotone in character. Sneering and sarcasm, for instance, are both difficult to disguise in our speech patterns.

Paralanguage will appear in written communications although in a more limited way, most often through punctuation, italics and capitalization. A lack of paralanguage can lead to communication difficulties, especially in e-mails.

## Non-verbal communication

This form of communication provides clues to the attitudes and feelings that lie behind the words a person is using and includes posture, facial expressions and gestures. As such, non-verbal communication can also be used on its own to communicate attitudes, emotions and feelings.

Non-verbal communication begins in the limbic brain, the part of the brain that reacts instinctively to the world around you. These instinctive or emotional responses are hardwired into our systems and so limbic responses are usually a genuine indication or reflection of your feelings, attitudes and intentions.

On the other hand, another part of the brain, the neo-cortex, is responsible for thinking, remembering and reasoning. It is this area that gives you the ability to evaluate and understand the thoughts and behaviours of both yourself and others, and which formulates and expresses your thoughts, ideas and opinions into verbal or written communications.

It is important to realize that if non-verbal communications are mostly unconscious and unintentional, then you are usually revealing your thoughts, feelings and emotions more genuinely than by what you are actually saying.

In the same way, when communicating with other people, you are reading or picking up on their non-verbal communication, often without being aware of it. This process is usually called 'intuition', which is the unconscious process of picking up and processing other people's non-verbal information, or, put into different terminology, your 'emotional intelligence'.

Highlighting the importance of non-verbal communication for us, as professionals, is the main theme of the work of Professor Albert Mehrabian in his book *Silent Messages: Implicit Communication of Emotions and Attitude*. His research found that in the expression or communication of emotions, attitudes and feelings, 7 per cent of that communication could be attributable to the words used, 38 per cent to the tone of voice expressed and 55 per cent to the body language displayed.[5] However, please do be aware that this research has been widely used by others and incorrectly attributed to all forms of communication.

As a professional, it is very important to have high levels of awareness of non-verbal communication as this will often provide the real story behind the words. For instance, it will help us to understand if somebody is telling us the whole story or whether they feel uncomfortable in telling us something.

Let's quickly look at some of the key non-verbal language signs that we can use:

- Facial expressions: these will often reveal what you are actually thinking, and a frown or a smile can be very expressive.
- Eye contact: the frequency of eye contact is very important and often very revealing. If somebody has lied to you they may avoid direct eye contact with you; on the other hand, they may overcompensate in order to assure you of their sincerity.
- Mouth: a smile may be genuine but it can also convey sarcasm, scepticism or cynicism. The range of 'smiley' faces (available to send in e-mails or texts) can, in themselves, be used to convey many different messages.
- Gestures: are integrally connected to speech and thought processes and are used to support or emphasize what is being said.

- Posture: how we sit, arm positions and the direction in which we are sitting all reveal feelings. An open posture will generally indicate a calm and approachable attitude, but a closed position can portray more negative feelings.

- Personal space: the physical space between people is extremely important, with intimate distance being up to half a metre, personal distance to just over a metre, and social distance being up to four and a half metres.

For instance, the fact that the other person's arms are folded may mean that they are being defensive about something. However, it could also mean that they are cold, or it could simply mean that it happens to be a comfortable position for them. So always look instead for clusters of behaviours fitting together to tell the same story. Look also for changes in body language, as levels of engagement with you may vary during a conversation or meeting.

Many professionals are analytical by nature and certainly that is a key part of their job specification, but a consequence of this is that they may find talking about feelings and emotions difficult. Almost certainly, lack of openness, or uncertainty, will manifest itself through non-verbal communication signals to the other person.

---

**Task:**

- Thinking back to your last client meeting, were your verbal and non-verbal communications in alignment? How good were you at picking up on the non-verbal messages from your client?

- For instance, did you feel that the client was being wholly straightforward with you?

- Was there something missing?

---

# A communication model – understanding the process of communication

When we are communicating with clients or colleagues we must make sure any communication has been translated into a form that can be transmitted and received clearly and unambiguously with an appropriate check-back procedure. Effective communication requires high levels of awareness and skills at each stage. How we manage the process is the key to effective communication, especially with clients.

Figure 2.1 reflects what we think is the simple process of communication. However, when we delve into each stage further, it starts to look a lot more complicated and potential communication barriers can pop up at every

**FIGURE 2.1**   A communication model

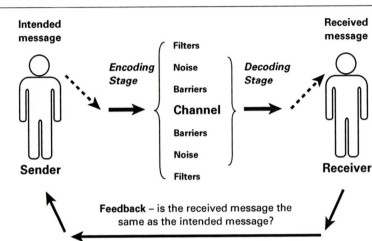

stage. Managing the process requires clear, concise, accurate and well-planned communication skills.

Let's take the opportunity of thinking about these stages in Figure 2.1 in a little more detail:

**The sender:** as the source of the message you need to be clear about what you are trying to communicate and why you are trying to communicate that message. In other words, you need to make sure that what you actually send accurately reflects the message you intended to send.

**The message:** this is the information that is to be communicated. It needs to be planned:

- Why are you sending the message and what is its purpose?
- Who is the intended recipient of the message and what information do they need?
- What do you want to say and how are you going to send it, ie through which channel?
- How are you going to know that your message was received?
- What feedback will be given to you and how receptive will you be to that feedback?

The acronym KISS ('keep it short and simple' or 'keep it simple, stupid!') is a good guide when planning your message.

**Encoding:** this is the process of converting the information that you want to communicate into a format that can be sent and correctly decoded by the receiver. So any message needs to be as simple, clear and accurate as possible and the sender also needs to be aware of and anticipate any potential miscommunications. This means that you need to understand to whom you are sending your message by:

- understanding what you want from the communication and what you want to say;
- anticipating the other person's reactions;
- choosing the right words, the right 'tone of voice' and the correct body language.

**Channel:** you must decide which of the potential channels will be the most appropriate to send your message through. Verbal channels include face-to-face meetings, phone calls, voice messages, Skype and video-conferencing as well as presentations. Written channels will include letters, e-mails, text messages, blogs, memos and reports.

**Barriers, filters or noise:** these are hindrances to communication and will include:

- unclear messages;
- messages that are too long or complicated;
- messages that are potentially wrong as to fact;
- messages that only tell half the story;
- messages where your body language does not actually reflect the message you are trying to send;
- messages being passed in a noisy open-plan office where there are lots of distractions.

Think about how often you take mobile-phone coverage for granted but when your signal becomes intermittent it can be very frustrating, with the result that the key purpose of a call can be easily lost in the confusion.

**Decoding:** this step will depend upon the skills, mood or attitude of the receiver as to whether they are actively listening or taking the time to carefully read the actual or intended message.

**Receiver:** the receiver does not know what you have prepared and will have their own ideas and feelings that will undoubtedly influence their understanding of the message you are sending, and will inform their own response. Being a savvy switched-on sender, you should have anticipated these potential responses.

**Feedback:** just sending a message is not enough and cannot guarantee that a message has been safely received or decoded by the receiver. Ideally, therefore, the receiver will provide you with feedback. The importance of feedback is that it gives you confidence that the intended message has been understood and, if not, gives you the opportunity to resend the message.

Having just been made aware of the difficulties inherent in the individual communication process let's just think about how many times these difficulties could be amplified within the business in which you work on a daily basis. For instance, if the message is too long, is disjointed or contains errors, then you can expect the message to be misunderstood or misinterpreted. If your verbal and non-verbal messages are confusing, then again this will result in miscommunication.

Similarly, we need to be mindful of sending information in bite-sized chunks, as sending too much information often has the same result as sending too little information.

However, there are many skills that the successful professional can learn, develop and improve to become a more skilled communicator and to anticipate some of these barriers. These skills are examined in the rest of this chapter.

# Listening skills

> To listen fully means to pay close attention to what is being said beneath the words. You listen not only to the 'music', but to the essence of the person speaking. You listen not only for what someone knows, but for what he or she is. Ears operate at the speed of sound, which is far slower than the speed of light the eyes take in. Generative listening is the art of developing deeper silences in yourself, so you can slow your mind's hearing to your ears' natural speed, and hear beneath the words to their meaning.[6]

This quotation comes from Peter Senge, one of the leading strategists in business organization, but which summarizes the essence of this section. When asked how well we listen, we will all probably assert that we are good listeners. After all, we do it all day long, don't we? But, what is going on in our minds when we are listening? For instance:

- Are we thinking about what we are going to say next?
- Do we jump to conclusions and close our minds to the remainder of what the speaker is saying?
- Are we thinking of what we will have for lunch?
- Do we interrupt before the speaker has finished?

The reality is that, although we probably *hear* a great deal, we sometimes fail to listen with our full concentration. Part of the reason for this is that the average person speaks at about 125 to 150 words per minute, whereas we can listen to and comprehend up to 600 words per minute. The result is that the listener's decoding channel can be underutilized by a factor of 4–5, unless we adopt generative or empathic listening, as directed by Peter Senge.

Hearing is itself a passive process undertaken by your auditory system; those sounds will have no significance until we give them some meaning. Listening, however, is an active process that uses our cognitive functions, including our attention, memory, thinking and reasoning. It also utilizes our emotional intelligence, as we have to interpret meaning from the messages we hear and see.

Set out below is a resume of the generally accepted layers of listening.

**Level 1: Passive/not listening** – this has also been referred to as 'noise in the background' when you are not concentrating on the sounds at all and nothing is registering with you – such as listening to somebody whilst also watching sport on the television.

**Level 2: Pretend listening** – also called responsive listening. You will be using nods or using stock answers such as 'Yes, Uh-huh, OK' but in reality you may be daydreaming or thinking about something else.

**Level 3: Selective or biased listening** – you are selectively listening and taking in a certain amount of information. However, because you have different views from the speaker, you are not allowing their information to influence you or you may not be thinking objectively, but rather simply fitting the words being used into your context. You will normally do this when you are being defensive or when you are under pressure.

**Level 4: Active listening** – this entails listening to words (including the attitudes or feelings behind those words), the intonation of the words, the body language and the facial expressions of the speaker as well as then giving some feedback. Active listening skills are about fact-finding and understanding feelings, but those feelings will not necessarily be incorporated into the feedback response.

**Level 5: Empathic (empathetic) listening** – this means listening with full attention to all the sounds and other relevant signals:

- tone of voice;
- other verbal aspects – pace, volume, breathlessness, flow, style, emphasis;
- facial expressions;
- body language;
- cultural, ethnic or other aspects;
- feelings;
- able to see and feel the situation.

By listening at this level you will also be reacting, giving feedback and checking your understanding with the speaker. You will be honest in expressing disagreement but also, at the same time, expressing genuine understanding.

There are further layers of listening above empathic listening such as facilitative and generative listening, which contain a much stronger element of being interested in helping the other person see and understand their options and choices. However, if you attain the empathic level of listening you will be listening with a very high standard, as it is an extremely difficult skill to master properly. The key client relationships in professional firms are based on this level of listening.

Active listening teaches us to focus attention on the speaker. Empathic listening skills take that technique further by using our emotional intelligence skills in order to develop deeper understanding. Empathic listening is about the giving of your advice in the client's framework or paradigm.

Figure 2.2 sets out a short guide to listening skills and techniques.

**FIGURE 2.2**    A short guide to listening skills and techniques

---

**Demonstrate 100 per cent attention:**
- Maintain good eye contact.
- Nod frequently to demonstrate interest and encourage the speaker.
- Keep an open mind – do not jump to early conclusions.
- Listen for, identify and write down key points and ideas.
- Avoid the temptation to interrupt.
- Be flexible – do not expect the detail to emerge in the way you want it to.
- Prevent distractions eg divert calls.
- Use appropriate body language – adopt an open posture.
- Use appropriate utterances, which will encourage the speaker and show that you are interested and listening – such as *OK, I see, Uh-huh, Oh really* etc,
- Use silence constructively.
- Read between the lines for what is not said.

**Reflect back information:**
- Reflect back what has been said eg 'So far, I've heard...'.
- Clarify key dates, actions, names, facts and figures.

**Reflect back feelings:**
- Adopt appropriate facial expressions to reflect the feelings and content of what the other person is saying.
- Give a reassuring or sympathetic look.
- Reflecting, paraphrasing or summarizing – which check meaning – show you are attempting to listen and help the development of empathy, such as 'What I think you are saying is... You feel that... You are obviously frustrated about... you seem very concerned about...'

**Clarify your understanding:**
- Ask questions only to confirm understanding.
- By reflecting back, we are able to correct any points that are incorrect.
- If unsure about a point, in order to avoid misunderstandings and clear the air, ask the speaker to confirm eg 'Let me check my understanding... If I understand what you are telling me correctly...'

**Task:**

- Relate your experiences to each of the above levels of listening in which either you have listened to other people, or other people have listened to you.

- What did it feel like and what was the effect?

So what does this mean in practice? In terms of our skills development, perhaps we should be thinking about directing our attention to our skills in listening or our 'reading of' a situation (the *demand* side of communication) just as much as making ourselves better speakers or writers (the *supply* side of the communication model).

There are two base elements to effective listening – acceptance and acknowledgment. Acceptance is a passive act – the ability to listen without attempting to negate what the other person is saying, by either interrupting, judging or dismissing them. This lays the foundations for feelings of confidence and trust. Acknowledgment, on the other hand, is a more active process and involves responding with recognition and consideration of what the other person has said – and further develops the feelings of confidence and trust.

Some writers, such as Stephen Covey in *The 7 Habits of Highly Effective People* (1989), suggest that empathic listening takes these two base elements further, by listening with intent to understand – and that this is an entirely different paradigm as it is getting inside another person's frame of reference.[7] You look through it, to see the world in the way that the other person sees it, so that you understand their frames of reference and how they feel.

The basis of empathic listening is, therefore, listening for feeling, meaning and behaviour – by sensing, intuiting and by feeling. In other words, using non-verbal communication as much as (or maybe more than) verbal communication (you have two ears and one mouth – so maybe the same ratio should be used here). This does not, however, mean that you have to agree with those ideas, opinions or feelings and nor do you have to make their situation your own. It is the understanding of the experiences that the other person is going through, and then framing your advice to best support that person, which is the key behaviour.

Empathy ultimately connects people and enables trust to build and can, therefore, make communication easier and quicker. It is a key constituent of the trust relationship that is an essential part of the client relationship.

Let the last words on listening skills go to one of the most famous Supreme Court justices in American history, Oliver Wendell Holmes, who said: 'It is the province of knowledge to speak and the privilege of wisdom to listen.'

# Clarifying communication – asking questions

Having listened with the intent to understand should enable us to substantially increase our understanding of any communicated message. But, having listened, we may not be clear about exactly what the other person has been telling us.

## *Types of question*

The three main types of question are known as open, closed and probing. Each has a purpose and they need to be used at the appropriate times in order to obtain as much information as possible. We will look at each of these in turn, as well as 'funnel' questions.

### Open questions

These questions are used to get new information or to help draw out more information from a person, as the answer will usually need to be much more than a simple 'yes' or 'no' answer. They usually begin with the words *where*, *what*, *when*, *why*, *how* and *who* or phrases such as 'tell me how' or 'describe what happened'. This will encourage the respondent to give more information about that person's knowledge, opinions or feelings.

Open questions are good for:

- developing an open conversation and obtaining new or general information;
- finding out the ideas and opinions of the speaker and their feelings;
- opening up and encouraging further conversation and giving control of the conversation to the speaker;
- finding out more detail.

### Closed questions

These are very useful to establish facts and to get a straightforward answer (often one word): 'Do you want x or y?' They are easier to answer than open questions, as they are not seeking an opinion from the other person.

Closed questions are good for:

- testing yours or the other person's understanding;
- concluding a discussion or making a decision;
- understanding.

There is a need to be careful with closed questions as they can be regarded as manipulative – as the framing of the question and the short answer may hide the real reasons for the answer. In addition, a closed question can shut off a conversation and lead to a difficult silence, and so are best avoided when conversations are in full flow.

## Probing questions

However careful we are in asking questions in the correct sequence, or choosing the wording to elicit all the required information, there will be times when we have to delve further.

Probing questions are good for: gaining clarification to ensure you have the whole story and that you understand it properly; drawing out information from people who are trying to avoid telling you something.

Probing questions must allow the respondent, within the context of the question, to provide further information thereby allowing the existing relationship to continue and not change the inherent meaning of the original question. Use probing questions to:

- Ascertain the accuracy of a statement – *'Are you sure that the sales representative confirmed that X was included within the contract?'* or *'What was said immediately afterwards?'*
- Allow the respondent to add further information – *'So what happened next?'*
- Gain better understanding – *'Why do you think it was excluded from the contract?'* or *'Why are you certain it was like that?'*
- Get a better overview of the situation – *'Can you think of an example that will illustrate...?'*
- Ask for justification of an answer – *'What do you think is the reason for that?'*

## Funnelling

Funnel questions are a series of questions that seek further information, which can either go into more detail (called the funnel) or become more general (the inverted funnel). A representation of the funnel is set out in Figure 2.3.

The funnel that increases detail gives you, the listener, more information about fewer topics. Starting with general questions, this technique narrows in on a point in each answer so that more information is provided by the other person at each stage of the funnel.

Funnel questions that become more general provide wider information about more topics. This can be useful when wanting a speaker to open up or to increase their confidence.

**FIGURE 2.3**    The funnel

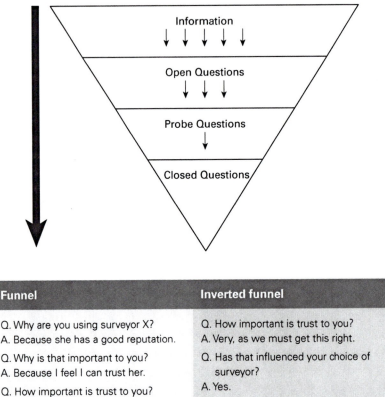

| Funnel | Inverted funnel |
|---|---|
| Q. Why are you using surveyor X? <br> A. Because she has a good reputation. | Q. How important is trust to you? <br> A. Very, as we must get this right. |
| Q. Why is that important to you? <br> A. Because I feel I can trust her. | Q. Has that influenced your choice of surveyor? <br> A. Yes. |
| Q. How important is trust to you? <br> A. Very, as we must get this right. | Q. Is that why you are using surveyor X? <br> A. Yes. |

# Emotional intelligence

Much of the discussion so far on communication has centred on feelings, attitudes, emotions and intuition. Another formulation or concept of these 'intuitive' concepts is that of emotional intelligence or 'EQ'.

In essence, emotional intelligence is about:

- knowing how you and others feel and what to do about it;
- knowing what feels instinctively right and what does not feel so good, and how to get from the not so good to the good;
- possessing emotional awareness, sensitivity and developing the personal management skills that will help us to maximize our goals.

EQ gained high profile by the work of Daniel Goleman in a 1995 book called *Emotional Intelligence* in which Goleman originally identified five (now rationalized to four) dimensions of emotional intelligence. They are:

- **Self-awareness:** how accurately you can identify your emotions and reactions in any particular situation.
- **Self-management:** how you can use awareness of those emotions to create the behaviour that you want.
- **Social awareness:** how well you can read the emotions of other people.
- **Relationship management:** how you can use the above three emotional intelligence skills to manage your interactions with other people.[8]

Helpful examples or ideas sitting behind these four areas are set out in Figure 2.4.

**FIGURE 2.4**    The four dimensions of emotional intelligence

**Personal competence**

**Self-awareness:**
- Emotional self-awareness – reading one's own emotions and recognizing their impact; using 'gut sense' to guide decisions.
- Accurate self-assessment – knowing one's strengths and limits.
- Self-confidence – a sound sense of one's self-worth and capabilities.

**Self-management:**
- Emotional self-control – keeping disruptive emotions and impulses under control.
- Transparency – displaying honesty and integrity; trustworthiness.
- Adaptability – flexibility in adapting to changing situations or overcoming obstacles.
- Achievement – the drive to improve performance to meet inner standards of excellence.
- Initiative – readiness to act and seize opportunities.
- Optimism – seeing the upside in events.

**Social competence**

**Social awareness:**
- Empathy – sensing others' emotions, understanding their perspective, and taking an active interest in their concerns.
- Organizational awareness – reading the currents, decision networks and politics at the organizational level.
- Service – recognizing and meeting follower, client or customer needs.

**Relationship management:**
- Inspirational leadership – guiding and motivating with a compelling vision.
- Influence – wielding a range of tactics for persuasion.
- Developing others – bolstering others' abilities through feedback and guidance.
- Change catalyst – initiating, managing and leading in a new direction.
- Conflict management – resolving disagreements.
- Building bonds – cultivating and maintaining a web of relationships.
- Teamwork and collaboration – cooperation and team building.

The EQ concept argues that IQ (the intelligence quotient), or conventional intelligence, is too narrow and that there are wider areas of emotional intelligence that support or limit how successful we become. IQ has become the traditional measure of intelligence but this ignores the essential behavioural and character elements that are key to building lasting relationships. We have all met people who are academically brilliant and yet are quite socially and interpersonally inept. And we know that despite possessing a high IQ rating, success does not automatically follow for them.

EQ is key to our present discussions on communication in the professional services environment. Some people seem to have a natural ability to communicate and generate a sense of rapport with virtually anyone they meet, whilst others will struggle to develop those relationships. The good news is that EQ can be learnt and developed. Some tips are:

- Observe how you react to other people. Do not stereotype people without making a slower and more studied assessment of them. Put yourself in their place or position.

- In the workplace don't seek attention for your achievements; share those achievements with your other team members.

- In stressful situations, do not become upset if things do not work out the way you want them to. Stay calm, keeping your emotions under control.

- If you have hurt somebody else's feelings, take responsibility for your actions; be upfront and discuss what had upset them and apologise, if necessary.

- Examine how your actions will affect others before the event, and if those actions will adversely affect others, then discuss the impact of those actions with them at the outset.

# Communicating with others in rapport

Rapport is a term used to describe the relationship of two or more people who are in sync or on the same wavelength with each other, because they feel similar feelings or relate well to each other. In professional terms, rapport is the ability to connect with others in a way that creates a climate of trust and understanding. This involves, as already discussed, the ability to appreciate one another's point of view (not always agreeing with it) and to understand and accept one another's feelings. You are more likely to agree with, support and buy professional services from someone to whom you feel a connection.

Many people think rapport is chatting about the weather, the family or the next big sports fixture. This may be part of it but only if that is what the people you are talking to wish the conversation to be about. Rapport is much more than this – it is about connecting with people in a way that supports all future communication. It is about creating a climate of openness.

Empathy and trust are a platform for effective understanding, effective communication and for developing stronger business relationships. They are both essential for developing business solutions for clients, to win and retain business, and then to avoid or defuse any potential conflicts or problems that might exist.

There are two key ways that you can build rapport: understanding the other person's perspective; matching your words, body language and voice tone.

First, if you are able to 'step into the other person's shoes' you will be able to identify what is important to them and spot areas of common ground. Understanding the other person's perspective is hugely important and is invaluable when building a client relationship.

Second, people in rapport typically adopt the same posture, movements and gestures. They are 'mirroring' each other's behaviours. This happens naturally when two or more people are in rapport. When you adopt the same body language, voice tone and words as someone else, you create the likelihood that you are engaging in the same thinking and feeling circuits.

Skilful communicators build rapport by:

- Seeking to connect with everyone with whom they come into contact in a way that demonstrates respect for difference. They respect beliefs, values and styles of others even though they may be different to their own.

- Being aware of the degree to which they and the other person are similar (or not) in any of the following (but at the same time recognizing that significant dissimilarity probably indicates a lack of rapport):

  - **posture:** position of the body, position of the legs and feet, weight distribution, position of arms and hands, shoulder tension, inclination of the head;
  - **expression:** direction of the look, movement of the gaze;
  - **breathing:** rate of breathing, position of breathing;
  - **movement:** fast, steady, slow, still;
  - **voice:** pace, volume, pitch, tone, type of words;
  - **language:** visual, auditory, feeling.

The more you can subtly get into the style of the person with whom you are communicating, the more you will begin to understand their motivation, attitudes, values and beliefs. However, deliberate mirroring can backfire on you. Rather, it is the awareness of the mirroring that is the important point.

# Communicating with clients

We now must place the importance of these skills into context.

Professional service businesses traditionally sell their knowledge and have the ability to focus their resources on narrow fields of expertise, gaining experience across a diverse range of clients. This means that both knowledge and relationships are the true sources of sustainable competitive advantage. This underpins the need for effective communication so that these knowledge-based relationships can be deepened by mutual trust.

In a *Financial Times* report in 2011 'A New Dawn: Lessons for Law Firm Management in the Post–crisis World', the 200 respondents from the leading law firms were asked about the factors that help their firms meet the needs of their clients more effectively. Two-thirds of replies pointed to two particular factors: a greater focus on a long-term relationship and better communication.[9]

Managing the expectations of the client is going to be the key to the relationship. All clients will have different needs and each corporate client will have a different corporate culture and ways of doing things. They will want to be communicated with in different ways. Then add on the need to explain complex issues – such as health care and long-term care information, complex tax matters or the intricacies of a boundary dispute – clearly and succinctly and in ways that resonate with the client so that they fully understand the issues. Misunderstandings down the line can undermine the confidence and trust that a client places in their professional adviser.

Here are some proven communication ideas that will help you develop your client and professional relationships:

1 **Understanding the client's needs or business:** this involves understanding their products or services, their corporate culture, their customer base and what their aims and objectives are. Taking time upfront for a full and open discussion should help build a more solid foundation for your relationship with them. However, clients will often be resistant to spending this time at the outset as they often just want to get started. Your influencing and persuasion skills will be needed to obtain this information.

2 **Listening and questioning:** understanding exactly what the client needs will bring into play all of the best-practice listening skills described earlier in this chapter. Empathic listening (including excellent questioning techniques) is particularly important in picking up on the client's real needs and/or the understanding of their particular business. Clients will usually understand the need for the transfer of hard facts about their case or their business, but not always about their individual needs, attitudes and emotions.

3 **Having a client induction system:** this brings together the discussions with the client and places all the information about the client in one place. It also acts as a risk filter. Keeping that database up to date is then very important and also ensures that when the particular project or service for the client has finished, contact into the future is not lost with that client.

   Some professions have very clear client induction procedures, which are set down by their regulators and, if not followed, could result in disciplinary action. Many view this process as a chore but it can be used very effectively as an opportunity to learn so much more about a client and to look, for instance, at cross-sell opportunities.

4 **Explanations:** as a professional adviser you should understand what you are advising on, but do not make assumptions that the client always understands all the issues, even if they give that appearance. A model that is often used in this context is the iceberg model. The key fact about an iceberg is that only 10 per cent of the iceberg is above the water whilst the rest is hidden below the surface. By analogy, a client may only understand a small proportion of the problem or project that they require advice upon, ie the visible portion of the iceberg. It is the job of the professional to dig down into the iceberg in order to extract that additional meaning, which will probably have an incalculable effect on that client's matter or project.

5 **Ongoing communication:** it is very important to keep a client informed at every stage of their matter and to explain fully the advice you are giving them. Clients will often want you to do something that you don't think is a good idea. It is very important that when such situations occur, you take time to demonstrate to the client why you think it is important and what the potential impact will be, rather than just doing it the way they want or doing it your way without any explanation. In other words, always acting in the client's best interests, which is not necessarily what they themselves may think of as being in their best interest.

6 **Avoid jargon and assumptions:** one of the biggest frustrations for clients is when their professionals talk to them in technical terms or incorrectly assume that the client has certain knowledge levels. So this is a question of knowing your individual client and adjusting your level of communication accordingly. However, you may talk on a different level to your co-professionals because there is a mutually shared knowledge and experience base. Use of examples to illustrate technical or easily misunderstood issues is always a useful tool to get your ideas and advice across.

7 **Make your communications count:** clients are busy and so are you. Making each communication count is really important to both of you. Plan and think through each communication in accordance with the communication model, selecting the appropriate channel. For instance, would it be better to discuss verbally a certain matter with a client rather than just e-mailing them?

8 **Put it in writing:** it is best practice from a client-care perspective to always record in writing any discussions or decisions made with a client, so that there is a clear record of what has been agreed. These records are also required for risk management purposes so that there is a clear audit trail. It is good practice at a meeting or during a telephone conversation to take a clear and contemporaneous attendance note of the discussions with your client, following this up with a clear written summary for the client.

# Conclusion

In this chapter we have discussed the crucial role of communication in gaining a better understanding of each person with whom we come into contact through our professional work (eg clients, other professionals and work colleagues). Communication lies at the heart of any relationship.

The hard truth is that if professionals do not meet the expectations of an increasingly knowledgeable and demanding client base, they are likely to lose their business to a provider that can.

The ability to view the world from the perspective of others is one of the most important professional skills for you to develop. A person who has difficulty in putting themselves in someone else's shoes in order to understand why they act in the way they do will usually have a hard time developing and sustaining close relationships. They will probably also generally find other social interactions (eg networking) difficult.

We shall build upon the basic skills and understanding learnt in this chapter in the following chapters. As a first step to being a better communicator, it is very important to understand and consider:

- How do I perceive myself?
- How do others perceive me?
- Is there a difference between how others perceive me and how I perceive myself?
- What consequences, if any, arise from this divergence of view?
- How will any difference impact upon my credibility as a relationship-builder and influencer?

This understanding will then inform your ability to deal effectively with different people. This will depend on:

- your ability to diagnose and understand differences;
- your awareness of and ability to select an appropriate response (eg communicate effectively);
- your ability to deal with your own feelings, and how to act appropriately.

# Personal organization

## Introduction

Personal organization is about organizing your time: this being the continuing sequence of events from the past through the present and into the future.

Time itself is fixed. There are 60 seconds in a minute, 60 minutes in an hour, 24 hours in a day, 365 days in a year (with an additional day every 4 years). Our lifespan itself is finite – so most of us want to pack in as much as possible. How you use and organize your time should be a real concern to you. At work you will need to be efficient, effective and profitable; the route to success is effective personal organization.

The advantages of being organized are:

- You can concentrate on the things that really matter to you.
- You can get more done in the time available.
- You can balance the demands of work, your personal needs, your family and friends, sports and recreation – in other words balancing the quality of your life.
- You would like to be in control and have a more relaxed approach to your life.

If you are not organized your life will be characterized by last-minute rushes to meet deadlines, days that somehow seem to slip by unproductively or crises that suddenly arise from nowhere.

How effectively you manage your time will, therefore, depend upon your attitude to time (and how you organize it). If you are not organized at work this can lead to lower levels of performance and higher levels of stress. The level of your personal organization can also have a considerable effect on your motivation and moods. If you feel well organized you will have a positive sense of well-being, you will feel 'on top of your work' and 'in control'.

Key to your approach to personal organization will, therefore, be who you are and the effect or influence of your personal attitudes, cultural heritage and values. These will all affect how you use or organize your time.

To be a successful organizer of your time requires a combination of: 1) a realistic knowledge, understanding and acceptance of who and what we are and how we react in different situations, especially when under pressure; 2) effectively using systems, lists and tools to underpin and support our work. This balance is represented within Figure 3.1.

**FIGURE 3.1**   Organizational systems and mindset

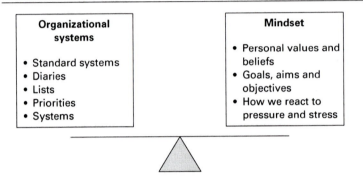

Organizational systems will never work unless we have the appropriate mindset

# The three circles of personal organization

To illustrate the key areas of personal organization we are going to use a three-circle model, as set out in Figure 3.2. Each circle interlinks and each one is equally as important as the others.

Circle A gives us direction; circle B is about how we organize ourselves to attain our goals; circle C highlights that we cannot achieve our goals without working closely and effectively with other people.

Key to working out whether we are as well organized, efficient and effective as we think we are will be our ability to reflect on what has happened. We will need to review this regularly (eg weekly), following key projects and over the longer term (eg six months).

## *Reflective practice*

Reflective practice is the capacity to reflect on something that has happened so that there is a continuous learning process. This concept was originally set out by Donald Schön in his book *The Reflective Practitioner: How Professionals Think in Action* (1984). The concept of reflection is widely regarded as being one of the defining characteristics of professionals and is a key differentiator in the way we all learn. In particular, trainees learn from their supervisors and more experienced practitioners in the day-to-day

**FIGURE 3.2**   The three circles of personal organization

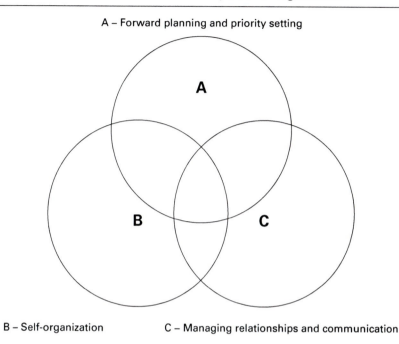

A – Forward planning and priority setting

A

B          C

B – Self-organization          C – Managing relationships and communication

working environment – through supervision, delegation and feedback – rather than just from formal training or knowledge transfer.[10]

A reflective model of 'experiential learning', known as the learning cycle, provides a helpful approach to how learning and skills development is linked with our experiences.

The learning cycle set out in Figure 3.3 below indicates that people learn through an integrated four-stage process:

**Step 1: Having an experience** – whilst undertaking a task or job, you will have different experiences and views of how you got on.

**Step 2: By reviewing how you got on** – did I complete the task competently? What scope is there for improvement? What did I do well? What didn't I do so well? What would I do differently next time? Through this review process you begin to identify the gap between your own know-how, skills and expertise and those needed to do the task to the appropriate standard.

**Step 3: By analysing the data gathered and the observations made** – you may reach conclusions based on reviewing the experience.

**Step 4: Modifying your behaviour or actions for the next time** – you can then plan how you will do the task again in the future.

**FIGURE 3.3**    The reflective process

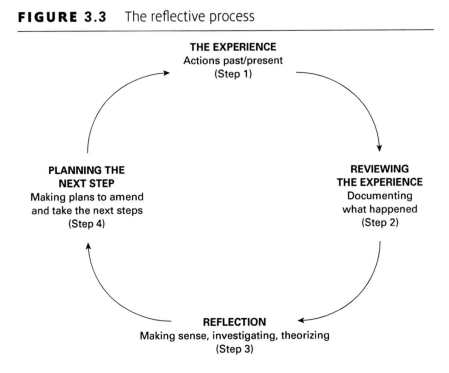

THE EXPERIENCE
Actions past/present
(Step 1)

PLANNING THE
NEXT STEP
Making plans to amend
and take the next steps
(Step 4)

REVIEWING
THE EXPERIENCE
Documenting
what happened
(Step 2)

REFLECTION
Making sense, investigating, theorizing
(Step 3)

# Circle A: forward planning and priority setting

'If you don't know where you are going, the chances are you will end up somewhere else.'

## Goal setting

We should never consider getting into our car and driving off without having, at least, some idea of our final destination and the route to it. All too often, people squander their precious resources of both time and energy by working with no clear idea of their goals or how they will achieve them.

Without a goal to focus on, it becomes increasingly impossible to prioritize work effectively or to make adjustments to maintain the most effective route towards achieving our goal(s).

Setting priorities is immensely important to both our work and our personal lives. It is important to have a balance between our working lives and our personal lives – and the planning principles and organizational tools are exactly the same.

The process of objective-setting and the use of the SMART model is covered in more detail within Chapter 10. The more clearly you can see your goal the more likely you are to achieve it.

However, not even the best goal in the world will help you if you are not committed to making it happen. The most effective goals are those that are set by ourselves rather than being imposed on us by others. Setting the objectives yourself relates each goal to things that you want to achieve rather than those you have to achieve.

## The planning process

'Most people don't plan to fail – they just fail to plan.'

Having worked out your goals, successful planning will help you to achieve them. Planning is the logistical part of meeting your goals. Planning should be both creative and flexible: creative because you are planning into the future and the unknown, and flexible enough to enable you to cope with inevitable changes.

Assuming that you are clear about your goals, you need to work out two things: 1) what percentage of your time can you actually plan? 2) how far ahead can you effectively plan?

In order to meet your goals you should plan in the long, medium and short term. It is important to have an idea of the most effective and realistic planning period for you. The short term is the here and now, but it does require longer-term planning in order to give it focus.

Set out below are six questions that you should ask yourself during the planning process:

**1** **Results:** what do I want to accomplish?
**2** **Activities:** what will I have to do to get those results?
**3** **Priorities:** what are my priorities?
**4** **Time:** how much time will each activity require?
**5** **Schedules:** when will I do each activity?
**6** **Flexibility:** how much flexibility is needed for events beyond my control?

Figure 3.4 provides examples of this planning process. Key planning guidelines are:

- Break down your goals into smaller more manageable elements.
- Work out the likely scenarios and any alternative strategies.
- Review your performance regularly and modify your planning accordingly. The main goals are unlikely to change but the ways of achieving them (ie the planning) may well alter.
- Do not overcommit yourself. This is a sure way of failing to meet your goals.

**FIGURE 3.4** The planning process

| Questions | Example 1 | Example 2 | Example 3 |
|---|---|---|---|
| Results | Completed first draft of the new agreement for client X | Prepare client engagement letter and accompanying documents | Update my CV on the intranet |
| Activities | a. Review the structure of the document<br>b. Review previous precedents<br>c. Check meeting notes<br>d. Type/dictate first draft | a. Carry out all due diligence activities<br>b. Check notes from client meeting<br>c. Prepare costs estimate + discuss with client partner<br>d. Complete engagement letter for signing by the client | a. Review the work done by me over the past six months – to update my skills and experiences<br>b. Review five other CVs for ideas<br>c. Update, check and then submit my new CV |
| Priorities | Client wants the draft by 1600 hrs tomorrow – first draft to be completed today. | Must be sent out today | Must be updated to support the preparation of a new tender – I want to be part of that tender, so my CV must be able to sell my skills in the best possible way. |
| Time | a. Review the structure of the document – 30 mins<br>b. Review previous precedents – 20 mins<br>c. Check meeting notes – 30 mins<br>d. Type/dictate first draft – 2.5 hrs | a. Carry out all due diligence activities – 30 mins<br>b. Check notes from client meeting – 10 mins<br>c. Prepare costs estimate + discuss with client partner – 20 mins<br>d. Complete engagement letter for signing by the client – 30 mins | a. Review the work done by me over the past six months – to update my skills and experiences – 30 mins<br>b. Review five other CVs for ideas – 15 mins<br>c. Update, check and then submit my new CV – 45 mins |
| Schedules | a. Review the structure of the document – 30 mins; 9–10am<br>b. Review previous precedents – 20 mins; 9–10am<br>c. Check meeting notes – 30 mins; 10–10.30am<br>d. Type/dictate first draft – 2.5 hrs; 10.30–1pm | a. Carry out all due diligence activities – 30 mins; 3–3.30pm<br>b. Check notes from client meeting – 10 mins; 3.30–4pm<br>c. Prepare costs estimate + discuss with client partner – 20 mins; 3.30–4pm<br>d. Complete engagement letter for signing by the client – 30 mins; 4–4.30pm | a. Review the work done by me over the past six months – to update my skills and experiences – 30 mins; 4.30–5.00pm<br>b. Review five other CVs for ideas – 15 mins; 5–5.15pm<br>c. Update, check and then submit my new CV – 45 mins; 5.15–6pm |
| Flexibility | If overrun have contingency 2–3pm | Limited flexibility – if client expectations are to be met | Needs to be done for selling myself |

- Remain flexible in your planning.
- Use a weekly/monthly/quarterly planning chart to help with your planning.

Having set your goals and planned accordingly you now need to look at how you organize yourself to achieve your goals.

---

**Task:**

- How frequently will you set goals (eg monthly/quarterly/half yearly)?
- When will you schedule in time to set your goals?
- What are your two or three medium-term goals in the next six months?

---

# Circle B: self-organization

Many of your self-organizational habits are just that: habits (things you are doing subconsciously). The key question is whether your habits are the right ones and whether you could be working in a better way. The same applies to the way in which you prioritize matters. Are you making the right decisions and does your planning support your goals?

Let's look first at the question of habits.

## *Habits*

We are all creatures of habit and we will have developed many of those habits over many years. As we already know from Chapter 2, many of our habits are a good thing and prevent our logical brain from having to process the masses of information that it could potentially have to deal with during each day.

The key issue is: are your habits good habits? How often do you lose your home or car keys? Researchers in the United States have suggested that we spend at least a year and a half of our lives searching for things we have lost!

The conscious competence model set out in Figure 3.5 (below) helps us to think about how and why we are doing things and how much attention we are or should be paying to the completion of certain tasks.

State 1 – unconscious incompetence: in this state you do not possess the skills (incompetent) and you are unaware of the fact that these skills even exist (unconscious). Example: before you learnt to drive, you were unaware of what the driver in a car actually does when driving.

State 2 – conscious incompetence: in this state you still do not possess the skills (incompetent) but you are now aware that the skills do exist

**FIGURE 3.5**   Changing habits – the four states of mind model

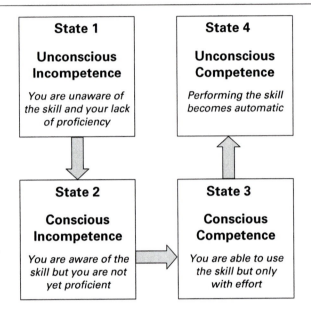

(conscious). This is healthy as it should encourage you to acquire the skills that you need, but your performance will generally still be of a low standard because of your incompetence. Example: your first driving lesson and the experience of 'kangaroo hopping' as you practise clutch control for the first time.

State 3 – conscious competence: you possess the skills and your performance has improved as you have been thinking carefully about how to put your skills into action. However, your standard of performance still requires conscious thought and concentration by continuing to engage the thinking part of your brain – the neo-cortex. Example: your first attempt at the driving test and thereafter when you were driving correctly, following the Highway Code 'to the letter' and undertaking all your hazard perceptions properly.

State 4 – unconscious competence: achieving this state of mind means that your performance should now be more natural, integrated and competent and you will be carrying out the skill without necessarily thinking about it – the emotional brain carrying out these functions. Example: driving on the motorway talking to somebody and being surprised when you are approaching the next motorway services and not having been conscious of having driven the last five miles. You hope and assume that you have been driving perfectly well, but you have been doing so unconsciously.

It could be that your decision making in this last state has become so un-thinking that you may start to make mistakes.

This awareness is really important for us as professionals, as we are potenti-ally more likely to make mistakes if we do not have the right level of com-petence or we are working too much in the unconscious competence stage. An example might be sending an e-mail but without the promised attach-ment and then having to send the e-mail again with an apology. These types of mistake can, however, affect your relationship with your clients, damage your reputation or even lead to potential negligence claims; they should be avoided.

It is important for you to know at which state of this model you are at any one time. It is also important to realize that you may be in different states for different types of work and the different degrees of responsibility you are being given. It will also be important to understand in which state your clients, your managers and your other team members will be on this model. For instance, if somebody undertakes a task in state 4, it will be much more difficult for them to explain to you how they are doing that task, as they are carrying it out unconsciously.

## Prioritization

The short-term planning process requires some form of 'to do' list so that you can group together tasks, set deadlines and estimate how long things will take. Prioritization is key to the planning process. Ironically, as we become more efficient, one of the effects is that our 'to do' list starts to grow, keeping pace with our increased efficiency. So this is a skill that you must get to grips with at an early stage.

One of the most effective ways to prioritize your time is to select the most important tasks that you must complete. Importance is to do with results. If something is important, it contributes to your mission, your values and your high-priority goals.

Urgency generally means that something requires your immediate attention. Examples would be taking a phone call, answering a text or answering an e-mail whilst in the middle of another activity. Urgent tasks are usually highly visible and insist on immediate action. A key personal skill is in recognizing and interpreting whether a call or message is actually urgent.

Prioritizing involves working out what is urgent and important from the viewpoint of other people, such as our clients or our supervisor/manager, and then balancing those demands against our own interpretation of what is important and urgent. Urgent for most people will probably be 'this morning' or by the end of the day. However, most professionals will have experienced situations where they have been asked to do something urgently and then, once completed by them, it has remained on their supervisor's desk for some days. Always find out what somebody means by 'urgent'.

A key target for efficiency must be to reduce the frequency of urgent tasks that you do in order to give yourself the opportunity to make important things happen. Peter F Drucker helps us think in the right way, by emphasizing the need for proactivity:

Effective people are not urgent minded

Effective people are opportunity minded

Effective people feed opportunities and starve problems

The prioritization quadrant in Figure 3.6 places both urgent and important tasks into four sectors, which we have called Do, Delay, Delegate and Drop tasks. The rationale of using this grid is to bring our decision making into the sphere of consciousness.

**FIGURE 3.6**    Prioritization grid (urgent and important)

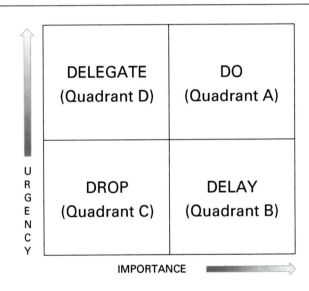

Do (quadrant A) tasks: are both urgent and important. These tasks could also be described as 'must do' or 'have to do'. These may be emergencies, crises, meetings, appointments or demands from managers or clients, reports that are imminent, and planned tasks or projects that are now due and must be done within a short time frame, ie this morning or afternoon. If you allow too much of your focus to be within this quadrant, it will dominate you and you will find it increasingly difficult to be proactive.

You should always look for ways of dividing urgent and important tasks into smaller parts and then carrying out that part of the task that is both important and urgent and then rescheduling the remaining parts of the task. This will involve discussing your plans with the other person so that you can manage their expectations by your suggested reprioritization.

**Delay (quadrant B) tasks:** are important but not necessarily urgent. These will be about planning, preparation, scheduling, systems, research, networking and relationship building, thinking and reflection as well as anticipation and prevention. All these are positive and proactive tasks and are about direction and strategy. Often they are critical to your individual success. So planning appropriate time slots and personal space for these tasks (and where you will be protected from interruptions so that you can complete them effectively) will be very beneficial. Take care not to allow these tasks to slip into the *Do* quadrant, where you may lose the element of choice.

**Delegate (quadrant C) tasks:** are urgent but not important. However, these tasks may involve a client or supervisor who is important, difficult, influential or capable of making life difficult for you. Therefore, their needs make these tasks important for you. Other types of activities could also include apparent emergencies, ad-hoc interruptions and distractions or pointless routines. As these tasks are about short-term focus they need to be controlled through sensitive negotiations with the other person.

**Drop (quadrant D) tasks:** are not important and are not urgent. These could involve unnecessary and sometimes unchallenged routines, habits or 'comfort' activities such as the overproduction of work. This quadrant will also include some less productive activities such as surfing the internet, chatting or gossiping, daydreaming, unnecessary adjusting of computer equipment. Staring into space – not sure what to do next – is a quadrant D task. These tasks are unproductive and you should plan to avoid, minimize and schedule them in at opportune times – or delegate them.

When prioritizing your tasks it is important to regularly refer back to either your goals or the result you want to achieve from the activity you are prioritizing. The categorization of the task of filing is an interesting example. We maintain that it is a quadrant B task as, from a risk management perspective, keeping files up to date is a priority. However, it often gets left and slips into quadrant A; some people categorize it as a quadrant D task, which means that it never gets done. Delegating the task would, of course, be one way of making sure the filing is carried out in a timely and effective manner.

## *Short-term planning – the 'to do' list*

Some people like to plan the next day the evening before, some plan on the day and some not at all. The problem with not planning at all is that you are likely to end up reacting to events when you should be directing them by being proactive. In addition, this is a clear risk issue as it is when mistakes happen.

Completing a 'to do' list is a very positive step. However, having made your list you will usually work through it in one of three ways:

- Start at the top and work your way through the list. However, this does not identify those tasks that are more urgent or important than others, and usually more tasks keep getting added to your list.

- Dealing with the urgent tasks first with the result that most of the tasks become urgent.

- Dealing with the easiest and quickest tasks first. This has some recompense in that you can cross a number of tasks off the list, but usually urgent or important tasks can get left out.

Set out below are some things to think about when planning your day:

- Priorities: plan into your day your highest-priority tasks.

- Your own efficiency levels during the day: your internal clock. We all have higher and lower performance periods during the day.

- Allow for your own underestimation of the time that a task will take: so initially try overestimating task times by 20 to 25 per cent. You should also be aware that when a task is being delegated to you, the person delegating the task will often underestimate how long that task will take. Always ask for a time estimate when work is being delegated to you.

- Plan backwards from the final deadline.

- Allow for contingencies: these can arise from many different sources, but always allow time for the unexpected. For instance, a client or your manager may not be available at a particular time or their previous meeting may have overrun. Allocate a catch-up period twice a day for these contingencies.

- Avoid arranging meetings back-to-back. A late finish to the first meeting will have a domino effect on the rest of your day. No client wants to be kept waiting.

- Give yourself debrief, catch-up and reflective time immediately after each meeting or task.

- Batch your e-mails and phone calls together into a specific time slot (a good time will be your least productive period).

- Plan some time to review your priorities and plan your workload. Give yourself 10 minutes' planning time at either the beginning or the end of each day. We suggest doing this planning at the end of each day so that you are fully prepared for the next day.
- If you have a secretary, regularly spend a few minutes updating her/him on your workload.
- Always try to finish the day on a positive note and, if possible, within the planned time frame.

However, what is really important is not to become a slave to your daily plan. It is only a guide and will probably require amending as you respond to changing events. The key is that having planned and established your priorities, you are in a much better position to make an informed decision as to how to change your plan.

Most young professionals when they start their careers will use a hand-written 'to-do' planning process or a diary system. Slightly more experienced professionals graduate onto using electronic organizers such as Microsoft Outlook or PDA systems, although some older professionals may still use systems such as Filofax or desk diaries.

**FIGURE 3.7**   'To do' list

| Activity | Priority | Time est. | Schedule |
|---|---|---|---|
| | 1 | mins + 25% | |
| | 2 | mins + 25% | |
| | 2 | mins + 25% | |
| | 2 | mins + 25% | |
| | 3 | mins + 25% | |

Figure 3.7 is an example of a more sophisticated 'to do' list as it incorporates a prioritization for the tasks, a time estimate and a rough scheduling for the task. The next step from using a 'to do' list is to use a diary system in which you can record all meetings and appointments as well as allocating periods of time to your priority tasks and for the batching of phone calls and e-mails. An example is illustrated in Figure 3.8.

**FIGURE 3.8**   Daily diary

| | Action | Priority | Time estimate | Notes |
|---|---|---|---|---|
| 09:00 | | | | |
| 09:15 | | | | |
| 09:30 | | | | |
| 09:45 | | | | |
| 10:00 | | | | |
| 10:15 | | | | |
| 10:30 | | | | |
| 10:45 | | | | |
| 11:00 | | | | |
| 11:15 | | | | |
| 11:30 | | | | |
| 11:45 | | | | |
| ......<br>......<br>18:00 | | | | |

Any item that hangs around in your 'to do' list for too long can go onto your 'to don't' list. If you spot the same task coming up time and again on your 'to do' list, yet it never gets done, then move it to the 'to don't' list, which includes all those things you have kept putting off. If any of the items on this list are truly important, they will crop up again, but often they will disappear as they are not important – and this will stop you worrying unnecessarily about them.

# Further tools and ideas

Let's look in more detail at some practical ideas that may support your drive to improve your organizational skills.

## Procrastination

Procrastination is the art of convincing yourself that you can put off until tomorrow what you should be doing today. However, procrastination will seldom lead to a decision becoming easier to make or a piece of work becoming easier to do. We all have tasks we would rather not do. Some helpful ideas to combat procrastination are:

- When procrastinating, the best thing you can do is admit it. Stop rationalizing and you are more likely to act.

- Do the toughest jobs first.

- Tackle unpleasant tasks in small pieces and short time segments. You can then do one small task that will get you moving in the right direction.

- Break complex tasks into smaller steps so that you focus on one step at a time.

- Commit yourself to action. Set deadlines, using your planner or 'to do list'. Promise results to others. The fear of losing face is a powerful motivator.

- Promise yourself a reward for completing the task. If you earn a reward, be sure to take it, eg a coffee or tea break.

## Maximizing your most efficient working period

Everybody has a natural daily rhythm to their energy patterns, rising to peaks of mental and physical performance and then experiencing troughs of low energy.

Your performance levels will fluctuate according to when you feel energetic and alert and when you feel tired. You need to understand the mental and physical cycles that your body follows each day if you are to prioritize and plan your workload effectively.

It makes great sense to allocate the most demanding tasks of the day to the times when you are at your physical and mental peak. For instance, if you are the sort of person who gets up early and goes jogging, you will probably find that you complete most of your important tasks early in the day. It might be different if you are a late riser or a 'night owl'.

In addition, the acquired wisdom is that most people are unlikely to be able to concentrate, without a break, for much more than an hour. Yet, left to our own devices, we often tend to work in unstructured blocks that can last all morning or all afternoon, and then be surprised by our own lack of motivation or concentration and that we have not achieved as much as we thought we would.

---

**Task:**
Work out your most efficient working period using the following steps:

1 Keep a daily record for one working week of how you feel when you wake up and then every two hours during the day until you go to bed.

2 Plot those results on a graph.

3 Remove any extreme results.

4 The plotted results will give you a good indication of your most alert or active time but also your downtime when you are least effective.

The next step will be to compare your most effective and least effective times to those of the other members of your working group and, more particularly, how they compare to the working rhythm of your supervisor. Anecdotally, most people perform better in the morning than in the afternoon, and hit a low point during the hour or so after lunch – 'the graveyard slot'.

## Providing additional focus

Although you cannot change your 'body clock', you can overwrite it temporarily. For instance, things that can boost your energy are:

- Slow-release carbohydrates such as brown rice (which will boost your energy over a period of hours).
- Sugar (short-term hit).
- Caffeine (short-term hit).
- Water (as your brain dehydrates, it gets less efficient and your thinking slows down, long before you notice tiredness or a headache).
- Chocolate (combines three powerful chemical types: cocoa, a legally available euphoriant; fats that give a sense of well-being; sugar, which will give a boost of energy).
- Getting up and moving around.
- Taking deep breaths.
- Fresh air: open a window if this is an option.

The problem of getting energy hits from sugar, caffeine and alcohol is that often the effect is only very short term and is then followed not long after by an even bigger low.

The human body is not designed to sit at a desk for hour after hour. So to avoid tense shoulders, stiff backs and lethargy it is a good idea to get up once an hour from your desk, stretch and walk about for a couple of minutes. This relieves stiffness and enhances your blood flow as the heart is having to pump faster, refreshing the brain as more oxygen is pumped to it through the reinvigorated blood supply.

It is also becoming common practice to work through lunchtimes. This allows little or no time to recharge your batteries. It is best practice to take at least a half-hour break (although preferably up to an hour) whilst also taking a walk, getting some fresh air and a change of scene, so that you are re-energized for the afternoon.

## Deadlines

Parkinson's Law formulated the idea that 'work expands to fill the time available for its completion'. For instance, if you have little work, or have little enthusiasm for this morning's main task, then that task can take the whole morning. If, on the other hand, you have a pressing deadline and so start the day with a difficult or important activity – with a lunch appointment or some similar reward at the end – this often means that the task will be completed on time. So, Parkinson's Law can work in reverse.

The Stock-Sanford Corollary to Parkinson's Law says that 'if you wait until the last minute, it only takes a minute to do'. We stress that this is not a method for time management, but it does provide a useful technique. When you set deadlines for yourself or for others, you create a powerful motivating force. If an activity or outcome has no deadline, there can be no failure as it simply has not yet been achieved. However, as soon as you introduce a deadline, you can motivate not only the people who find success a powerful driver, but also those who are motivated to avoid failure.

This is particularly true when you accompany a deadline with a commitment. When we commit to a deadline, the little voice in our head will worry away at us as the deadline gets nearer. Our conscience does not like the conflict between a promise made and the prospect of breaking it – even when we made that promise to ourselves.

People who work to deadlines should, however, be aware that always producing work at the last minute is a potentially risky strategy. First, you have to perform but, second, this can also be stressful for your supervisor or your clients, who may not work in the same way as you and so may find it stressful.

## Managing interruptions

Interruptions can come from many different sources: your boss, colleagues, your clients or maybe your friends, whether that be in person, by e-mail, text, Facebook or some other source. Sometimes those interruptions can be welcome, but not all the time. We have already discussed that there are times when we need to work undisturbed. The key skill is how you handle those interruptions, otherwise they become 'time stealers'.

A key question to be answered by everybody in considering their own personal organization and effectiveness is whether it is necessary to be available all of the time. Everybody is entitled to some protected time every day in order to carry out those tasks that are important for the business and for them personally.

It is also important to stress that we must find ways of managing or controlling interruptions, not preventing them. The examples of interruptions given above are from external sources but the biggest source of interruptions may be yourself, especially when you try to multitask, ie do more than one task at any one time.

Set out below are some pointers for best practice in managing interruptions.

## Let others know you do not want to be interrupted

- Let others know why you are unavailable and explain the priority of the work you are doing. Keep your supervisor 'updated'.
- Close your door for portions of the day (if you have a door); if you are in an open-plan office then use a quiet area to achieve the same objective.

## Why are you being interrupted?

- Find out why you are being interrupted and try to eliminate the reasons for the interruption.
- Question your own behaviour with your colleagues – in other words do you interrupt them in the same way?
- Make client files and any general or client information easily available to other people, so they do not interrupt you to gain the information they need.
- Learn to delegate more effectively; brief people more fully.
- Ask other people to think about possible solutions rather than just raise problems with you.

## While you are being interrupted

- Discourage the other person from sitting down by deliberately standing up yourself.
- Show interest in the person and the reason for their interruption.
- Ask the other person how long they need and, if necessary, schedule an alternative time.
- Delegate the discussion to the person most able to deal with it.
- Set a time limit on the interruption and stick to it.
- Learn to say no without alienating the other person (using your assertiveness skills).

If you are going to interrupt somebody else then it is important that you, in turn, respect their need to manage interruptions. So some useful thoughts are:

- Call or e-mail first or ask if it is convenient for you to speak to them.
- If you have to wait, do not bother anyone else.
- Take work with you in case you are kept waiting.
- Agree the time available for the interruption and an agenda and then stick to both.
- Always offer solutions when discussing problems.
- Stop asking others to help you – find out information for yourself.
- Prioritize the need for your interruption, eg does it need doing now, who is the best person to approach and how time-critical is it?

## Managing e-mail and your phones

The high volume of e-mail that everybody now receives means that more thought should be given to the content of the e-mail message, to whom it is being sent and, more importantly, whether the message is necessary.

Some people can spend up to half of their working day going through their inbox and becoming tired, frustrated and unproductive as a result. Recent studies have also suggested that up to one-third of office workers suffer from e-mail stress.

Key ideas of how to deal with e-mails are given below.

### Personal discipline

- Keep your inbox small and empty it regularly.
- Only keep current, live e-mails within your main inbox.
- On-screen e-mail alerts – do not be a slave to them and, if necessary, turn off the alerts, if possible at certain times.
- Avoid junk e-mail – eg including newsletters/marketing information (unless relevant to your work), gossip or 'look how busy I am' messages.
- Think about whom you include in an e-mail – do they need to be included?
- Understand how to use your e-mailing programme properly, including all its available tools.

### Using the tools

- Create task/calendar entries for e-mails for outstanding actions.
- Create rules and use flags to deal with incoming e-mails, eg colours to highlight messages from key people or placing the e-mails into a client subfolder.
- Use your out-of-office message to manage expectations.
- Think carefully about security for those files containing confidential information.

### Communication

- Make your e-mails as succinct as possible (ideally less than half a screen in length).
- Do not use e-mails when issues are overly complex.
- Make sure that your messages are clear and think about inserting an executive summary at the start of the message.
- Be careful of e-mail chains that may contain some information that the other person should not see.
- For urgent matters, use the phone.

- Do not use e-mails to cover up your own poor management or delay.
- It may be more effective communication to speak by phone rather than send an e-mail.

## Best practice

- Set aside quality time to deal with your e-mails.
- Avoid dipping in and out of your inbox all day.
- Do not feel that you must provide answers immediately (prioritization grid).
- Make sure that somebody else has access to your mailbox.

## Practise the 4 Ds

Making the correct decision the first time you open an e-mail is crucial for your effective time management. The 4 Ds of e-mail decision-making have been developed to help support this decision-making process:

- **Delete:** half of the e-mails you get can probably be deleted immediately.
- **Do:** if the e-mail is urgent or can be completed quickly.
- **Delegate:** if the e-mail can be better dealt with by someone else.
- **Defer:** set aside a planned time to spend on e-mails that require longer action.

Ideas on how to deal with your phone are also set out below:

## Managing your phones (including your mobile)

- Use call divert when able.
- Reply and respond to phone messages as a 'filler' task – your downtime.
- Respond to all messages as agreed so that trust and confidence is built.
- Tell a caller how much time you have at the beginning of a call; ask someone you have called if it is convenient to speak and how long they have available.
- Keep track of how much time you are taking on each call.

# Circle C: managing relationships and communication

Inevitably, our review of effective personal organizational skills within Circle B has highlighted, at every stage, the importance of high levels of communication and the need to manage relationships. However, we consider these skills to be so important that they merit a circle of their own – Circle C. Without these skills, it becomes much more difficult to manage the expectations of others, eg clients.

Delegation is an excellent example of these skills, as well as an essential organizational tool.

# Delegation

Managers get things done through other people. This description recognizes that there are limits to any manager's time and knowledge. Eventually, no matter how well a manager is using their time, they will hit a limit to the amount they can get done in the time available to them.

The manager must, therefore, find ways of freeing up their resources in order to move up to the next level of productivity. If you are a manager, or an aspiring manager, then this involves not just managing your own time but also the need to manage other people's time as well. Effective professionals need to understand the value of delegation, which is one of the most important and challenging management skills.

## What is delegation?

Delegation of work is giving somebody else the responsibility to carry out a specific activity that was originally your own responsibility. But, at the same time, you must give them the authority they need to do the task and to make any necessary decisions about the job according to the agreed level of delegation given to that person.

It is important that the person who delegates the work must also retain overall accountability for the outcome of the work, whilst allowing the person who is doing the task to make appropriate decisions.

Delegation, if it is to be done properly, must not be either abdication (where there is little or no direction or feedback), nor should it be micromanagement (where a manager provides too much input and direction). Deciding on the levels of control exercised by the manager and the levels of responsibility being given to the other person will be crucial to the success of the task. A full discussion of these areas of control and responsibility lies outside the skills being talked about in this book.

A useful definition of delegation is: '*Getting the right things done, by the right people, at the right time to the required quality standard.*' This means that, in order to achieve the required quality of output, the person delegating the work must understand and effectively communicate the following:

- which tasks are to be delegated;
- to whom;
- on what basis (ie clear instructions);

**FIGURE 3.9**  How to delegate effectively

# Effective Delegation in 4 Stages

## The Delegator

**WHAT**
- What does the client want?
- Timetable and deadlines
- Scoping of matter
- Skills/knowledge needed
- Format of response needed
- Delegate complete tasks

**WHO**
- Identify who can help
- Who can be trained to do this?
- Relationship with the client
- Capacity and availability
- What must you retain?
- Costs implications on whole task

**HOW**
- Level of guidance and control
- Face-to-face or written briefing

**CHECKLIST**
- Check availability
- Do not assume knowledge
- Do not assume experience level
- Brief fully – set context and scene
- Describe the required end result
- Discuss the end result
- Identify know-how and precedents
- Identify resources
- Discuss timescale
- Discuss interim and final deadline(s)
- Agree level of monitoring

**BEST PRACTICE SUPERVISION**
- Be accessible
- Update any changes to delegatee
- Set up reviews – if required
- Encourage feedback
- Encourage suggestions
- Give support
- Give direction
- Give empathic support
- Avoid taking work back
- Monitor time taken
- Monitor overall cost

**REFLECT and REVIEW**
- Review the whole task
- Acknowledge what went well
- Explain any changes made
- Give constructive feedback
- Feedback on substance not style
- Discuss other possible methods
- Key learning points
- Suggest how can work together better next time

**Stage 1 Planning**  →  **Stage 2 Briefing**  →  **Stage 3 Doing**  →  **Stage 4 Reviewing**

**UNDERSTAND YOUR CURRENT WORKLOAD**
- Be realistic – do not take on too much
- Give informed consent or say 'no'
- Clarify priorities with supervisor
- Be positive and enthusiastic
- Raise your profile, confidence and expertise by gaining work experience

**UNDERSTAND THE TASK**
- Take clear and effective notes
- Be honest about current experience
- Ask questions to aid understanding
- Clarify deadlines
- Clarify work parameters
- Check level of detail
- Check background information
- Agree review process
- Summarize your understanding

**PLAN YOUR WORK**
- Avoid last minute work
- Plan for contingencies
- Seek further direction (if necessary)
- Feedback on your progress
- Raise potential problems asap
- Monitor your time
- Group questions together
- Progress matters as far as possible

**REFLECT and REVIEW**
- Be able to understand and explain your approach
- Ask for feedback
- Avoid being defensive
- Reflect on the learning
- Plan what you will do differently next time

## The Delegatee

© Sally Sanderson, Profox Consultancy Ltd

- to be completed by deadline (time and date);
- to the required quality standard.

As a giver of delegated tasks you must ensure delegation happens effectively. It is important that the recipient of the delegated task also has the opportunity to 'manage upwards', by suggesting improvements to the delegation process and the way in which the task was delegated – especially if the person delegating could use the help to make the process more effective. Managing the way you *receive* a delegated task is one of the central skills of 'managing upwards'.

## The four stages of delegation

There are four key stages to effective delegation and these are set out in Figure 3.9.

The checklist sets out a useful approach for both the giver and the recipient of the delegation. The delegation system will have failed if, having delegated a task, you end up redoing the task yourself because the person you gave the task to never really understood the task and didn't do what you thought you had asked them to do. This is often called reverse delegation and should not happen.

## Lateral and upward delegation of tasks

Some tasks or issues need to be delegated upwards or laterally. This must not, however, be confused with 'abdication of responsibility' or 'passing the buck', neither of which is acceptable behaviour for a young professional who is expected to take responsibility. By laterally or upwardly delegating, you are seeking the involvement and cooperation of the other person, whether they are your team leader, a specialist, or a colleague in another team or different office. In this situation you cannot delegate in the traditional way, ie with authority. Accordingly, you should take responsibility by seeking to complete the task/achieve the objective, but at the same time you are asking or requesting the other person to take responsibility by making a contribution to achieving the same objective, eg by contributing specialist skills, or by reviewing/signing off your work.

Because of this element of request, lateral delegation is sometimes called 'delegation without authority'. So, when delegating laterally and upwards it is important to have built up your own credibility and a good working relationship with supervisors, colleagues, specialists etc.

Set out below are some helpful thought processes.

---

### Planning:

- Consider why you are asking for help – prepare your justification.
- Prepare your request for assistance well and consider how you will motivate the other person to carry out the task.
- Always be open and honest with the other person.
- Get the support (and preferably authority) from your team leader/supervisor for involving the other person before you do so. If this is not possible, always inform your supervisor/team leader of your actions.
- Communicate effectively by choosing the appropriate channel of communication – e-mail is not always the best approach.
- Be assertive without being too pushy, using your persuasion and influencing skills to gain cooperation.
- Follow up by doing what you have agreed to do as part of this process.

### How to:

1  Agree objective and ASK for cooperation.
2  Agree timescale and completion time/date.
3  Gain agreement and transfer responsibility for the task.
4  Agree the next contact or any progress checkpoints.
5  Thanks and credit.

### Never:

- manipulate the situation to avoid doing the task yourself;
- exploit the goodwill of others;
- oversell the job either in terms of its importance or what the task actually is.

---

# Conclusion

Personal organization is crucial to the role of the professional. Your clients are placing trust and confidence in you. If you are not in control of your workload it will soon manifest itself to the client and harm your client relationship.

The skills we have been discussing in this chapter are personal skills; they need to be underpinned by the right approach and mindset. We have used the three circles as a guide. You may need some direction in developing your career to provide challenge, focus and direction – circle A. You then need to organize yourself – circle B. You then need excellent relationship and communication skills – circle C in order to make sure you achieve your goals.

Regularly reflecting on your personal organization skills is crucial because, as Peter F Drucker has pointed out: 'Until we can manage time, we can manage nothing else.'

# Effective business writing

## Introduction

All writing, whether it is for business or any other purpose, strives for an effect of some kind. In this chapter we will look at what effects you try to have on your readers, and how to achieve them. We will also warn you on the matter of how careless writing can have unexpected negative effects.

You are presenting yourself as someone of integrity, knowledge, and careful judgement so you need to protect your image as a trustworthy authority. Any kind of error or inattention will undermine that authority, and writing is no exception. In fact, writing is particularly important as the texts that you produce – whether they be letters, reports, contracts, prescriptions, surveys or day-to-day e-mails – are documents of crucial importance to clients.

The key things to consider are:

- structure;
- accuracy;
- clarity;
- tone.

## What we want to avoid

It is unlikely that you are fully aware of the flaws in your writing and the impact they can have on your message. There are dangers in adopting the wrong structure (or lacking any) and using the wrong tone. When it comes to accuracy, even those with good degrees and great career prospects are often ignorant of the rules for common words and punctuation. What may be acceptable in social communication, staff room notices and so on will not pass muster at the highest level. Looking more closely at what is at stake, there are three main consequences to avoid:

- mistrust;
- incomprehension;
- professional negligence.

## Mistrust

Inaccuracy of any kind affects trust, and trust is central to the reputation of any professional. Perhaps it is not rational that people would doubt your expert opinion just because you spelt 'tomorrow' with two 'm's or wrote 'Neither of them are...' instead of 'Neither of them is...'. After all, these little errors don't affect the meaning of the text in any significant way, but the problem is that they give the impression that the writer is slipshod. The reader may start wondering beyond the punctuation to what else has been missed – some vital detail in research that will affect the project's outcome, perhaps?

It is rather like the way that some people pass judgement on restaurants according to the state of the toilets. They think: if the toilets – which the customer can see – have not been kept spotless, how dirty might the kitchen – which is behind closed doors – turn out to be?

## Incomprehension

Written communications that are not quickly and easily comprehensible are ineffective. As a client, I want to be left with no doubt as to the facts you are conveying and the course of action you are suggesting – and I want to get this in one reading, not four.

The worst-case outcome is that I might decide to engage someone else – someone who takes care that I understand everything first time round. This is especially likely if I am considering which firm to go with on a new project.

Even supposing the client was tolerant – or committed already to your organization – then he or she would have to write back, or call and ask for clarification. This will cost extra time and money – dissatisfaction guaranteed.

## Professional negligence

This is obviously serious. It might result from leaving out vital information, including erroneous information, or misleading the clients to such an extent that their business or welfare is harmed. It goes without saying that this would be disastrous for your career and the reputation of your organization. It sometimes happens, and it mustn't happen to you.

# Your writing strategy

You don't want to approach every writing task as if it is the first one you've ever done, figuring out how to do it as you go along. Neither do you want to spill out all the points you think might be important and hope that everything will be covered somewhere on the way; what you want is a strategy that works for everything all the time. It needs to be something you can remember and apply effortlessly. Over time you may come up with your own strategy, but the route followed in Figure 4.1 is a good one to start with.

**FIGURE 4.1**   A logical writing strategy

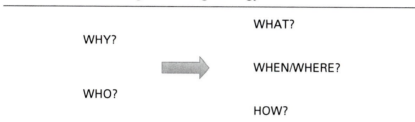

*Why?* and *Who?* are the most important questions, yet they are the most likely to be forgotten (just think how often we sit down and say to ourselves 'Now... what shall I write?' before thinking about our reader and reason for writing). But if we can answer those first two questions then the answers to the others fall smoothly into place. We'll explain this below, and then show how it works with an example.

# Action: making something happen

Generally, the difference between clear and unclear writing is that clear writing has a definite purpose and the writer never loses sight of it. So our advice is ultimately very simple: know your aim and stick to it. If you lose your way, go back and look for that original aim.

## Why am I writing this?

This is the question that everyone should start with, but people often rush in without asking it, usually because they are busy and feel that sitting back for a moment's reflection is a waste of time. But a lot more time is wasted if your text is not fit for purpose.

The second problem is that many people answer the question in the wrong way. They tend to say things like this: *I have to write a report for the board; The clients asked for this information in full; We need a memo to go out across the whole division; Because the deadline for my report is Wednesday and I need to get their figures.*

The problem is that these are just ways of saying 'I am writing this because I have to'. That doesn't help because it doesn't focus on what outcome you want to achieve. And this is the key thing: that when people read what you have written, you want them to go on to do something: follow your instructions, answer your question, take up your recommendation, and so on. You are unlikely to achieve this objective if you haven't got it clear in your own mind. So stop and think it through. Then write it down.

And be particularly careful of expressing your outcome just in terms of 'informing' people; if you are giving someone information, you presumably want that person to do something with it – what, exactly? Our tip for getting right to the heart of your task is to jot down a sentence like this one: I want *[insert name of reader/s]* to *[insert verb]*.

Completed examples might be: I want *the client* to *call* me and *ask* about this solution; I want *the two colleagues to whom I've given this task* to *finish it by Thursday night and do it properly* so that I don't have to redo it on Friday morning. The key thing here is the verb. As you probably know, a verb stands for an action. In the examples given, the verbs are clear and simple: *call, ask, finish,* and *do*. The simpler the language you use for this, the more likely you are to hit the nail on the head, and have the focus squarely on what the reader will do as a result of your message.

In addition to the direct results of your message, there are always feelings and beliefs that you would like the reader to be aware of. Things you might write down here are: *I want all the recipients of this e-mail to feel that the work we do here is important to what they do;* or, *I want my manager to think that I would be a good person to promote and the wrong person to lay off.* Of course you can't magically produce these feelings and beliefs in one routine communication, but the cumulative effect of consistently effective and impressive communication can be exactly those things.

Once you have defined the effects that you are trying to bring about, your writing task is already getting a lot easier. But the second vital question that is often forgotten at this stage is: Who? Who am I writing to? By this we don't just mean someone's name and position but everything you might know about them in relation to your task. Think about these 10 questions:

1  What is this person's duty/role? (Colleagues have job descriptions, clients may need to submit to procedures.)

2  What does this person already know about this topic?

3  What motivates this person? (Think of what they actually care about and how it can coincide with what you want.)

4  What does this person need from the whole process? (They may want to exit quickly, or work painstakingly – show how your goals help to achieve this.)

5  What objections or obstacles might they see? (These may be real or imagined, but see if you can lay them to rest in your first message.)

6  What beliefs do they have about this process or my profession that affect their actions? (eg are they impatient with/suspicious of all people who do my job, or people from our team?)

7  Is this person fully able to comply with my wishes? (Do they have the executive power, the budget, the information?)

8  Does my reader have a different first language?

9  Is my reader going to focus on the detail or the big picture?

10  How much time will my reader have in which to read this?

Not all of these questions will matter to each thing you write, but something will almost always come to light that will influence your planning.

Incidentally, the most common mistake is to see things *just* in terms of the first question: 'What is the person's duty/role?'. This is perhaps because we believe it is our right to expect others to do their jobs, and clients to behave in their own best interests by complying with our requests at key points in the process. That would be rational, after all. But very often it is not the case: colleagues and clients will let you down. You could, of course, write it off as their fault, and you'd be right. But the professional attitude is to look for some way to motivate them to comply with your request.

Bear in mind that none of this thinking means that you then go on to write a lot of extra things as a result – quite the opposite. Considering your reader's point of view will help you to filter out irrelevance and decide what to emphasize – alerting your readers to the points that matter to them, which is what counts. You appeal to what *they* want so they do what *you* want.

Before we move on to looking at this in practice, here's another tip: the last question on the list above will always have the same answer. When you ask how much time the reader has for your message, the answer is: none at all. They do not have a two-minute or two-hour gap in the day when they will be drumming their fingers on the desk whereupon your e-mail or report arrives as a welcome way to fill the empty time. On the contrary, all their days are already full – just like yours – and that demands two things of you. First, they need you to get to the point quickly and keep your message as concise as possible. Second, you need to show them immediately that the message is worth reading and that they should put aside their other urgent tasks in order to read it.

Now let's take a real-life example to illustrate how this works.

You have been told to obtain some data from a client, Ms Kristeva, that is vital to the work your firm is doing on her behalf. She was notified of the need to provide this information some time ago when the firm was engaged. However, it hasn't arrived and Ms Kristeva has a reputation for being awkward. When you were on the phone to her a few days ago she mentioned she would be out of the country until the end of the week. You need your data before that. You also got the impression that the client feels you are too junior and only wants to speak to your manager, an older man. If you don't get anywhere then you could go back to your manager and say that Ms Kristeva won't cooperate, but you don't like the idea of him stepping in.

So your first move is to take 30 seconds to think clearly what you want, and you write down: I want Ms Kristeva to send the data to me within two days. Thinking about it more deeply, you also add: I want my manager to believe that I get things done and don't bother him unnecessarily. I want Ms Kristeva to believe that she will get the best possible service by dealing with me directly.

So that is what *you* want; what about the client? Look back at the 10 *Who* questions above. What do you think the answers might be in Ms Kristeva's case? None of us is a mind-reader but here are some reasonable suppositions:

**1a** She should know these documents are required but seems to have overlooked the request in the earlier letter.

**2a** She should be happy – in principle – to provide what is needed for us to do a good job.

**3a** She seems to like to feel important, and she must want a positive outcome from our work.

**4a** She needs a speedy and effective service.

**5a** She might feel that we should have asked for this before, not realizing that we had done. She may claim that she can't do it at the moment.

**6a** She fears she's being fobbed off with a junior.

**7a** If she is out of the country, accessibility of data and delay could be a problem.

**8a** She speaks excellent English but it is her second language.

**9a** Judging by the fact that she has overlooked the need to send this – she is not focused on detail.

**10a** She has even less time than normal because she is travelling.

Now that you have established why you are writing and who you are writing to, you have very little else to do; it all flows from what you've done already. You are ready for the What, When/Where, and How:

**1 What** will I say?

**2 When** and **where** in my message will I say it? (ie Which is the best order to present the content?)

**3 How** will I say it? (ie The choice of words and tone.)

To decide what to say, all you need to do is to look down the lists you have already made. You might end up with something like this:

## What to say:

- Which data I need and why it will help us to do a good job.
- When we need it by.
- When we first asked for it.
- That I have been asked by my manager to send this e-mail.
- That I realize time and accessibility could be a problem.

## When and where (the order)

Looking at the notes above, and knowing what you do about Ms Kristeva, your best opening might be to say that your manager asked you to get in touch – that way she'll feel more connected to him, will be more likely to see the message as important, and is clear about who to reply to. Immediately you should then state the desired outcome, which mustn't get lost further down. The tricky issue after that is to say that the data was requested some time ago (the hold-up is on her side not yours). You need to mention this otherwise she may reply that she is being given insufficient notice, but you don't want to offend or irritate her when you point it out, so try to mention this information in passing, without seeming to want to make much of it. Perhaps the final order could look like this:

1 That I have been asked by my manager to send this e-mail.
2 Why these documents will help us to do a good job.
3 We need the documents and when we need them by.
4 What the documents are and when we first asked for them.
5 That I understand time and accessibility could be a problem.

## How will I say it? (the choice of words and tone)

You've decided that the client likes to feel important so make sure that the tone does not sound peremptory; formal writing, which is objective and impersonal, often does – especially if the writer is slightly irked and allows it to show through. Emphasize that you understand how busy she is, and that you would be willing to help in any way. As an example:

Dear Ms Kristeva
My manager Anthony Knowles asked me to contact you, so that we can prepare your documentation for submission by 8 June, as agreed. In order to do this, we will need to make certified copies of three documents by Wednesday 6 June.
I have copied below the list of documents from our letter to you of 14 May for your convenience:

1 Current statements of VAT exemption for the companies that you own in the UK.
2 Lease agreements on all UK properties leased by your UK companies.
3 The name and address of the audit accountant(s) for all UK companies.

I recall from our telephone conversation earlier this week that you will now be abroad and hope that this will not create any difficulty for you in despatching the necessary documents within the required time.

If there is anything I can do to provide assistance please contact me directly by e-mail or on + 44 20 737 4747.

I look forward to hearing from you.

Reading this simple letter, your reaction might be to say 'That's more or less what I would have done anyway.' That may well be the case, but take a moment to think whether you might actually have written a letter something like this:

Dear Ms Kristeva

Further to your submission to the Department for Business, Innovation and Skills, for which we received the instruction on 14 May, I am writing to remind you of the need for certified documents as specified in our letter of that date, which we have not yet received.

Unless we receive the documents in question by close of business on Wednesday 6 June, we will be unable to process the submission by the agreed date of 8 June.

Thank you for your understanding in this matter.

Regards

Perhaps you will be able to anticipate the potential problems we will find with this version? Here are some of them:

- The first sentence is long and overcomplex, making it unclear and overformal (remember she is reading in her second language, so don't make her work to understand you).
- The reference to the date of instruction is irrelevant.
- Although there is no emotional language in the message, the reader is likely to feel scolded.
- The documents have not been reiterated here, which may cause delay.
- The letter emphasises the client's obligation to comply, not the writer's dedication to help.
- There is the air of a threat ('Unless...') not to complete on time.
- There is no offer of assistance or contact – again, the onus is on the client.

The first few times that you structure your writing by thinking in this way, it may feel contrived or slow, but you'll soon find that it speeds you more quickly to your goal – partly because the total number of messages exchanged is reduced. The process will soon become second nature, with the result that you will develop a smooth, crisp style of writing that you and your readers are happy with.

# Structuring longer documents

We will now look at more extended documents, which may have many readers – including people not known to you. Reports, proposals and plans fall into this category. For these, you should still consider the purpose and whatever you know about the reader as we have just done, but there are also decisions to make about how to order large amounts of information. Outlined below are five of the options available to you: logical argument, chronological, value-based, adopted structure, and question and answer.

## Logical argument

This will be familiar to you if you have written academic essays. Writers use it when they need to: 1) make an assessment based on evidence and argument; 2) show that they have considered both sides and come to an objective conclusion.

The structure is as follows:

**1** Introduction – outline your reasons for writing and your objectives.

**2** Main body – list and discuss the pros and cons, evaluating as you go.

**3** Conclusion – make a recommendation or judgement.

You would follow this model if you were writing a report for people to use when making decisions or to familiarize themselves with subject areas unknown to them. You need to be aware of how much you are required to make a recommendation in the conclusion, or whether you should hold back from expressing an opinion and merely summarize the key points to consider. If you do have a strong conclusion to draw, consider whether or not to announce it in your introduction. The advantage of this is that people can skim-read the rest more efficiently – which may suit your needs. The alternative is to keep the reader waiting until the end for your opinion. This can often be more engaging or persuasive, but presupposes that the reader is patient or committed.

## Chronological

This may work with reports of an incident or a series of events. It may also work for project planning. Use it to: 1) set out how something occurred; 2) show how something will take shape over time.

The structure is simple – you list the events/actions in the order they happen. This will require some kind of numbering system (eg dates, or a numbered list) and you should think about whether this is appropriate for your audience. If not, consider making the chronology an appendix.

There is also a risk that the more important points may go unnoticed by the reader. A summary of some kind may be needed, either at the beginning or the end, to highlight key points.

## Value-based

This is when you order the topics to be discussed according to priority – your reader's priority. It will be appropriate when you want to: 1) persuade someone towards a particular decision; 2) direct their attention to the facts that will influence them. An example structure is: benefits, costs, preconditions. Note the difference between this and a more objective or informative text, which might mention the preconditions earlier. You also need to remember that this kind of structure relies on your knowledge of the reader's priorities.

## Adopted structure

An example of this would be when your document is a commentary on an existing contract. It allows the writer to:

- confine comments to what is strictly relevant;
- eliminate unnecessary linking and preamble;
- aid comparison between documents;
- ensure precision of reference (ie the reader knows exactly which sentence/paragraph in another document you are talking about).

One danger is that the reader cannot quickly separate the major details from the minor ones. A summary or covering letter might be needed.

## Question and answer

Websites and information guides often have a section in this style. Choose this to: 1) present a helpful and approachable image; 2) deal with questions that you can easily anticipate.

This format is not usually intended to be comprehensive or definitive. It would work well within your own trusted team or as a way of 'softening' information that is available in a more precise but less accessible form elsewhere: as when long news articles contain a box with some Q&A on the topic.

Whether you use one of these five formats or not, there are also some general structural principles that always apply. The introduction and conclusion must be direct and clear, capturing the gist of the whole document. In the introduction, grab the reader's attention with a statement or question that will intrigue them and quickly show that the text to come is worth reading. Your conclusion should not introduce anything new, but don't let it be a bland repetition of what you've already said. Use it as an opportunity to reiterate your main points in a shorter, punchy style that will imprint your main ideas on the memory.

Make the structure you are using explicit, so that the reader knows exactly how the part they are currently reading relates to the other parts, and the whole. In most cases you can do that with headings, so use them carefully to show the reader the thread of the argument. If headings are not appropriate (for example, if you've seen other similar types of document that don't use headings), the first sentence in each paragraph should make clear to the reader the topic that will follow.

# Sitting down to write

Now that you have planned out your piece of work, you are ready to begin. No matter what the content of the piece, and the context in which you work, there are guidelines that apply. We've divided this section into words, sentences and paragraphs.

## Words

Possibly the most common type of writing error is the wrong choice of word, where someone uses a word that doesn't have the meaning they think it does. It is often a word they have read or heard, but only partly grasped. Here is an example from everyday speech: *'They're going to deliver it today, allegedly.'*

The speaker here is using the word 'allegedly' to mean that there is some doubt about the truth of the claim. But the word should be used only in a legal context, when someone is being accused of something, eg: *'This is the car that she allegedly stole.'*

The speaker would have done better to use 'supposedly' or 'apparently'.

If this is a common problem, how do we avoid falling into it? After all, we *think* we know the meanings of all the words we use, so how can we know which ones we are mistaken about? The answer is to use simple language. Pick the simplest and most common word that fits, and avoid any words or expressions you have heard a lot lately, as these are often the ones that are misused.

And anyway it is always better to use words that most people understand. Don't load the text with jargon to come across as 'in the know'. Within your field there will be certain specialist terms in constant use, but use them only when you have to, not excessively; think about whether the reader is likely to be familiar with them.

Avoid slang, and social and jokey phrases. Where you are writing to a colleague with whom you have an informal rapport, you can relax a little, but not too much – imagine that everything you write will be open for the whole company, or even the whole world, to read; one day it might be – as countless people have found to their cost.

Never allow a word that is potentially offensive or abusive into your communication. Don't even forward on something like that; delete it from your inbox. If someone repeatedly uses questionable language in messages to you, call them and tell them to stop. If that doesn't work, you will have to report them. Even if you are not a prejudiced or abusive person, you don't ever want to have to defend yourself against such accusations.

## *Sentences*

Here are some tips to ensure that your writing is made up of effective, engaging sentences:

### Vary the length

If the sense of what you are saying flows naturally then join up sentences to keep the reader moving. But alternate them with shorter ones. Very short sentences are especially effective in persuasive writing.

### Vary the construction

There are many ways of stringing ideas into a sentence. Don't get stuck in a rut where you keep repeating the same pattern. Here is the same sentence constructed in different ways to remind you of some of the variations that are possible:

- *Because the samples were contaminated the product had to be withdrawn from sale.*
- *The product was withdrawn from sale as the samples were contaminated.*
- *As soon as it became aware of the contaminated samples the company withdrew the product from sale.*
- *Sale of the product was withdrawn due to the discovery of contaminated samples.*
- *Contaminated samples led to the product being withdrawn.*
- *The withdrawal of the product followed hard on the discovery of contaminated samples.*

To come up with variations for yourself, pick out a key word from your sentence and see if you can construct the sentence again with that word at the beginning.

### Don't overload your sentence

Overloaded sentences sound clever, and you can find them in all kinds of published writing, but they are there to impress or intimidate the reader, not to aid communication. Take this example:

*The resurgent Apple corporation, in contrast to rivals who believed themselves to have a comfortably dominant position in a market that was still years away from saturation, prioritized leisure and entertainment functions over the kind of core functionality on which those competitors had staked not just their brands, but their entire conception of their own R&D.*

Presumably there are individuals out there who can digest a chunk of verbiage like this at pace, but they are few and far between. For most of us, following the sense of this sentence takes mental energy and we have to read it twice or more. A more digestible version would be:

*The resurgent Apple corporation prioritized leisure and entertainment over basic functions. This was in contrast to its dominant rivals at the time, who were relying on their existing products, marketing and development. Those rivals were confident of the market and their position within it.*

This second version is less sophisticated in its use of English syntax, but it is easier to understand in the first reading. It has more sentences, but fewer words.

## Paragraphs

There are a few simple tips to follow:

- Don't make paragraphs too long. Too many short paragraphs together would result in a disjointed effect, though, so give each one just enough length to make its point.

- Start a new paragraph for a new idea. Don't stray into other ideas as they occur to you.

- Make use of headings. It is vital that readers can relate the ideas together as they read.

- All the paragraphs should be linked. Headings can help with this, but phrases like *The next point to consider...* or *One disadvantage of this approach...* are helpful to the reader.

- Use bullets and numbered lists. Items are hard to remember when listed in a sentence, and are much more memorable in a vertical list.

- Consider putting your key sentence of the paragraph at the start, and then adding any supporting details as you go down. It is not always the best solution, but often leads to a clear flow of ideas through the document.

# Accuracy: spelling, grammar and punctuation

Let's suppose for a moment that your document had some statistical or numerical information in it. How would you feel if you found out that someone who read it had noticed errors in your numbers? Probably, like most people, you'd feel foolish and you'd be determined not to let it happen again. You certainly wouldn't shrug and say 'I'm no good with maths.'

Yet when it comes to language, we can see mistakes all over the place. In the local supermarket car park there is a notice declaring: *No trolley's beyond this point.* Somebody in a reasonably responsible position ordered that sign, and someone else printed it up, with no one bothering to check it. It doesn't create a good impression of the company and its attention to detail.

Of course, everyone makes mistakes from time to time. And there are some areas of language where no definite rule applies. In addition, people's literacy is being affected by web writing, because whereas in the past all printed material was proofread by a professional, now we can all publish our own content directly onto the web, complete with all our errors. These errors are then read by other people, and start to spread contagiously. But whatever the reason, there is no excuse for ignorance or carelessness on your part, and that's what the majority of errors stem from.

It is not our aim here to teach all the rules of spelling, grammar and punctuation; there are whole books devoted to the subject, and after reading this section you may decide to go in search of one. What we can do is point out some of the most common mistakes and why people make them.

## *Spelling*

Make sure your spellcheck function is active – and set to the correct variety of English (UK or US as appropriate). If you have misspelt a word by confusing it with another (eg their and there) the computer won't notice, so look out for those, especially the ones you know you've made before.

Rereading your text carefully will probably show up a few typing errors, and perhaps a few spelling mistakes as well. Print out your document – you will invariably spot one or two that you missed on the screen.

There are a few 'usual suspects' that everyone should be wary of. The chances are that you spell at least one of the following words incorrectly: accommodation, commitment, committee, embarrass, harass, recommend, parallel, privilege, definitely, separate, relevant.

Note that each of the first seven words has doubled consonants somewhere, and the confusion arises over whether there are two sets of doubled consonants or one (eg *committee* or *commitee?*). The last four words are examples where it is not obvious from the sound of the word which vowel we should use – e, i or a.

Here are some words whose spellings are often confused. They are dangerous because mistakes will not be picked up by the spell check: lose/loose, every day/everyday, passed/past, affect/effect, quiet/quite, they're/their/there, who's/whose, lie/lay (and their past forms – lay, lain and laid.)

## *Grammar*

English speakers do not usually learn grammar formally at school. This is partly because the language has less formal grammar than many other languages. Unfortunately, there are a few grey areas in the minds of most educated people. If you don't overcomplicate your sentences you shouldn't go too far wrong, but there are a few well-known grammatical errors to look out for. Here are some of them:

- *None of them are...* – 'None' means 'not one'. It is singular, so you should use 'is' not 'are'.

- *Neither of them have...* – This is the same rule as above. 'Neither' is singular and so you should use 'has'.

- *Everyone loves their mother.* – Again, 'everyone' is singular, whereas 'their' is plural. You can say 'his or her mother'. Better perhaps to rethink and use something like 'We all love our mothers' or 'It's usual to love one's mother' etc.

- *Revenue was higher, however, higher operating costs swallowed these gains.* – This should be two separate sentences. One way to get this right is to remember that 'however' and 'but' have the same meaning, but different grammar: 'but' links two halves of a single sentence whereas 'however' shows the relation between two separate sentences.

- *There were less people and less cars.* – 'People' and 'cars' are plural so you should say 'fewer' not 'less'. (You could say 'less traffic' because 'traffic' is always singular.)

- *The person you should speak to is myself.* – The last word should be 'me'. Use 'myself' when you are both the subject and object of the verb, as in 'I can laugh at myself'. It is also possible to use 'myself' for emphasis as in 'I myself would never consider such a thing' but it is not necessary. The same rules apply to 'yourself', 'herself' and 'himself'.

- *Sharon and me will be able to handle any problems.* – This should be 'Sharon and I'. The easiest way to see why is to remove 'Sharon and' from the sentence: you wouldn't say 'Me will be able...', and so there is no reason to switch to 'me' when you talk about two people. But be careful, because some people overcorrect as follows: *If there are any problems, just speak to Sharon and I.* – This time 'me' is the correct choice. Again, if you remove the 'Sharon and' part, you would get 'speak to I', which is clearly wrong!

This is just a selection of the most commonly seen errors. Another thing to be aware of before we leave this topic is that there are some areas of grammar where people disagree. You could say that there is an 'old school', whose members are keen to uphold traditional rules that are falling into disuse.

Against them, you have modernizers who argue that some of these old rules should be dropped. Here are some examples, where all the 'modern' versions would be regarded as errors by some:

**Modern / traditional:**

*If this was a privately owned company... / If this were a privately owned company.*

*I'd like to quickly explain. / I'd like to explain quickly.*

*We can smoke in the garden. / We may smoke in the garden.*

*Each person will have their own room. / Each person will have his own room.*

*Who are you writing to? / To whom are you writing?*

*We spell it like the Americans do. / We spell it as the Americans do.*

*Hopefully it will arrive on time. / We hope that it will arrive on time.*

If you suspect that your reader might have traditional ideas about language, you can either use the traditional forms or write the sentence in a different way altogether so that the issue doesn't arise. It is also worth noting that the more traditional forms do have a more elegant, classical sound.

## *Punctuation*

It is well worth getting hold of a punctuation guide and keeping it close to your desk. It is also easy to find most of the important rules on the internet with a simple search, but there are areas where people very often slip up and we will examine two of them: the apostrophe and the comma.

The apostrophe has two functions. One is to show possession, as in 'Steve's bike'. The second is to show missing letters, as in 'he's' – this is known as a contraction. To complicate matters, we add an 's' (but no apostrophe) to make plurals and also on verbs after 'he', 'she' and 'it'. So people get confused between the four. Here they all are again:

- *Mr Hoover's wife.* (possessive)
- *Mr Hoover's a good husband.* (contraction)
- *There are two hoovers.* (plural)
- *He hoovers the floor every day.* (verb + s)

It is possible that you might need a possessive and a plural at the same time. This would be when a number of people possess something, as in the following example: *That is the Hoovers' house.* As you can see, the apostrophe goes after the 's' in this case. Some common plurals (men, women, children, people) don't end in an 's', so in this case you just add the possessive 's' as normal: *The children's teacher; Some people's attitudes.*

The other thing you have to remember – and perhaps the most common mistake of all – is a rather strange little rule. Look at the two sentences: '*It's a long way from here.*' and 'The *animal got separated from its herd.*' Notice that the first 'it's' has an apostrophe while the second 'its' doesn't. The first one is a contraction of 'it is'; always use the apostrophe for this contraction. The second is a possessive (like my, your, his etc) and doesn't have an apostrophe. You now have all the facts you need in order to use this punctuation mark correctly in the vast majority of situations.

The use of the comma, on the other hand, is harder to pin down. It is used in lots of ways, though a good rule of thumb is to remember that its main purpose is to show the reader where to break up the sentence to pause, or take a breath. Two common issues are:

1 Separating two independent sentences with a comma: *He didn't go to the party, he didn't have the money.* Grammatically, these two parts make separate sentences. You should separate them with a full stop or a semi-colon. So either of these would be fine: '*He didn't go to the party. He didn't have the money.*' or '*He didn't go to the party; he didn't have the money.*' Semi-colons are useful when two sentences follow close together and one explains the other, as in the example given.

2 Don't use a comma after conjunctions such as *and, but, when,* or *because.* For example: *They need to pay the invoice by the end of the month but, they don't have the money.* In speech we often pause there for a little dramatic effect but it will only confuse your reader. Neither should you put any comma before the conjunction: *They need to pay the invoice by the end of the month, but they don't have the money.* However, this is not such a serious matter, and if your sentence is quite long, the comma may actually be appropriate. A comma is acceptable in the middle of your sentence if your conjunction is at the beginning: *When he comes through the door, we want everyone to cheer.* Also: *If she calls, I'm not here.*

This is just a taster. If you find this too brief, or generally confusing, you should go over it in more detail with the aid of a style guide. There are some very comprehensive ones for the use of journalists and publishers, as well as handy tips on the internet.

Best of all would be a colleague or family member who is knowledgeable and willing to proofread your work. Good feedback will improve your performance far more quickly than private study.

# Conclusion

We said at the beginning that you need to count structure, accuracy, clarity and tone as your strengths, and we have given you some indications of how to achieve this:

1 Define your purpose.

2 Assess your reader's wants and needs.

3 Structure your content in the order that best fits your purpose, audience and professional context.

4 Aim for clarity and simplicity as you write – use language that you and your reader understand easily.

5 Eliminate common errors and make yourself aware of the rules of grammar and punctuation.

The time you spend developing good habits will pay off in a number of ways. First, you will save time by writing more succinctly and avoiding confusion. Your clients and colleagues will also see you as effective and methodical, rather than disorganized and careless. Most importantly, people will respond to your messages more promptly and helpfully, and you will have more power to influence people to do what's best for you and for themselves.

If you would like to take an online assessment in written English and business writing, please go to **www.freshpd.com** and follow the links you find there.

# Presentation skills

## Introduction

Your ability to influence others, as a professional, will certainly be enhanced if you have good presentation skills. What do we mean by 'good presentation skills'? Essentially it comes down to two things: first, getting your ideas across with simplicity and clarity; second, being able to answer confidently any questions that arise. These two things are probably not new to you, and you may well have practised them in other contexts: debating, presenting topics at school or university, giving speeches at social events such as weddings or anniversaries. In this skill area, however, we have seen many people find difficulty in translating their experience gained outside work into a good presentation style at work. When you presented a seminar at university you felt perhaps that it was all part of the learning experience, but when presenting in a work context you may feel there is much more pressure – from your managers, peers and clients – to get things exactly right. And when you feel under pressure, it is even harder to perform well.

In today's environment, being able to present well is an important skill to have. You might be asked to lead or contribute to a training session, either internally or externally. You may be speaking at a conference or a seminar, or you may be asked to present to a client meeting some aspect of what is being worked on. You could be given the task of introducing a speaker at an event, and managing the question and answer session. Or you could be leading or taking part in a formal pitch for new work. These are just a few examples of the times when presentation skills will be called upon in your professional life. There are many others.

The good news is that, with practice and application, everyone can improve their presentation skills and can learn to feel confident about this aspect of work. Figure 5.1 below sets out the steps required to give a good presentation. We will touch upon each of these in this chapter, but at this point it is interesting to note that the actual delivery of the presentation is only one part of a much bigger process. Many people focus all their attention on their delivery – how they look, sound and feel when they are up at the front speaking. What we would like you to see is that your delivery is part of a bigger picture and that if you also focus on the steps beforehand, you will see the rewards. You should ensure that you have great content that is appropriate for your audience, well structured and simply put. The confidence you gain from knowing that your material is good will be reflected in how you look and sound on the day – we have seen this come true time and time again.

**FIGURE 5.1**   Presentation skills

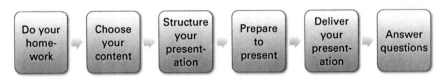

# Do your homework

This is about understanding as much as you can about your audience and the practicalities before you even start to think about putting your presentation together. Ask some straightforward questions in good time and ensure that you get the answers. Professionals can sometimes assume that having an area of specialist knowledge is enough to get them through a presentation, but to be really polished and effective, you will need to put in some effort.

Why? Take an example: addressing a group of 100 people at a conference who are well versed in your topic and for whom it is within their area of expertise will require a completely different approach to addressing 20 new graduate trainees who know little or nothing about the subject. The number of people invited and their level of knowledge about your topic are usually simple enough things to find out. They will have a huge impact on your presentation. So think about the following:

## Who will be there?

Think about the people who are coming. You may be able to find out more than just the overall number and their level of prior knowledge. See if you can glean why they will be at your presentation and what they are hoping to find out. This gives you useful information when you're considering what content to include and how to structure it – and prevents you from wasting time on a presentation that won't meet the needs of your audience. If you know people who will be in the audience you could ask them about what they would like you to include or to concentrate on. Anything you can glean in advance will be helpful.

## Practicalities

Research the practicalities surrounding your presentation. You'll need to know exactly how much time you have, and the kind of room and set-up you'll be using. If possible, have a look at the venue beforehand so that you can envisage where you will be and how your audience will be seated. There is nothing more stressful on the day than walking into a room for the first time and feeling intimidated by its size, or by the way the chairs are arranged, or by the distance between you and your audience. Perhaps you are only presenting to 10 people in a small meeting room. In that case, check whether there is enough space for everyone to sit comfortably, and to hold any laptops and other equipment you or they may use.

## Technical considerations

Check what technical facilities you will have access to and what you need to provide beforehand, or bring with you on the day. You need to be familiar with the technology you will be using, and feel comfortable with it, so that you can focus on your presentation without being distracted. If you know that you get nervous with new technology, see whether you can arrange a quick run-through with it before the day of your presentation.

## Time of day

Be clear about what time of day your presentation will be. Is it first thing in the morning, or after the working day has finished? How will your audience be feeling at that time? Notoriously, the time straight after lunch is one when people find it very hard to maintain concentration, so if that is when you are presenting you might have to work even harder than usual to grab – and keep – attention. And is yours the first of the presentations or the last? If you are first, your audience should be fresh, but if not you need to bear in mind that the audience has been listening to others for some time.

## Example

Let's take an example. You have been asked to make a speech at a friend's wedding – you have said yes and now you are a little nervous about it. You already know the date (so you know how long you have in which to prepare) and you probably know roughly how many people are coming. That's all you know so far, but ask yourself: is there any other information I could get? You could find out exactly how many guests will be there, and also what the age range will be, which will help you craft a speech with broad appeal. Are you expected to talk for 5 minutes or 15? You'll want to speak for long enough but not too long – nobody wants your speech to go over time! How many speeches are there in total and where are you in the line-up? You may be giving the only speech, or you may be one of five. In each case you should try to imagine yourself as one of the guests listening. What is the venue like and where will you be speaking from? If you are speaking from your seat at the table, as sometimes happens, it may help you to feel more relaxed. On the other hand, if there is a podium for the speakers at the front of the room it would be useful to know about this in good time (and not simply to find out on the day, when you may already be feeling nervous).

From this example, you should be able to see that there is a lot of background information you can easily find out. This will help you to decide what kind of speech will be suitable. Then you can start to plan what you will say, put your speech together and rehearse a little. In this way, you can do something to minimize your nerves beforehand and on the day. You can apply the same principles to any presentation you ever have to give.

Set out below is a checklist of information to obtain before you start planning your presentation.

---

### Checklist of background information

**My audience:**

- How many people are likely to be there?

- Why are they coming? Are they volunteers or is it compulsory?

- What is their level of knowledge about the subject? Are they expert? Are they beginners? Will there be a range of knowledge?

- Do I know some or all of the audience?

**Audience expectations:**

- What are people expecting to learn from my presentation?

- If I have a mixed audience, will individuals have different expectations?

- What will the attitude of my audience be to this topic, and to me?

**Basics:**

- How much time is allocated to me?

- What time is my presentation?

- Am I the first, the last or in the middle? Or am I giving the sole presentation?

**Venue:**

- Where will I be presenting from?

- How will the audience be seated?

- What technology is available? Do I know how to use it?

# Choose your content

The key to a good presentation is having the right content. Through doing your homework, as recommended above, you should have a good idea of what the audience is expecting and are interested in, and what their attitude will be to your material. You can use that information to pick the appropriate content for this audience. Remember that if you are presenting to other professionals you will need to make different content choices than when presenting to a general audience, because of levels of background knowledge on your subject.

## What does my audience need to know?

Start by thinking about what your audience needs, and wants, to know. This is probably only a small part of what you personally know about this topic. For example, if you are giving a talk on an unusual piece of work you have done recently, the audience is going to be interested much more in the unusual aspect of that piece of work, and its practical application – in other words, the insight you have gained and can pass on – than they are in all the specifics of the work. So in this case, you might choose to give just a little background on the piece of work for context, and then spend most of your time on what the audience is really there to find out. Remember that it often feels more comfortable to focus on what you know best (in this case, the details of the work you did) but this may not be what the audience is there to hear.

## What is my key message?

Having decided what your audience wants to know from your presentation, you now need to think about your key message. What one, simple, thought underlies everything you will be saying? Can you express this to yourself in one sentence? It is important at this stage, before you do anything else, to be very clear about your key message – because if you lack clarity this will be reflected in your presentation. In this example, you might decide that your key message is: 'the most important thing that comes out of this piece of work is how a small change in our communication within the team can make a huge difference to our clients'. You would then choose your content to back up this message, demonstrating how you changed the communication within the team, how it made a difference to your client, and how this might have wider application.

## What information conveys my key message?

You know what your key message should be, based on audience needs and expectations. You now have to choose – out of all the information you have

– what pieces of information to use to make the case for your key message. This is no easy task, so prepare to spend some time on it. Challenge yourself: does my content really put my message across? Is any of my content unnecessary to my message? In the example above, all your content should be focused on demonstrating how communication within the team changed for this piece of work, how it made a difference to your client, and how this might have wider application. You might choose to say very little about the piece of work itself, only using details that illustrate your other points, and you might choose to concentrate on how you think this new way of working could make a difference to everyone in the room. In other words, this presentation might be less about the past and more about the future.

## How interactive do I want this to be?

At this stage you should also think about how interactive you want to be with the audience. Is there any opportunity to engage the audience by asking them questions or starting a general discussion? You should consider here the benefits versus the drawbacks of an interactive approach. If you are not familiar with facilitating a discussion with the audience, then as the presenter it is all too easy to lose control of your content and focus, and to find time galloping away. People in the audience may want to hold the floor, or may get involved in heated debates with each other, making it hard for you to carry on as planned. However, the big advantage of this approach is that you involve, and interact with, your audience, which makes the audience more engaged with what you are saying.

In the wedding example above, you would not expect much interactivity because the audience wants to hear *you* and will not be expecting to answer questions. On the other hand, in most work contexts you will be expected to engage the audience. If you are running a training session, interactivity and engagement are essential, so in that case make sure you yourself have had some training in how to facilitate discussion. Even if you are presenting on a particular piece of work you have done, or are speaking at a conference, you can still look for opportunities in your presentation to facilitate discussions and engage those you are talking to.

## Have I got too much material?

Before you start to structure your content, do a final sense check to see whether the content you have chosen will fit into your allotted time. Remember that you should allow enough time for questions from the audience at the end of the presentation, and also any time for questions you might be asking the audience. This all reduces the amount of time you can speak for. If you think you have too much content, then go back to your key message – and be brutal: cut out anything that does not make your key message clearer.

# Structure your content

Now that you know what your key message is, and how you can back this up with content, you will be able to structure your presentation. Aim to put your message across with clarity and simplicity, so that it is easy to understand and remember.

## *Using diagrams*

Some people find a spider diagram is a useful tool – this is a visual representation of what you are trying to say. If you are a person who finds it useful to have visual material (like charts, or diagrams) to help you understand, then you are likely to find a spider diagram helps you to make choices about your material. To make a spider diagram, take a blank sheet of paper and write down the title of your presentation in the centre. Then draw spokes coming out from the centre and use these to record all the facts, ideas and knowledge you want to use. Don't worry if the sheet looks scrawled and untidy. Now look at all the information on the sheet and think about a logical order or sequence you can put it into. What does the audience need to know first, and how should you build on that initial content? Use the spider diagram to group content together (you can use circles for this), to cross things out if they are not going to be included, and to work on a logical flow for your material.

---

**Structure checklist**

- Always aim to make your key message clear and memorable for the audience.

- Break down your content into manageable chunks.

- Signal the beginning of a chunk by telling the audience what you are going to say in that chunk; at the end of the chunk summarize what you have told them. Generally, people need to hear a message a few times, so do not be afraid to repeat your main points.

- Where will you build-in questions for the audience? Think about how you will phrase your questions to make them unambiguous and clear.

- What will you say in your introduction and your conclusion? It is often easiest to craft these at the end, when you are happy with the flow of your content.

- When you have put your structure in place, check that it does put your key message across.

## Example

Let's take an example. You have been asked to go to a local sixth-form college and take part in a careers event, talking about your professional career to date. You have a short slot of 20 minutes and you will have 15 people in the audience. You have decided that your key message for this audience is that your job is varied, interesting and exciting, with great opportunities (but is highly competitive to get into, so the sixth formers should make a start now on getting the right CV). How can you get this across in a very short time and still leave room for questions?

You decide that you should spend 10 minutes talking and allow 10 minutes for discussion, as the organizer has told you that several members of the group are very keen to learn more about your job. After trying out various structures you decide on the following:

1 Introduction: who I am, what my career path has been to date, my key message.

2 First section: anecdotes about my day-to-day work that illustrate its variety and interest.

3 Second section: examples of some of the great opportunities I have had in my job to travel and to develop my skills.

4 Third section: my advice for sixth formers based on the current entry requirements for the job and my experiences helping with graduate recruitment.

5 Summary: where to get more information and advice, recap of key message.

6 Questions.

Looking at this structure it is clear that you cannot spend as long as you would like to on each section, so you decide to spend more time on the anecdotes about your day-to-day work, which you know will bring your job to life, and also on your advice to sixth formers based on your experience of current recruitment, which is a piece of insight you know they will value. You will cover the other sections only briefly. You are happy with this structure; you can see how it puts your key message across and feel you can now go on to prepare for the presentation.

# Prepare to present

Preparation should include making your notes; preparing slides, handouts and other materials; rehearsing. Make sure you start these in plenty of time.

## Make your notes

Full scripts are rarely the best form of notes as they lack sparkle and spontaneity. If you have ever been to a presentation that consisted of someone reading from their notes, you will know how dry it can be. The audience loses interest quickly and the key message is lost. Because professionals are used to giving advice in written form, they can sometimes adopt a familiar practice by writing full presentation notes. Rather than a full script, make the kind of notes that are going to help you to be confident and in control of your material on the day. One popular method of preparing notes is to use blank postcards; if you are doing this, here are some tips:

- Have one heading only on each card.
- Back up the main heading with a key word or phrase, a story or an example – whatever the main piece of content is.
- Write in capitals and use colours to highlight anything particularly important.
- Use a staple or a tag to keep your cards together and in the right order.
- Keep the cards simple – they are there to jog your memory rather than hold all of your content.

## Prepare other materials

At this point, you should also prepare your slides and any other materials. Try to apply the same principles with slides as with your notes. The slides are there to help the audience to understand your message, so they should be simple, well chosen and linked to what you will be saying. Avoid the temptation to have large numbers of slides – if you do, you are likely to bore the audience – and make each slide simple so that it does not detract from what you are saying. Remember: less is more.

Will you have any handouts? Handouts have three main purposes: 1) as a reminder of your presentation; 2) as a place for audience members to write during your presentation; 3) as a place to provide facts and figures that you cannot deal with in your verbal presentation. Often a handout is not necessary. If you are considering a handout, think carefully about what the audience will really want or need – and produce something that matches those wants and needs. Keep it short and simple. Make sure your handout has all of your contact details on it.

Something often overlooked is the relationship between what you are saying verbally, your slides and your handouts. These should all complement each other. They should be in the same language, and should deal with the same material in a way that makes them harmonious. Do not make new points in your handout or slides that you do not deal with in your presentation, and try to ensure that the key points of your presentation are all reinforced in your slides and handouts. Check your slides and handouts carefully before your rehearsal.

## Rehearse

You have now assembled everything you are going to use for your presentation and are ready to rehearse. Time spent rehearsing is never time wasted, so try to have at least one rehearsal. If you can find a friend or colleague to act as your audience and provide feedback, all the better. If not, find a quiet room and practise your presentation out loud (and if you can, record yourself). It is really important that you practise aloud rather than reading quietly to yourself, because you need to hear how your material will sound, and you need to time yourself to see how long your presentation lasts.

At the rehearsal, run through your presentation from start to finish with no stops, just as you will deliver it on the day. Try to make the conditions as similar as you can to those you will experience on the day – stand up, be at the front of the room looking into the audience, present at the pace you intend to use, use your slides and handouts, even rehearse at the venue itself if possible. If you have a friend or colleague watching you, ask them to bear certain feedback points in mind, for example:

- How long was my presentation?
- What did you think was my key message? Was it clear?
- Was my content logically structured and easy to follow?
- Did my slides help or hinder your understanding of my message?
- How was my pace and volume?
- How was my body language?
- Is there anything I should cut out?
- How might I improve the overall presentation?

Once you have had the feedback, or analysed these points yourself, make any necessary changes (such as cutting down your presentation to fit within your time allocation, or restructuring the order of your content if it is too hard to follow). Do a final check on your slides, handouts and notes to ensure that they all complement each other, as detailed above.

## Anticipate questions

During your preparation phase, anticipate some of the questions that you are sure will be raised. You can prepare for these and have an answer ready, or at least some key points that you will make. Then think more laterally of questions that might come up from a difficult member of the audience who is trying to test you. How will you deal with these? Prepare an answer if you can, or a way of dealing with the question if you do not have an answer. Finally, how will you deal with a question that you have not anticipated, and which is a complete surprise? Practise how you will respond. One way of dealing with such a question is: acknowledge it, comment that it is an interesting question that you haven't considered before, then say you will need to look into it and will get back to the person if they give you their contact details at the end of the presentation.

# Deliver your presentation

Most people have nerves on the day of their presentation, no matter how good their preparation – and the bigger the occasion, the greater the nervous tension. Your aim is to control your nerves and stop them from getting the better of you. To do this, try one or more of the ideas suggested in this checklist.

## Checklist for controlling nerves

**Preparation:**

- Be fully prepared and rehearsed.
- Be confident that because of your preparation nothing will let you down.
- Do some breathing exercises before you start.
- Decide what you will do with your notes – either hold them or put them on the table.

**Make a good start:**

- Know your first sentence or paragraph.
- Start slowly.
- Avoid humour to begin with.
- Have an opening that really captures the attention of your audience and makes them want to listen.

**Posture and body language:**

- Hold on to something such as a pen if you need to.
- Pay attention to your stance early on.
- Decide what you are doing with your arms before you start.
- Maintain good eye contact with your audience.
- Smile when appropriate.

### First impressions

You should make a good first impression. If you feel confident, you will look confident – so make sure you have done whatever preparation you need and are well organized on the day. Be aware of your posture – try to be relaxed and natural, with no gestures that could be distracting to the audience (such as twisting a pen or piece of jewellery). Even if you know you are blushing and feel nervous, don't focus on that. Take a few deep breaths and start in a confident voice (it's a good idea to know your first few lines so that you can deliver them at a good pace and without needing to think about them). Make sure you look at your audience, rather than at the ceiling, floor or back of the room – but scan the audience rather than focusing your gaze on one person.

### Vocal technique

Make your delivery as polished as you can. If you watch any well-known public speaker you can pick up a number of speaking techniques, some of which will fit in with your own presentation style. The best speakers vary their speaking pace and volume throughout their presentation, because delivery at an even speed and with a constant volume is monotonous for the audience. Try to build in variety, for example by slowing your pace at times – especially to emphasize a really key point. If you have a quiet voice, you should also try making some sections louder, and if you are a confident speaker then let some sections be spoken more quietly, for extra effect. Remember not to speak too fast or the audience will find it hard to follow what you are saying – this is something to get feedback on during your rehearsal.

One technique that you should practise and use is the pause, which has several advantages. A pause will never seem as long to the audience as it does to you. It will help you to gather your thoughts for what you will say next, and will let you breathe properly. For the audience, a pause signals that a particular point has been concluded, and allows people to absorb what they have been hearing. And a pause, used effectively, can create suspense and keep people listening. Finally, pausing can prevent you from the habit of saying 'err' or 'umm' at the end of a sentence, since these are substitutes for a natural pause.

# Dealing with the unexpected

You should expect, and be ready to deal with, some surprises on the day of your presentation. A common thing to happen is that you do not have as much time as you thought you would, perhaps because people turn up late (so that you start late) or because the previous speaker overran. What will you do if this happens? The worst thing you could do would be to speed up your delivery and try to get through the entire presentation more quickly. This would make you look out of control and unprepared, and would decrease the chance of your message being understood. It is far better to cut some of your material so that your presentation fits into the available time. You will have to make some speedy decisions, so it is a good idea to decide beforehand what you will leave out if you need to. Perhaps you could cut down the number of examples, or just give the headlines of one section without going into too much detail. If on the day you know you have to shorten your presentation, make a decision early as to your approach and stick to it, then spend the rest of your mental energy on giving a good presentation.

Another issue you could face is presenting to a very different number of people to the number you were expecting. Perhaps there were due to be 20 people and, because of weather and transport problems, only four people have made it. Your presentation was going to be formal, with you standing up at the front of the room, but with just four people in the audience how will you switch your style? You will probably want everyone to move so that you are all sitting round a table (or at least together) and move from a formal presentation into a much more discursive style. Again, this is something to think about in your preparation. Then, if that happens on the day, you will know how to deal with it. In the same vein, think about what you will do if more people turn up than you were expecting – will people need to stand at the back? Have you got sufficient handouts? Will you change your presentation in any way?

Occasionally, someone may ask a question during your presentation. Consider how you will deal with this. Will you answer the question when it is asked, or will you acknowledge the question, make a note of it and answer it at the end? Either method can work, so you just need to know what approach you will use if this happens.

The examples above show that you can deal with almost any unexpected surprises on the day if you are well prepared and have given yourself some options. Try to anticipate some of the things that could happen and what you will do. This is particularly relevant if you know that you get nervous and could be put off your stride if the unexpected happens.

# Answer questions

In Chapter 2 (Communicating with clients, professionals and third parties) we dealt with questioning techniques when it is you who is asking the questions. If questions arise in the context of your presentation, it may be that you are asking the questions, but more often you will be answering them. If you are asking questions of the audience, be clear about why you are asking. If you want to do a very quick straw poll, then you will need a closed question with a yes/no answer. To open up discussion and debate you need an open question, but one that is short and clear so that the audience will understand at once what you want. For example, a closed question after a statement you have made would be: 'do you agree with that statement?' but to open up debate you might ask: 'what do you think is wrong with that statement?'

## Dealing with audience questions

Professionals who are asked to present often say beforehand that their greatest worry is being caught out by a difficult question from the audience. But the same presenters often relax visibly when it comes to questions, because they can be less formal and more themselves – paradoxically, this means that during questions they feel more confident and perform better than in the presentation. In your preparation phase you have already anticipated many of the questions likely to arise, which will help you to feel more confident. Here is a sequence for dealing with any question that you get:

- Listen carefully to the question, focusing on the person asking it.
- If you did not hear the question properly, or haven't taken it all in, ask the person to repeat it (perhaps jotting down the key words to help you).
- If the question is complex, check your understanding of it by paraphrasing it. You could say: 'So if I have understood correctly, you are asking whether...'
- Make sure everyone in the audience has heard the question properly (if not, repeat the question for them by saying: 'The question was...'
- Pause if you need to consider the answer. Do not feel you have to answer as soon as the questioner has stopped speaking.
- Answer the question succinctly and try to make your answer relevant for the whole audience.
- If you don't know what the answer is, don't bluff. It's better to admit it is something you haven't considered before and then either ask if anyone else in the audience has a view, or say that you will check on the answer and get back to the person who asked the question.

Remember that questions allow you to show how professional you are. Not only do you use your professional knowledge in your answers, but in the way that you deal with individuals in the audience you show how courteously you can deal with others. In the way you handle yourself you show how confident you can be, even in a stressful situation.

# Conclusion

Using one example, let's draw all of the points in this chapter together. You have recently written an article and have been asked to present on the subject matter of the article at a small conference, which you know will be good for your network and your own profile. The conference is in three months' time. How can you get ready to deliver the most effective presentation possible?

First, do your homework. You have plenty of time to speak to the conference organizers to find out about the venue arrangements as well as who will be at the conference, what the expected audience for your session is, and what level of knowledge they are likely to have. The people attending have filled in a questionnaire about what they would like to learn at the conference, and you ask to see the results. You look at the names of the people who have already agreed to attend, and realize that you know a few people. So you ask them what aspects of your topic interests them the most, and what would be most useful to hear about. At the end of this information-gathering phase, you feel you have more understanding of what you should focus on.

Now you choose your content. As the author of an article on the subject, you know far more content about your topic than you can deal with at your conference session. So you need to be quite ruthless in deciding on your key message and picking content accordingly. Your article was about a new piece of legislation and how it directly affects the work that you do, and you originally wanted to rehash the article for the conference. But you realize that most people will have read it, and will want something different and immediately useful. You decide to leave out the detail of the new legislation. Your key message is about the practical impact of this legislation and what steps need to be taken now.

Having chosen your content, you need to order it. You summarize all your ideas on a piece of paper, using a spider diagram, and think about the most logical way to organize them. You work out that you can divide the content into four chunks and you decide on the most logical order to follow. You add in a very short introduction and conclusion, both of which state your key message and why it is important for your audience.

Now you work on your notes. You decide to use postcards and to keep them short and clear, with one idea per card. You create your slide presentation in the same way, with one simple message on each slide. You rehearse your presentation in front of a colleague who knows nothing about your topic and get some interesting feedback. Despite your decision to leave out the details of the legislation, your colleague feels too much of that detail has crept in, and there is not enough about the practical impact. This has watered down your key message and, in addition, you have gone 10 minutes over your allotted time, without allowing for questions.

You need to do a fairly dramatic reworking of the presentation, so you go back to your spider diagram again. You try to put yourself into the shoes of an audience member, and conclude that one whole section can be dropped, and that you need more anecdotes and practical examples, but less theory. You rewrite the presentation and record yourself running through it, using your mobile. Your timing is much better and you feel that the content is about right. You are confident that you have prepared well and you send your slides and other materials to the conference organizers.

The final thing for you to do before the day is to anticipate surprises. You decide what material you will cut if you have less than your allotted time, and how you will adapt your presentation if you have a bigger or smaller audience than expected. You also decide that if nobody asks you any questions at the end, you will use a small case study that you have prepared, to get some discussion going.

On the day, you feel you have prepared well and you present confidently and deal with all the questions asked. You leave the conference knowing from the audience reaction and questions that you have delivered your key message very clearly and pitched your presentation at the right level.

This example illustrates the preparation process outlined in the earlier parts of this chapter, building from information gathering, to choosing and structuring your content, preparing well and finally delivering your presentation and answering questions. It is intended to show how everything you do beforehand makes a difference to how you perform on the day. For example, preparing for different eventualities makes you more confident that you can deal with them if they come up, even if they never do, and this means you feel more confident generally on the day. If you follow the steps set out here, then you will be on the way to being the most effective presenter you can be.

# Meetings: making an effective contribution

## 06

## Introduction

Meetings take up many hours of our working lives. If you spend an hour each working day in meetings, over the period of a year this will total around 225 hours, the equivalent of 32 working days in meetings. As a professional, because of your specialized knowledge and expertise, and the nature of your work as an adviser, you will have meetings with colleagues, clients and third parties – and you may also attend other work-related meetings, for example of industry bodies or with partners that your organization is involved with. You are likely to spend a significant proportion of every month in meetings, so developing your meeting skills is a good investment of your time and energy. The aim is to make your most effective contribution to each meeting you go to.

You are likely to have experience of meetings outside work. Perhaps you have been on a sports committee, or have taken part in a big project with others that needed significant planning. All of those involved met together, discussed ideas and exchanged information, made plans and took decisions. The meetings you had for those committees or projects needed exactly the same skills as are required for work-related meetings. So this chapter will build on the knowledge and skills you already have. By the end of the chapter you will know how to make an effective contribution, whether you are leading the meeting or are there as a participant. You will know what kind of preparation to do, how to be effective at a meeting, and what you should do following the meeting.

Throughout this chapter we will use a case study: your organization wants to partner with two charities this year, raising funds for the charities in a coordinated way, and allowing people in your organization to get to know the charities really well and feel a sense of helping them. You have been asked to be part of the committee that puts all of this in place and oversees it when it is up and running. You have agreed, because you are genuinely interested in this initiative and want it to work.

# Before the meeting

## *Basics*

Every meeting you go to has unique characteristics: it is a combination of several different aspects. Before you start your meeting preparation you will need to know about each of the following:

### What is the purpose of the meeting?

- Presenting or exchanging information?
- Negotiating?
- Making decisions?
- Allocating actions and tasks?
- Checking progress from previous meetings?

Most meetings are a combination of some, or all, of these things. Everyone coming to the meeting is responsible for making sure that the purpose of the meeting makes sense. For example, if the purpose is just to present or exchange information, could this be done by e-mail instead? Or could information be sent beforehand so that the meeting time is used for questions and challenge? Or to take another example, if the meeting is just to check on progress, could the leader or chair do this by contacting individually those who were taking actions?

Remember that exactly the same techniques can be used for a meeting that is likely to have a positive atmosphere (a meeting with colleagues, say, or with an outside organization) as for a negotiation meeting, which could become more difficult.

### What kind of meeting is it?

- Face to face.
- By telephone.
- By videoconference.
- A virtual meeting.

The type of meeting can make a big difference to how people feel and, therefore, how well they contribute. As an example, a meeting by telephone is often far more convenient than a face-to-face meeting, if the participants would otherwise have to travel. However, because people cannot see each other, they cannot read body language, and do not know if they are about to speak at the same time as someone else. Their concentration may lapse and their attention may drift, because it doesn't feel as formal as a face-to-face meeting. So the meeting has to be far more carefully managed by the chair, and the participants have to pay extra attention to ensure the meeting runs smoothly and achieves its aims.

### What is my role in the meeting?

- Am I the chair of the meeting?
- Am I supporting the chair?
- Am I taking notes or minutes?
- Do I have a point to raise or an item on the agenda?

Again, the role you are playing will differ from meeting to meeting. In some cases you will have called the meeting and will be responsible for setting the agenda and for leading the meeting itself. Sometimes you will be supporting the person who is leading the meeting, and may have helped them to set the agenda, think through the relevant issues to be discussed and decisions to be taken, and to circulate beforehand all the right information. Sometimes you will be taking notes or leading discussion on an item on the agenda. Making an effective contribution will mean different things in each of these cases.

In this chapter we use the word 'chair' to refer to anyone who is leading a meeting. At some meetings there is no official chair, but the person who called the meeting is likely to be leading it and should prepare to do so, because meetings will never function effectively unless someone is in that role.

### Who else is coming to the meeting?

The number of participants and their status in the hierarchy will change the dynamics of a meeting. For example, a one-off meeting with 15 people, ranging from the most experienced in your organization to the least experienced – is likely to feel quite different to a weekly team meeting of five people. In the former, participants may feel more constrained by the size of the meeting and by the more experienced people in the room. In the latter, participants may feel so comfortable that they do not prepare properly and the meeting time is wasted. At any meeting you go to, there may be a mixture of people from your organization and people from outside it, and there may be some that you know and some that you do not. If you can find this information out beforehand it will help you to be prepared.

**CASE STUDY**   Finding out the basics

In our case study, you are attending the first meeting of the Charities Group and you have received an invitation by e-mail from the chair. This tells you that it will be a face-to-face meeting for 90 minutes. You can see that the other participants are a mixture of people at different levels in your organization, including a couple of the senior management. You know some of the people in the group well, but there are others that you do not know at all. You have also been sent a short agenda and it is clear that the purpose of the meeting is introducing the team and discussing the project in general terms.

# Effective preparation

Once you know about the characteristics of the meeting you are going to, there are a number of things you can do to prepare. Have a look at the checklists below for preparation if you are a participant, or the chair.

## Meeting preparation checklist if you are a participant

- Where is the meeting being held and how long will it last? If I need to travel, how long will it take me to get there?
- Have I received the agenda and the supporting papers and documents? Have I read everything?
- Do I have any comments on the agenda or any additions to make to it? Have I given these to the chair in good time?
- Do I understand every agenda item? Does it require an exchange of information, a decision or an action?
- Who else is coming to the meeting and what are their priorities? How could their priorities affect the outcome of the meeting?
- What are the key points that I need to make at this meeting? How will I make them effectively? Should I talk to other members of the meeting beforehand to get support for my key points?
- Have I made good notes to help me in the meeting? Have I done any research I need to do beforehand to improve my understanding?

## Meeting preparation checklist if you are the chair

- Do we need to have a meeting at all? If so, should it be face-to-face or by another method?

- What is the purpose of this meeting?

- Have I put the right things on the agenda? Can anything be dealt with beforehand or outside the meeting?

- Is the meeting length sufficient to deal with everything on the agenda?

- Are the right people coming to the meeting? Is everyone necessary?

- Have I circulated the agenda (and supporting documents) in good time? Have I agreed the agenda with the participants?

- Have I made the arrangements for the meeting?

- Who will take notes and what do we need to circulate after the meeting?

- How will I open the meeting?

## Being efficient

There are a few simple things that will prevent inefficiency at the meeting, and whatever your role you should always consider them, as they are often overlooked.

First, should you be at the meeting at all? Is your presence necessary to achieve the aims? If you think not, then talk to the chair of the meeting.

Second, is the agenda really the right one? Think about the following:

- Can anything be removed from the agenda?
- Does anything need to be added to the agenda?
- Are the points in a logical order?
- Is there enough time to cover all the agenda points properly? Be realistic about how much can be covered in the time available and take items off the agenda if necessary.
- Order the agenda so that the least important items are last and can be dropped if you run out of time. Give your points to the chair in time for the agenda to be changed prior to the meeting.

Third, is everyone coming prepared to be on time for a prompt start to the meeting?

In Chapter 8 we discuss negotiation strategy; if your meeting will contain negotiation then ensure that you have done your strategic preparation beforehand.

**CASE STUDY**    Doing your preparation

In our case study, you now want to do your best preparation for this first meeting. What can you do? A starting point would be to think about the purpose of the meeting. It seems to be introductions – so you could try to find out a little about those participants you don't know. Are they at your level, or above, or below? Do they have a particular interest in this area, or any experience in this area? Are they likely to have a lot of time to commit, or will they be leaving the actions to others?

You find out that many people in the group have a lot of management responsibility already and will not have much time to spare outside the meetings, so you are likely to be asked to share the action points with a few others. This leads you to your next piece of preparation: thinking about how this project might work and what element of it you would like to be given. You can see that there will be two distinct parts to the project: first, choosing the charities for the organization to support; second, managing the fundraising and partnership. You decide that you are more interested in managing the fundraising and partnership, but can see you will also need to have some input into the first stage. You read the short briefing paper from the chair and realize that you have a friend in another organization that has put in place a similar arrangement with a charity recently, so you let the chair know about this. You don't hear anything back but you talk to your friend about how her organization got started with their project. Your friend knows the person who led the team and offers to put you in touch.

# At the meeting

## *The make-up and process of a meeting*

Every meeting has the same basic make-up and process. It will start with an introduction or opening from the chair, who should briefly remind everyone of the purpose of the meeting and clarify the agenda items and the order in which things will be discussed. The chair will also designate roles for the meeting (for example, who will take notes) and outline any rules to be followed.

For each agenda item, there will be a sequence:

- The person proposing the item will put their proposal or outline the information to be given.
- The chair will invite contributions from others and points of view on the agenda item.
- Discussion of views and issues.
- The chair puts options to the meeting to try to gain consensus and agreement.

- Review of consensus and agreement for the agenda item, or, if there is no consensus possible, the item may be put aside to be revisited later in the meeting or at another meeting.
- A quick summary of the agreed decisions and action points from the chair.

At the end, the chair should summarize and close the meeting. This may involve a recap of agreed decisions and action points, gaining agreement on the time, date and venue for the next meeting, clarifying any other follow-up action and thanking the participants for their time.

## The influence of the chair in the meeting

If you are the chair of the meeting, you will see from the above that you play a vital role in setting the tone, managing the contributions from others and helping to gain consensus. A successful chair ensures that everyone has the chance to share his or her views, without one person dominating. He or she knows when to move the discussion on (diplomatically) if it has become stuck, and how to focus on areas of agreement in order to build a consensus, or recognize honestly if no consensus is possible. The role of the chair is not an easy one, but carried out properly it will make a meeting productive and ensure participants remain well-mannered and courteous, even if they disagree with each other.

## The changing dynamics of meetings

When you are agreeing the agenda, be aware that it is a strategic tool. The positioning of certain points can have a huge impact on the achievement – or otherwise – of the meeting's purpose.

As the chair, start off with a couple of easy things to build rapport and trust amongst participants, for example, who will take notes or the timing of breaks. These are usually not contentious and get people thinking in terms of agreement early on. If people do not all know each other, ask them to introduce themselves, as this also helps to build rapport.

Tackle difficult items next and try to allocate sufficient time to items that will need a lot of discussion or where you know (or suspect) that there will be a wide range of views. Allow everyone to speak, eliciting contributions from those who are quieter. Try to encourage consensus before you run out of time – time alone should never be the critical factor in the decision-making process. Remember, you can use the placing of items on the agenda to influence the outcome and to achieve the purpose you want to achieve.

Whatever your role in a meeting, be sure to concentrate all the time, and be aware that you may need to alter your planned approach if the meeting dynamics change. For example, despite good planning, the meeting may run out of time because of unexpectedly lengthy discussion on an issue. People may arrive late or leave early, and this change may disrupt the meeting for a while. Participants may realize through discussion that there is a fundamental issue that needs to be dealt with before any of the agenda items can be sorted out, and this could turn the whole course of the meeting down another path. The meeting may give rise to anger or emotion, and people could become difficult. If any kind of disruption occurs, it may influence the discussions, the decision-making process and the final outcome (and action points). All the participants have a role to play in salvaging the meeting.

**CASE STUDY** The first meeting

In our case study, the chair opens the meeting and then asks everyone to introduce themselves. She reminds everyone of the purpose of the meeting – to start planning for the two charities project – and then asks if everyone has read her briefing paper and is happy to discuss it. Unexpectedly, one of the other participants raises an objection. He mentions that he has been speaking to a number of people he knows in the wider organization and that there is a lot of disapproval of the 'two charities' idea. People have been fundraising for a number of different charities over the years and don't like the idea that there will be official support for only two charities. The chair asks if anyone else has had the same experience, and a few other people agree that they have had the same feedback.

You are then able to say that your friend's organization experienced the same challenge, and can talk about how it was overcome there. There is discussion about whether the same could be done in your workplace, and it is generally agreed that the appropriate solutions to this challenge need careful thought, but that the meeting should proceed as planned. The chair will go back to senior management after the meeting to ensure they want to continue with this initiative. And the charities group will make sure that it spends time and thought on how to get people to support the idea.

The chair now only has 30 minutes left for the rest of the meeting so she suggests that, rather than rush the discussion, a smaller team should produce a timetable and project plan for discussion at the next meeting. It is agreed, and you volunteer to be one of this smaller team and to draw on the experience of your friend's organization if possible. The date and time of the next meeting are set and the chair concludes the meeting.

# Participating in meetings effectively

Whatever your role in meetings, there are ways to participate that ensure you are a helpful member of the group, even if you disagree with others. See the following chart for a list of meeting dos and don'ts.

| Do | Don't |
|---|---|
| • Prepare your points. | • Be late. |
| • Be ready to make a constructive contribution and build on what others have said. | • Interrupt other participants or speak over them. |
| • Be diplomatic and courteous. Make notes of the key points you need to put across. | • Waffle. |
| | • Mislead. |
| | • Make assumptions without checking them. |
| • Have clear reasons and evidence for what you are saying, and be prepared to discuss them. | • Speak about something you know little or nothing about. |
| • Be aware of your own body language and that of others, particularly: | • Lose your composure. If you feel this happening, find a way to take a few breaths or have a short break, and calm down. |
|   – eye contact; | • Be afraid to ask questions in case you look stupid. If you have been listening carefully and don't understand something, chances are that others also won't understand it. |
|   – facial expression; | |
|   – head movements; | |
|   – posture and stance; | |
|   – gestures; | |
|   – hands. | |
| • Take notes of what others have said. | |
| • Ask good questions to clarify understanding. | |
| • Speak in a clear voice, in good sentences, and sound confident. | |
| • Listen to others carefully. | |
| • Anticipate objections and know what you will say in response. | |

## What is my message?

You should be able to summarize the key points that you would like those present at the meeting to go away with. The message should always be clear in your mind when thinking about your contribution to the meeting, then you can make sure that the message is convincingly put across and that what you want people to do as a result is easily understood.

## *Delivering the message*

When you are speaking, try to put your message across eloquently and in plain language – for professionals, this can be more difficult than it sounds, as there is often an unconscious temptation to use jargon. Doctors and lawyers, for example, deal with the special language of their professions all the time, and in meetings may be tempted to use jargon. However, those at the meeting who are not doctors or lawyers are likely to miss some or all of the message – and even others from the same profession may not completely understand the message if they do not ascribe the same meaning to the piece of jargon, or do not know what it means. The consequence is that the recipient now has an incorrect understanding of the message. It is your responsibility to ensure that people at the meeting understand what you are saying – summaries, and asking for feedback from others on your points, are good ways to check that people are following and understanding you.

**CASE STUDY**    Participating in meetings

You are now at the second meeting of the charity group and the purpose of the meeting is to present and discuss the timetable and project plan. You have agreed to lead the discussion on this, and you know it will be tricky as the timetable is quite tight. To achieve it, everybody will need to agree to take on some of the work.

Your key message is how this project fits into your organization's values. One of its values is supporting the local community, so you believe that the two charities should be local, and that as much as possible should be done to get people from your organization and the charities to get to know each other. You feel that this is the way to get support for the project. You have spent time before the meeting thinking about how best to put this message across so that it appeals to others in the charities group, and you convey your message confidently. You also have some examples of other community projects that have had wide appeal and which people have enjoyed being part of.

This is a great way to preface discussion of the project plan, as everyone feels they have a common goal, and one that fits into what the organization is about. You briefly talk through the project plan and expect everyone to be enthusiastic, but to your surprise you encounter a lot of opposition. Others feel it is too ambitious in its timing, has more work in it than the group can manage, and is too complicated. You then feel very deflated as you have spent a lot of time on it; your first instinct is to defend yourself against the criticism. But the chair sees this and, before you can say anything, asks everyone in turn to summarize their objections to the plan, with reasons, and asks you to make notes. It transpires that the main criticism boils down to this: people are extremely busy, and cannot commit the amount of time it would need to achieve your timetable. You calm down. The chair asks if your small group could replan the timetable with a list of tasks that can be divided among the group, and you agree.

From this meeting you see that you have achieved something positive – everyone agreed with your key message. You have also learnt from your experience: you should have asked people for their feedback, and listened carefully, rather than assuming they would agree. You could even have showed the plan to a few people before the meeting in order to check it with them, and you decide to do this next time round.

## Taking notes

It is a good idea to make notes at meetings, or at the very least as soon as you can after the meeting while discussions are fresh in your mind. Professionals are busy and have many things to juggle, and with so much going on it is impossible to remember the detail of every meeting unless you have some notes to refer to. You will see that even very seasoned chairs are taking notes – and it is a good habit to get into.

If you are the nominated note taker, or know that you will be asked to prepare a summary after the meeting, your notes are even more important. Do not be afraid to ask someone to repeat a point if you did not hear it properly, or to clarify exactly what was meant if you did not understand – without doing so, you will not be able to keep an effective note. Make your notes concise but accurate and, where actions are agreed, keep a note of the tasks, who is carrying them out and the timescales. Remember that, for important meetings, your notes may be relied on some time later, so it is important that they are complete and clear.

---

### Checklist for taking effective notes

- Take a notebook with you, or your laptop, and get yourself set up before the start of the meeting.
- Make a note of everyone who is present.
- Don't try to write everything down word for word – listen carefully and summarize.
- Ask questions to clarify your understanding.
- Ask the speaker to repeat a point if you need to hear it again in order to make an effective note.
- Use headings and numbers to give your notes structure.
- Where actions are agreed, make a clear note of:
  - action points;
  - designated tasks;

- who is responsible for carrying them out;
- the timescale for completion.

- If you are leading on a particular point and cannot take notes at the time because you are contributing, make sure you write your notes on that point as soon as possible following the meeting.

- Read your notes after the meeting to make sure you haven't missed anything and that they are clear.

## *The role of the note taker*

In many formal meetings, the role of the note taker is critical. This is especially true where notes are needed to show compliance – if it is not written down, there is no way to prove how the discussion went. People will remember different parts of the discussion. As a result, months (or years) later there may be no agreement on what happened. If a regulator, court or other enquiry ever needs to know what happened, the importance of the notes cannot be overemphasized. So if you are the note taker in a formal meeting, make careful notes in a formal and impersonal style, keep them structured according to the agenda of the meeting and, where you know that an important point is being debated, ensure your notes cover the discussion in full.

# Dealing with difficult people in meetings

Most professionals will have to deal with difficult people in meetings from time to time. It could be a difficult client who is pushy and aggressive and will not listen to your advice. It could be a colleague who says very little and holds back their opinions until things go wrong – and then you are blamed. It could be a particular and notorious participant who constantly interrupts others and is always waiting to speak, rather than listening.

Table 6.1 sets out some common meeting behaviours, and suggests some strategies for how to deal with them.

**TABLE 6.1** Strategies for managing difficult behaviour in meetings

| Type of behaviour | What you will see | Strategies on how to deal with this |
|---|---|---|
| **Bully or dominator** | This person is pushy and ruthless, and can be either openly aggressive or quietly intense. Does not listen to other points of view and wants to dominate the discussion. | Be assertive and hold your ground. Stay calm and listen carefully. When the person has finished, summarize the point made and then propose how to deal with it. Be brief and businesslike. |
| **Sniper** | Will try to undermine the discussion by using sarcasm or loaded statements at strategic moments. This is an attempt to control. | Make eye contact. Use open questions for clarification of remarks/statements and to bring out the real issue and expose tactics. In private, suggest alternative behaviour in future. |
| **Know-it-all** | Holds forth on issues and perceives new ideas as a challenge. Others do not bother to put forward their views, or if they do, are made to feel that their views are not valuable. | Be prepared – your goal is to open up this person to new information. Summarize his or her views well, show understanding and then show how the new ideas can take these into account. Perhaps make your suggestions sound hypothetical: 'perhaps if we looked at it this way...' |
| **Silent person** | Does not give anything away. Does not provide feedback or views. If it goes wrong may blame everyone else for doing it their way. | Plan enough time to deal with this person and the issues. Ask open questions and make it clear that his or her views would be valuable. Lighten up the discussion as much as possible. |

**TABLE 6.1** *continued*

| Type of behaviour | What you will see | Strategies on how to deal with this |
|---|---|---|
| **Waffler** | Says a lot but is not good at being concise. Cannot stick to the point. Their good ideas may get lost. | Ask closed questions to identify specific ideas or issues and acknowledge the issue or point being made. If appropriate, invite others to comment on the idea or issue, or deal with it yourself. Move the discussion on by raising the next point. |
| **Negative person** | Very focused on tasks and motivated by getting things right and avoiding mistakes. Perfection becomes the standard to reach and everything else falls short. Is doleful and depressing and can dampen the atmosphere of the meeting. | Listen – sometimes this person has spotted something important. Allow him or her to be negative and give him or her time to think, leaving the door open to return to the discussion. Acknowledge his or her good intentions in pointing out problems but maintain your perspective and confidence. |
| **Interrupter** | Does not let other people finish before coming in with his/her own points. Is not listening but is just waiting to speak. | Control potential interruptions by ensuring that the interrupter knows you have seen him or her and that he or she will have a chance to speak. |

**TABLE 6.1** *continued*

| Type of behaviour | What you will see | Strategies on how to deal with this |
| --- | --- | --- |
| Yes person | Will agree to anything and takes on too much to be able to deliver. Tries to please everyone but can become resentful of the burden of work they have got. | Try to ensure that he or she verbalizes their understanding of the work and commitment involved. If necessary, outside the meeting examine whether he or she can really deliver what has been agreed. Reassure him or her that it is much better to be realistic than optimistic when taking on tasks. |
| Maybe person | Wants to get along with people. Will keep putting off crucial decisions in case the consequences are unpopular – until it is too late. | Reassure this person that open communication is helpful, then explore the options and obstacles. Listen carefully for signals of hesitancy and then dig deeper. Stay calm and help him or her to reach a decision. |

## Assertive behaviour

The key to managing these difficult people is to stay calm and polite, being assertive but never aggressive. If you are being assertive you are standing up for your own rights and opinions in such a way that you do not undermine another person's rights or opinions. Being aggressive, on the other hand, means ignoring other people's rights or opinions in order to get your own way or dominate.

Some tips for assertive communication:

- Ensure that your statements are brief and to the point. Use 'I' statements and requests, for example: *I would like you to...*; *I think that...*
- Acknowledge other points of view. Use cooperative statements and questions, for example: *Let's see what everyone else thinks...*; *What do you suggest?*; *How can we resolve this?*

- Use empathetic statements, for example: *I can see that you feel very strongly about this; I can see that you seem worried...*
- Stay calm and do not take things personally.
- Be prepared to compromise.

---

**CASE STUDY**    Difficult people

You are now at the third meeting of the charity group and are presenting the new project plan. You have circulated this before the meeting and have also spoken to the chair about it. She seems fairly happy with it. In the meeting, you come up against a negative person (see the table above) who points out everything wrong with the plan, which is exasperating. This is a fairly senior person in the hierarchy and you do not feel comfortable challenging her. You are not sure what to do. The chair sees this and steps in, acknowledging that the negative person seems worried about the direction the project is taking. The chair has made a note of all the objections and they are discussed in turn – a few of the points are easily disposed of and a few raise real issues. The chair also asks the negative person at some point: 'What do you suggest?'

As the discussion progresses, the negative person can see that her views are being incorporated into the plan and that the plan is better as a result. The remainder of the meeting goes more smoothly and positively. You can see how the chair has used assertive behaviour – empathy, directness, calmness, listening and moving towards action – to get the best from the situation.

# After the meeting

Remember to do your follow-up after the meeting. A few things to remember are:

- Look through your notes and make a list of everything you need to do between now and the next meeting.
- If you are sending out a note of the meeting, or a list of action points, do that as soon as possible.
- Inform anyone else who needs to know what happened at the meeting.
- Have a good personal filing system so you can find your notes easily if you need them.
- Ensure that action points are followed up.
- Prepare for the next meeting.

**CASE STUDY**    After the meeting

At the third meeting of the charity group a number of amendments were agreed to the project plan, and various people agreed to take on pieces of work. You amend the project plan and send it to the group, together with a list of tasks and responsibilities. You also say that you will be following up with each person separately to see if they need any further help or support from you – this is a good opportunity for you to check with each person that they will actually be able to do what they have taken on. You follow up and find out that one or two people cannot make the deadlines you have suggested, so you discuss and agree new dates and agree to follow up with them again in two weeks' time. You put a note in your diary to do this – this means that you will have all the information you need in order to give a progress report at the next meeting.

# Video and telephone meetings

## Tips for different types of meeting

Meetings today come in a variety of forms. Many meetings are still face to face, with everyone in the same room. But increasingly, technology has a part to play in meetings, and they can just as readily become telephone meetings, or video meetings, or even virtual meetings. In these cases, participants are not in the same room and may, or may not, be able to see each other/hear each other.

Professionals use these new technologies because it makes life easier. Perhaps you are based in one city and your client is based in another. Perhaps there are a number of people who must attend the meeting from different countries, and a conference call would be cheaper and would save travel time for many. Perhaps your organization has a number of locations and videoconferencing is the norm. However, despite the advantages, meetings in which the participants are not in the same room present their own challenges. The chair and all the participants will have to work harder to make the meeting successful. Here are a few things to remember:

- Try to make sure that participants have met face to face if possible before moving to a telephone or video meeting. It is easier to build rapport, initially, if you have met in person.

- It is important not to have too many people at a telephone or video meeting. If you are the chair, consider carefully who you have invited; if you are a participant, consider whether or not you need to be present.

- Try to ensure that, just as for a face-to-face meeting, it starts on time and finishes on time. If you are a participant, dial in to the conference call or get to the videoconference promptly.

- Concentrate throughout the meeting. If you are on a conference call you will have less information than usual, as you will not be able to see the body language or facial expressions of other people, so you need to listen hard to verbal contributions. Keep notes.

- Have some kind of system so that people are not talking over each other. The chair will need to be a strong presence and may need to manage the order in which people speak, if there are many people at the meeting.

- If you are in a videoconference, be aware that others can see you remotely even though you are not in the same room. Behave as you would if you were all in the room together (so, for example, if you need to leave the room, let everyone know you are going out).

- Think about what you can send to people in advance to assist them in processing what they are hearing on the telephone or by videoconference. Structure charts, diagrams and summary documents are all helpful.

See the following list of key points to bear in mind if you are participating in a meeting by telephone or in a meeting by videoconference or Skype.

**TABLE 6.2** Participating in a meeting by telephone, video conference or Skype

| Key points for a telephone meeting | Key points for a meeting by videoconference or through an internet facility |
| --- | --- |
| • Prepare your key points before the meeting. Write them down and have them in front of you.<br><br>• Make sure you have the agenda to hand so that you can follow the order of the meeting.<br><br>• Dial in to the meeting on time.<br><br>• Listen actively throughout the whole meeting.<br><br>• Keep your own notes of what is being said and who is speaking.<br><br>• Do not speak over anyone else – try to make it clear you have a point to make and then wait for a suitable moment.<br><br>• Mute your telephone if you are in a noisy environment.<br><br>• Stay on the line for the whole of a meeting, as you would stay in the room until the end of a face-to-face meeting. | • Make sure you know how to use the technology (audio and video).<br><br>• Be at the meeting at the start.<br><br>• If you can be seen, then your posture and demeanour should be exactly the same as in a formal meeting.<br><br>• Listen actively throughout the whole meeting.<br><br>• Keep your own notes of what is being said and who is speaking.<br><br>• Do not speak over anyone else – try to make it clear you have a point to make and then wait for a suitable moment.<br><br>• Speak a little more slowly than you would in a face-to-face meeting, and try to structure your points very clearly to aid understanding.<br><br>• If you can be seen, try to look at the camera when you are talking, rather than down at your notes. |

# Conclusion

Whether you are the leader of the meeting or a participant in the meeting, an effective contribution involves much more than merely turning up to the meeting on time with all the papers. As a professional, there will be times when you are overloaded with work, and have back-to-back meetings, with little time to prepare or to do follow-up. This is part of life, but where possible you should try to carve out a little time (even if it is only 10 minutes) to do some meeting preparation. You will have seen from this chapter the kind of preparation that can make your contribution to the meeting effective and useful.

In the meeting itself, be prepared both to make your key points and to deal with the unexpected. As we have seen, you may encounter changing dynamics in a meeting and be faced with difficult people – be flexible and adaptable, and have strategies to deal with these. Above all, remember to stay calm and professional and to leave a good impression of yourself and your capabilities on those who were at the meeting.

Finally, do not forget to follow up. There is little point in having a meeting if no one attends to the action points afterwards – do not assume that someone else will be responsible for this and will chase you on your own action points. Make sure that you take responsibility for them and are able to report back on progress by the time of the next meeting.

If you follow these simple rules then you are sure to make an effective contribution, whatever your role in a meeting.

# Networking

## 07

## Introduction

The most successful professionals tend to be those who continually cultivate and maintain productive relationships both inside and outside their workplace. In a professional services business it is important to maintain effective communications and high quality relationships with:

- existing clients of the business;
- prospective clients – those who might use the business in the future;
- current and prospective referral sources (eg banks and financial advisers) that could introduce prospective clients to the business;
- intermediaries (eg other professionals) who could introduce prospective clients to the business.

These are the people that you should be networking with. Although very few people are 'naturally gifted' networkers, the good news is that networking is a skill you can learn. Effective networking shows that you are taking responsibility for your own career and seeking to develop new business. It also demonstrates that you are involved and interested in the development of new business – because an effective professional does not sit and wait for things to happen.

Networking is a natural, common-sense process made up of activities that are familiar to you already. You already have to cultivate contacts and find information in your day-to-day work and in your life generally. So do not think of networking as something that is different to how you operate already – it is not. It is simply putting the same skills and processes into the working environment, but in a structured way. Facebook, LinkedIn and Twitter are examples of new-media communication tools (of which there are many) that make it much easier to connect and network with greater frequency and fluency and with many more people.

In this chapter we are going to concentrate on identifying your network; developing and strengthening it, as well as looking at some of the core skills of networking.

# What is networking?

Networking is about how visible you are, or how many other people know that you exist and that you have (or have access to within the business that you work for) certain areas of expertise and depth of experience.

You already have a large network of contacts in existence – this is often forgotten, neglected or overlooked. What you have to do is to learn how to access that network as effectively as possible.

Carried out in the right way, networking is an invaluable business development tool. For instance, did you know that:

- A referral generates 80 per cent more results than a cold call.
- More than half of all jobs are found through networking.
- Most people you meet have at least 200 contacts.

In other words:

> *Truly effective networking is based on relationships that are cultivated and nurtured so that a mutual exchange of information, advice and support is given and received.*
>
> L M Tullier, *Networking for Everyone!* (1998)[11]

Networking is about knowing who you are and the skills you have – and ensuring that others know the same. It is also about your being aware of the expertise and resources you have access to in the business in which you work and ensuring that others are made aware of your access to that expertise and those resources – *I may not be able to do this for you but X in our Y team will.* Enlist the help of others, eg make sure you have read all promotional materials for the business in which you work and network with the members of other teams.

Networking is not something that is the sole responsibility of the owners of the business; they may lead networking activities, for example, by initiating lunches or approving client events, but you will be expected to play a role in ensuring their success.

# What is a network?

A network can be described as a set of individual people, organizations (or families) and the relationships that hold them together. The basis of those relationships is an interchange or exchange of information, data, goods and services, social or financial support. The strength of what holds the network together depends on the number and types of contact, the frequency of those exchanges and the degree of proximity or intimacy involved.

Networks have always existed: humans have always built relationships and formed groups as they have communicated and collaborated. Your network is based on personal relationships. These may exist within a business or organization or across organizational borders. The main purpose of the network is to share information and advice, although not necessarily just in the context of work.

An example of using a personal network would be when you have been given a new project in an unknown area. One of the first things that you would do is to contact people who know and understand that area and who can provide background information or give advice on how to solve any potential problems.

A number of formal network groups already exist, eg more traditional groupings such as Rotary and Round Table. There are also modern groupings such as BNI Business Networking Groups where you have to create your own individual network, developing individual contacts.

## What does your individual network look like?

You should put your existing network into a visual form and assess where you are and where gaps may exist in your network. To do this you will need to take stock of the people you know, or to whom you could have access. It is helpful to think of broad categories of contacts, including: personal, work, education, professional groups and multimedia, eg websites, e-mail, news groups, chat rooms etc. These broad categories can then be subdivided into subcategories, (eg 'personal' can be broken down into family, friends/acquaintances, clubs/organizations, community groups etc). Follow the instructions set out below to create your own network spider diagram:

1 Take a sheet of paper, draw a small circle in the middle and insert the word 'me'.

2 Now think of the spheres of influence in your life and draw a spoke out from the circle with the name of each sphere of influence (personal contacts, professional groups, work, multimedia, professional service contacts etc)

3 From each sphere draw branches with the names of the key people with whom you have a relationship within each sphere of influence.

4 Draw connections from these people showing the links they have to other contacts.

To assist you in creating your network diagram, listed below are examples of possible headings for your contacts and 'sample' categories. This list is not exhaustive.

**Personal contacts**

- family friend/acquaintances;
- clubs/organizations (eg gym, sports clubs, cultural groups etc);
- community groups (eg charities, governing bodies, neighbourhood groups etc).

**Multimedia contacts**

- internet newsgroups;
- websites;
- e-mail contacts;
- Facebook;
- LinkedIn;
- other media contacts.

**Education contacts**

- fellow students in school/higher education;
- teachers/lecturers/professors; advisers (eg career advisers, personal tutors etc);
- professional development/ continuing education (tutors, delegates at seminars, workshops etc).

**Work contacts**

- colleagues and co-workers (present and past);
- supervisors/bosses (present and past);
- third-party contacts (eg freelancers, counsel, experts, agents, etc);
- volunteer work colleagues (eg pro bono units, CABs etc).

**Personal and professional services contacts**

- doctors;
- dentists;
- lawyers;
- accountants;
- financial advisers/experts;
- bankers;
- insurance experts;
- property experts (estate agents, surveyors etc).

**Professional group contacts**

- membership of professional/trade organizations (eg RICS, RIBA etc);
- networking groups (eg business clubs, breakfast clubs etc);
- fellow trade union members and contacts made through the union.

## Testing the strengths and weaknesses of your network

Once you have identified the sources of people for your network then it is time to take stock of where you stand. You can use the following checklist as a starting point (feel free to amend it to include any specific categories relevant to you).

| Personal contacts | Strengths | Weaknesses |
|---|---|---|
| Family | | |
| Friends / acquaintances | | |
| Social groups | | |
| Community groups | | |
| Neighbours | | |
| Sports groups | | |
| Work contacts | | |
| Co-workers | | |
| Supervisors | | |
| Colleagues | | |
| Clients | | |
| Volunteer work | | |
| Education | | |
| Fellow students | | |
| Teachers/lecturers | | |
| Advisers | | |

| Personal contacts | Strengths | Weaknesses |
|---|---|---|
| Continuing professional development | | |
| Professional groups | | |
| Professional/trade associations | | |
| Networking groups | | |
| Professional advisers | | |
| Multimedia | | |
| Internet | | |

Having established what your unique network actually is you can then decide how to develop it. Like any business, nothing stands still and your network will be constantly changing.

# Planning your networking strategy

## Establishing clear goals

The first step in networking is to know why you are doing it. Without a goal in mind, networking is undirected and a poor use of your time.

Strategic networking is high-quality networking. It is based on getting to know the people who can support you in reaching your goals. Think of goals as the results you want to achieve in any given situation. An example of a goal may be to expand your contacts in a particular industry sector in order to generate new business.

## Setting objectives to reach your goals

The next step will be to set objectives that will help you reach your goals. Objectives are milestones along the path to meeting your goal. They should be specific, measurable, agreed, realistic and a timely means to a desired end. If, for example, your objective is to extend your contacts in a particular industry sector, key objectives in reaching that overall objective should include:

1 Reviewing existing work for clients in that industry sector by the business as a whole and looking to see where demand does or may exist for the services that the business can offer.

2 Reviewing the position of a competitor business in that sector.

3 Reviewing sector trends showing where demand is likely to grow or where it may decline.

## Creating a plan to meet your objectives

A plan in this context will be a list of networking activities (connecting with people and information) that will lead to successful completion of your overall objectives – in other words an effective 'to do' list.

A plan to meet the second objective listed above (reviewing a competitor's position in the sector) would include a review of:

- the trade press, directories and websites;

- competitor marketing (eg their websites, newsletters, blogs etc);

- discussions with clients in the industry sector and colleagues currently doing work for clients in the target sector.

## Characteristics of a successful networking plan

- It should be systematic and support your overall objectives. Planned networking activities should be focused on the outcomes you want to achieve.

- It balances quality and quantity. An effective strategy should enable you to connect with those people with whom you can develop quality relationships.

- It fits your personal style. An effective strategy will not require you to do too many things you are not comfortable with (although this is not a reason to stick within your comfort zone) but will enable you to make the most of your strengths.

Your networking plan should be based on thorough preparation. Even the best networking plan will fail if you have not done your homework, eg researching a business development idea, researching the prospective market and perfecting your communication skills etc.

# Developing your network – places to meet

Networking can happen just about anywhere: face-to-face, by telephone and via the internet (eg from casual telephone conversations to formal client entertaining or events). It is not simply attending client events or taking clients for lunch.

Whether you are interacting with people in an informal or a formal setting, there are key ways to make the most of the encounter.

## Structured networking events and working a room

Some of the best places to meet new contacts or reconnect with existing contacts are events where networking is either directly or indirectly part of the agenda, including conferences, professional association meetings, professional groupings (young professional groups) and 'launch events' set up to inform people of a new service or product. These events offer key opportunities to meet different people, cultivate relationships and gather valuable information about your work area and the business you work for. It should, however, be said that some groupings can end up existing solely of professionals with no other prospective clients.

## Unstructured networking events

Unstructured networking settings offer valuable opportunities to connect with others because, although networking is not the main focus, there are likely to be common interests. In a workshop setting, for example, you have the opportunity to connect with people with the same or similar interests – that is why you are there. Solid relationships can be cultivated in this way and are often longer lasting than those made at structured networking events, which can be quite superficial.

These events are also opportunities to meet others in a non-pressured environment where the emphasis is social or connected to some form of learning or transmission of information rather than just business.

## Networking with existing and prospective clients

Networking with clients creates some unique challenges, which rely on putting into effect key networking skills. Clients will expect you to have certain skills and expertise even when you are a less-experienced professional. Simply saying that you have these skills or this expertise will not be enough. Remember, you may think you are a good networker but that may not actually be the reality.

The aim of any client relationship is to build a long-term, mutually beneficial relationship, not a one-off 'sale'. This is the key to successful networking and the justification of the time you invest in it. Think about why an existing or prospective client should ask you to undertake the work rather than someone from another professional services business who can do the same work for what is likely to be a comparable cost. Ask yourself:

- What unique selling points do I, or the business that I work for, have?
- What is my relevant expertise and experience?
- What is the depth and breadth of expertise and experience of the business that I work for?
- What benefits are there for the client in instructing me or the business that I work for?

# The networking event

## *Your personal pitch*

### Introductions

Attendance at a networking event should be planned to gain maximum advantage. A checklist is set out on page 137 to help your personal planning for the event and your follow up after the event. The checklist also gives you some dos and don'ts for when you are at the event itself.

Key to your success will be how you introduce yourself and your ability to circulate and meet other people – further guidance in these areas is set out below.

It may only take 10 seconds to introduce yourself so getting your introduction right is vital to make an impact. However, get it wrong and you can turn people off or leave them cold. So it is important to capitalize on every opportunity you have to promote yourself and the firm. Remember: you are your own best PR.

A powerful self-introduction should be:

- **Clear:** make sure people know what you do. You want people to be interested but not confused.

- **Concise:** follow the KISS rule – keep it short and simple. Develop an introduction that says what you want to say in 7 to 10 seconds otherwise the other person may lose interest.

- **Distinctive:** be catchy enough to distinguish yourself from others whilst also being professional. You can do this by, for example, telling people what you love about what you do, your commitment to your clients or what is special about the way you do business.

- **Relatable:** use plain English – rather than technical jargon or complex phrases, use words or examples that people can easily relate to in order to help the development of rapport.

- **Engaging:** your words, tone of voice, body language and eye contact all contribute to making other people intrigued, interested and drawn to you. People remember warmth, openness, enthusiasm, interest – and people who smile.

In developing your self-introduction, practise different approaches until you find the best words to represent you whilst getting your message across in a way people will remember. Once you identify the words and phrases that best represent how you want to introduce yourself, you can adjust your introduction to fit any situation. It is a good idea to write a general version of your own self-introduction, which fulfils the powerful self-introduction criteria described above. You may also find it helpful to practise your introduction in front of friends/colleagues or in front of a mirror.

## Generating conversation

The skill of generating conversation can be a great asset in networking situations. Conversation generators are icebreakers to which people can respond easily. A conversation generator usually relates to something you have in common with the other person (and you will always have something in common – you may be at the same event, work in the same building, be a member of the same professional body, live in the same city/town etc). Examples of conversation generators:

- *'This is my first time at a Women in Business Network meeting. Is this your first meeting too?'*
- *'What an interesting venue. Have you been here before?'*
- *'Tell me a little more about your organization?'*
- *'The wine is excellent. Have you tried some?'*

## *Breaking away and circulating*

At networking events you need to meet people, identify realistic opportunities for mutual benefit and then move on, circulate and meet more people. Breaking away from one conversation and moving on is a networking skill. There are a number of ways in which you can do this politely and effectively:

- Ask the person you are speaking to if they would like another drink and offer to get one for them – the chances are they will refuse and you can then go and refresh your glass.
- Ask the person you are speaking to if you might introduce them to another contact you have spotted in the room. Either they will say yes and you make the introduction, or they say no and you excuse yourself.
- Ask the other person who else they know at the event and if they have contacts you would like to meet – ask if they could possibly introduce you.
- The arrival of food (eg the buffet) at an event creates opportunities to circulate, by getting a plate for the person you are speaking to, helping others etc.

There are many ways in which to circulate and move on; after all, this is the purpose of the event and people expect you to do this.

Two keys to being confident when meeting people are preparation and practice. Plan your conversation generators in the same way that you plan your self-introduction so that you are comfortable when approaching and talking to people.

## Networking of clients – checklist

**Prior to the event – preparation:**

- Identify targets – people you want to meet – in advance.
- Set goals about the type and number of people you want to meet and why.
- Research any target/prospective target in advance.
- Prepare and practise your personal pitch beforehand.
- Take plenty of business cards with you.
- Wear your badge on the right hand side – it is easier for the other person to view when shaking hands.

**Your role at the event – dos:**

- Take the lead by introducing yourself to other people.
- Use your personal pitch.
- Always give a firm handshake and maintain eye contact (but do check appropriate cultures).
- Bring other people into your group and introduce them to the other group members.
- Spot people on their own and introduce yourself or introduce them to another group.
- Ask open questions and listen empathetically to the answers.

**Your role at the event – don'ts:**

- be late;
- cling to the guests/people you know;
- discuss no-go areas that might be too personal or political;
- become too pushy or try to sell too hard;
- start with a negative point or critical point... *not much food is there?*

**Post event:**

- Go through collected business cards and note key information as a reminder.
- Make a 'to do' list of follow-up tasks.
- Use e-mail to keep in touch with a large number of contacts quickly, easily and cost effectively.
- Do what you said you would – follow up after the event.
- Review goals /objectives to measure success.
- Review and update your network of contacts.

# What prevents us from networking?

## *Previous bad experiences*

Uncomfortable or unpleasant networking experiences arise from the misuse of networking. For example:

- being talked at by someone completely focused on their agenda;
- inappropriate selling;
- being walked over or being used.

## *Going it alone*

> '*if you want the job done right...*'

Thinking we have to achieve everything on our own is a common fault. Instead of thinking: '*I don't want to bother x with...*' or '*I should be able to do this on my own*' think: '*People appreciate the opportunity to share their expertise and I am smart enough to use the resources and relationships in my network for support and help.*' Learn to be interdependent, not independent.

## *Being uneasy or worried about the networking process*

Many people are shy or reserved and for them networking can be frightening and onerous. No one likes entering a crowded room alone, and many professionals are uncomfortable at the thought of promoting themselves or their business. How many people have you heard saying: '*I didn't become a professional... to be a marketing expert*'?

Given the potential for successful outcomes from effective networking – and that is part of the requisite armoury of a good professional – you have little option but to learn to be more comfortable in networking situations. It is not what you know that counts: *it is who knows that you know what you know.* Visibility is the key.

## *Coping mechanisms for shy networkers*

- Take one step at a time. Build your confidence slowly. Do not expect miracles straight away: networking is a skill that requires practice.
- Do not assume that you are being a pest or bothering people. Most people will be glad to hear from you.
- Rely on your supporters to help your motivation and keep your thoughts positive, even when you are discouraged or rejected.

- Think about your successes. Keep in the front of your mind the times you have enjoyed meeting new people both inside and outside work. Be positive in your approach. Positive attitudes get positive results.

- Do not go it alone. Ask a friend or colleague to attend events etc with you. Use them as a safe harbour.

- Do not underestimate the power of listening. Networking may seem as if it is all about talking. Listening is invaluable in identifying the needs of clients and prospective clients. You do not have to have the gift of the gab to be a successful networker.

- Enlist a spokesperson to make initial contact for you if you need to.

- Do not get stressed by the small stuff. Small talk is exactly that, 'small'. You do not need to be witty or profound. Mundane questions and comments can break the ice, eg *'this is a good turnout'* or *'what do you know about the speaker?'* etc. Opening conversations with a question is a good way to get the ball rolling.

- Like minds. If you find group interactions difficult, others will too. Look out for like-minded people and approach them (rather than opposites) first.

- Make the most of what you say. Remember, what you know is just as important as who you know. Shy types are likely to have all sorts of information, given that their natural tendency is to work alone and spend a lot of time gathering information through reading etc. Make the most of that resource.

- Rehearse again and again. You are likely to have the same types of conversations repeatedly when you are networking, eg conveying information about your firm.

- Streamline what you say. For example, prepare a personal pitch in advance but be prepared to tailor it for the particular person/occasion.

- Share your information and knowledge and work collaboratively. Do not think you have to be self-sufficient.

- Attend events that have a purpose and be strategic in selecting them, eg training, lectures etc rather than pure networking events.

- Write. If you find oral communication difficult, write instead (make the most of your strengths).

- Be comfortable in your own skin, who you are and how you appear to others. If you have concerns about, for example, your appearance, ask for help from friends or others (even image consultants).

- Just do it. Move out of your comfort zone. Make time to meet and practise interacting with people in different environments.

# Dealing with difficult people and situations

Since networking is all about human nature, you are always likely to come across difficult people and situations. Some people are simply rude or arrogant, others may have had a bad day or it may just be a case of 'wrong place, wrong time'.

## *Difficult people*

- **Elusive people:** either personally elusive or because they surround themselves with guards to prevent you from getting through to them. Tips for dealing with these people include:
  - Keep trying: do not give up too easily.
  - Make your objectives clear and simple: people may not respond because they are unclear about what you want from them or think you are wasting their time.
  - Offer something in return or use the name of a mutual contact as a means of validation.
  - Charm the guards: eg the PA who guards their boss very efficiently.
- **False promisers:** people who simply do not deliver on promises made to you. This is a difficult group to deal with. In particular, it may be difficult to know how assertive to be. Tips for dealing with these people include:
  - Maintaining as much control as possible from the start as this often prevents the problem from happening in the first place.
  - Look again at your own networking technique – are you asking the right person or are you being clear about what you need? (Note that most people do not respond because of time pressures.)
- **The rejectors:** every networking effort brings the occasional rejection. The trick is not to take it personally and to put it in perspective. Tips for dealing with rejection include:
  - Keep a balanced perspective, eg recall positive experiences.
  - Do not internalize the rejection or take it too personally.
  - See rejection as a natural, albeit occasional result of networking, not as a character flaw.

- **Pains in the neck:** people who are rude, inconsiderate and impossible to deal with do exist and you will come across them. Tips for dealing with these people:
  - Consider whether they are essential to your network. If not, do not deal with them.
  - If they are crucial to your network, feed their ego. This may grate but it is often the best way to deal with them: they often behave as they do because they are insecure and striving for power.

## Difficult situations

- **Foot and mouth:** occasionally you will say or do the wrong thing. Tips when you say or do the wrong thing include:
  - Maintain your composure.
  - Make sure you have indeed made a mistake and evaluate its impact: do not panic.
  - Apologize, correct and move on.
  - Learn from the experience.
- **We just do not click:** sometimes we meet people we simply do not get on with. Tips for dealing with this situation include:
  - Remain objective and make sure you are not misreading the situation.
  - Think of ways around the problem. Try focusing on mutual interests or using enthusiasm.

# Managing your network and yourself

Being organized with your contact details, databases (whether computerized or paper-based) and the allocation of your time is as critical to success in networking as in the other aspects of your professional life.

## Keeping track of who you know

Keeping an accurate, organized record of contacts (those you know as well as those you would like to know) is essential to successful networking. The first step is to develop a contact management system that works for you. This system can be on paper or on a computer database. The best paper system is an index card (not notebooks or files) as this simulates a database and can be added to and updated fairly easily. Computer systems (such as contacts in Microsoft Outlook or Access) are more efficient and often easier to maintain. You could include the following data in relation to any contact:

- first name;
- last name;
- title;
- job title;
- employer;
- address (office, home, other);
- telephone (office, home, other);
- e-mail (office, home, other).

- business sector;
- referred to you by;
- meetings /contact and results;
- date of birth;
- other relevant information (eg secretary's name and contact number, personal interests, membership of relevant network groups etc);
- notes (for any other relevant information);
- website.

Set up key people files for those individuals you have regular contact with. These should contain copies of correspondence, notes and other relevant papers so that you have a record of all communication, with a key contact.

Whichever type of contact management system you use, make sure it works well for you and can be accessed by others should the need arise and that it is updated regularly.

## Keeping track of what you know

Networking will always involve a significant amount of research. Keeping up to date with relevant information is key to maintaining and building your network. The easiest way of keeping track of this information is to set up topic and resource files. Topic files contain articles, handouts from training sessions and other information relevant to a particular topic (for example, topics within your specialist field of practice or topics of interest etc).

Resource files are arranged around a function rather than a topic. They may contain flyers, brochures etc on people and services. For example, resource files can include people/organizations that you may need to refer clients to.

## Keeping track of your networking activities

Effective networking is about quality not quantity. There is some value in keeping track of how much networking you have done, either by project through a project log, or by contact through a record-of-contact log. Each log should include date, contact details, type of communication and follow-up undertaken. This will also be useful for you to prove to your supervisor or partner the amount of client development work you have been undertaking.

## Finding time to network – managing your time

A common concern people have is to find time to network. Set realistic targets and prioritize. Do the networking that is needed to get things done and achieve your key goals and objectives.

Spread your networking activity. Avoid falling into the comfort trap of speaking to or meeting with the same people. Think about defining your contacts as frequent, moderate or occasional and look at the priority you need to give to maintaining contact with each group.

Establish a 'to be contacted' system. This is a useful tool that can be linked to a diary forward system. Contacting a number of people as a one-off task is a good way of prioritizing your time and efforts.

Establish a 'research to do' list so that you can focus on one task at a time rather than doing bits and pieces of research over a number of occasions.

Scheduling these tasks is a simple but highly effective way of managing your time. It transforms 'to do' lists into actions. General time management principles, as highlighted in Chapter 3, apply to the way that you network, just as much as they apply to the way you work generally.

# Measuring success – evaluation

As networking should be seen as a strategic activity and one that is a vital business development tool, it is important to assess the results achieved. In the early years of a career you should build the foundations of effective networking practices in order to enhance your career progression. This evaluation process is important in reviewing a one-off activity but also in reviewing your networking activity overall. Reviewing your network in the ways suggested in this chapter allows you to measure the success of developing your network of contacts.

The key tip is to make sure that all your networking is strategic. Give yourself SMART (specific, measurable, achievable, realistic and timed) criteria to review success in analysing your general networking goals, objectives and targets and those for more specific one-off events. When reviewing the things that have not been so successful, assess why that is so in order to avoid unnecessary repetition in the future.

When reviewing achievements and successful outcomes, remember to consider what went well so that you can continue to build on patterns of behaviour and a networking style that gives you results. Focus on the positive in order to raise the effectiveness of your networking activity.

Networking does not always give you immediate results, so be patient. If you are focused in your networking activities and invest time in it, with specific goals and targets in mind, you will reap the rewards.

# Conclusion

In this chapter we have tried to get you thinking about your existing network of contacts, how productive they are and how you can maximize the efficiency and effectiveness of your networking activity.

Effective networking is an essential skill for all professionals – it feeds their professional practice with contacts, prospective clients and helps to strengthen relationships with existing clients.

A key to effective networking will be your ability to maintain contact with existing clients at those times when you may not actually be doing any 'active' work for them. Professionals have a tendency to ignore clients they are not actually acting for on a 'live matter'. This is not intentional as professionals have many clients, all of whose needs are important and pressing. However, sporadic communication may be perceived negatively by clients who think their adviser is not interested in them other than for the fees their work provides. Effective networking is the antidote to this. If you network with clients and maintain your relationships regularly then this is indicative of your interest in the client and helps build a stronger relationship. At the same time, it is always important to build new client and business relationships and to have an ongoing stream of potential new business. Effective and systematic networking is a useful tool to enable you to manage both of these objectives.

# Negotiation skills

## Introduction

This chapter is designed to build on and strengthen the negotiation skills that you already have. We will look at the competitive and cooperative styles of negotiation. Then we will consider the positional and problem-solving approaches to negotiation and look at how they link with the competitive and cooperative styles.

It is important to be able to identify the 'zone of potential agreement' (ZOPA) in a negotiation; we will help you to understand the importance of this concept and enable you to identify when you are entering the zone. We will look at principled negotiation, how it differs from the competitive and cooperative styles, and how the 'best alternative to a negotiated agreement' (BATNA) forms an integral part of it.

An effective negotiator always prepares for each negotiation. We will look at how you might prepare, as well as the toolkit and the tactics you could use during a negotiation. A negotiation is not over until it has been properly concluded – we will look at what you need to do to finish off a negotiation effectively. Many of the negotiations that you will undertake will be via telephone and e-mail: we will look at the issues that are specific to telephone negotiations.

In this chapter we focus on negotiating as a professional adviser, when acting on behalf of a client. These skills are useful when communicating with the 'other side's' adviser, with your own client and with third parties. However, the skills that we discuss are equally applicable when negotiating with work colleagues, eg with the IT help desk.

## Styles of negotiation

The fundamental styles of negotiation are the competitive style, the cooperative style and the principled style. After you have read this section, you should be able to identify each negotiation style, understand the key attributes of each and be aware of the pros and cons of using each style.

## *The competitive style*

Competitive negotiators are adversarial in their approach. Competitive negotiators are combative. It goes with the role and is often seen as a badge of courage, by them and the clients who choose to instruct them on their behalf. Competitive negotiators are argumentative rather than conciliatory in approach, focusing on narrow issues for negotiation and having little if any empathy with the other side's points or approach to the negotiation. To some competitive negotiators it is as stark as 'good versus evil' or 'right versus wrong'.

A competitive style of negotiation is characterized by the negotiator opening with high demands. Typically these demands will be unrealistic, which will in itself cause antipathy and lead the other side to 'dig in' and make a very low counter-offer, or no offer of settlement at all. This is sometimes described as the 'over and under' scenario.

A second feature of competitive negotiation is the taking up of strong or specific positions and standing firm without making any (or few) concessions. This is often perceived as being a 'tough negotiator'.

The question to ask is: has this helped the negotiation to move forward? Often the answer is: no, it has not. What is often achieved is entrenchment – the party making the demand 'sticks by their guns' and repeats the demand, while the other party repeatedly responds by refusing to agree to the demand. This can lead to delay, embittered parties to the negotiation and little hope of any future or ongoing relationship between the parties to the negotiation. In business this can be a 'lose–lose' situation for both parties, assuming that they could both benefit from further dealings with each other.

A competitive negotiator will reveal little information or provide scant detail in response to any questions asked of them. They work on the basis that if the other side knows little or nothing, then they cannot use that information against them. This lack of openness is antagonistic if the questions asked by the other party to the negotiation are legitimate and there isn't any reason not to answer them.

Why do professionals provoke the other side in this way? Some see it as part of their role, ie to protect their client and 'stonewall' any requests for information. Yet it is rarely effective to take this approach in business negotiations.

However, many clients like this approach when taken by their own professional adviser – the adviser is 'fighting the client's corner' and that is what the client pays them to do. When the adviser on the 'other side' takes such an approach, your client will undoubtedly say 'They are being unreasonable'. So what is seen as a positive when used in one direction is often perceived in a negative way by the same person when they are on the receiving end of it.

Whilst a competitive negotiator is loath either to provide information or make concessions, this does not stop them from demanding either information or concessions from their opponent. However, without any reciprocity on their part (ie their lack of preparedness to provide either information or concessions) this will not work.

When you are negotiating, you can identify an opponent who is taking a competitive approach by asking yourself the following 10 questions:

1 Is your opponent seeking confrontation and conflict between the parties to the negotiation?

2 Is there a single issue (or no more than three issues) on which your opponent is focused?

3 Does the outcome of the negotiation hinge on this issue(s)?

4 Is victory your opponent's only goal?

5 Does your opponent give the appearance of being tough and uncompromising?

6 Is your opponent taking key initiatives in the negotiation (eg to precipitate a crisis)?

7 Is your opponent eager to retain control and maintain pressure on you and your client?

8 Is your opponent always stressing the strengths of their position and emphasizing the weaknesses of your points and the position of your client?

9 Is your opponent using aggression, accusation and intimidation as tools; seeking to cause discomfort to you and your client?

10 Is your opponent trying to wear you down and undermine your client's resolve, so that they are prepared to instruct you to make concessions?

## The cooperative style

The approach taken by a cooperative negotiator is quite different to that of the competitive negotiator. Whilst a cooperative negotiator will seek to put their interests and those of their client first, they do so in a way that is fair to the party with whom they are negotiating and they will also seek to maintain good relations with them.

Advocates of cooperative negotiation say that this style of approach has potential to produce the greatest benefit for both sides. When it works this is undoubtedly true.

When you are negotiating, you can identify an opponent who is taking a cooperative approach by asking yourself the following five questions:

1 Is your opponent actively looking for common ground between the parties to the negotiation?

2 Does your opponent consider the needs and interests of you and your client to see if they can be accommodated? (Empathy and understanding are part of the armoury used by the cooperative negotiator.)

**3** Is your opponent demonstrating empathy and understanding towards you and your client?

**4** Is your opponent making reasonable concessions and offers towards settling the negotiation?

**5** Is your opponent looking for a way whereby both parties to the negotiation gain something?

If you are working with a cooperative negotiator there is a high probability of reaching settlement, provided both parties to the negotiation cooperate. However, if your assessment of the situation is wrong and you are actually negotiating with a competitive negotiator you will not succeed using a co-operative style, unless you can persuade the competitive negotiator to change to a cooperative style (which is very unlikely).

If a cooperative negotiation can be achieved, relations between the parties to the negotiation are normally maintained. They can even be strengthened because both parties know that if something should go wrong in the future they will be able to deal with it in a cooperative way. This is an incredibly powerful point when the parties have an ongoing commercial relationship or are very likely to be working with each other on a future project.

Because cooperative negotiations tend to be reasonable and fair, they also promote ease of enforcement, with both parties cooperating to ensure that the agreed outcome is achieved.

## The positional approach to negotiation

This approach is favoured by the competitive negotiator and is closely linked to bargaining. A three-step approach:

- **First step:** determine the bottom line.
- **Second step:** ascertain your opening position.
- **Third step:** negotiate, trying to maintain starting point and avoiding, as far as possible, movement towards the bottom line.

All of these have to be planned in advance and discussed with your client, so that they can instruct you on how to proceed. Skill is required in not only selecting the first, second and third steps but also in deciding how to proceed during the negotiation. Your mission is to give as few concessions as possible, ie stick as close as possible to your opening position.

You need to judge which concessions to make (and the order in which to concede them) in order to gain agreement without either reaching your bottom line too quickly or at all. A skilful negotiator should still be some distance from their bottom line when agreement is reached.

## The zone of potential agreement

The zone of potential agreement (ZOPA) describes the 'space' within which the parties to the negotiation have the opportunity to reach agreement. The parties need to recognize that agreement can be reached on terms that can be accepted by all (even though the terms are not those they had hoped for).

In any negotiation you should:

1 accurately identify the ZOPA for that particular negotiation;
2 be able to identify if the other side to the negotiation has also identified the ZOPA;
3 be able to identify when you have entered the ZOPA;
4 be able to identify when the other side has entered the ZOPA and whether the other side recognizes that they have done so.

You also need to consider your approach to communicating the ZOPA to the other side in a negotiation. Identifying and setting out the ZOPA may be a useful tool to move the negotiation towards a successful conclusion. Where this is done, it will help you identify whether the other side is going to be flexible in their approach and move towards agreement.

## The problem-solving approach

This approach is favoured by cooperative negotiators and centres on all aspects of the negotiation, not just those favourable to one, or other of the parties. A problem-solving approach considers all the possible factors that will enable a successful conclusion to the negotiation.

When using this approach the primary objective is to achieve the most possible for both sides, maximizing gains all round. The idea here is to add to the sum total through a process of dialogue and full consideration of the available options, and of all factors that may influence a successful outcome.

# Principled negotiation

Roger Fisher and William Ury, in their book *Getting To Yes*, advocate a particular style and approach termed 'principled negotiation'.[12] This is a hybrid style of negotiation: a third way of negotiating that comprises the following elements.

## Separate the people from the problem

A competitive negotiator will use their personality as a negotiation tool (or the personality of their client), if it works to their advantage in the negotiation. Equally, they may exploit a real or perceived weakness in the personality of an opponent or their client if that will help them succeed in the negotiation. The first principle of principled negotiation is to take all of this out of the negotiation arena: 'separate the people from the problem'.

## Focus on interests, not on positions

The competitive style of negotiation uses the taking of positions: opening position and bottom line. This can lead to 'digging in' and entrenchment, which is not productive and should be avoided. The taking of positions may also mean that the negotiation focuses on the wrong things and a potential way forward is overlooked or dismissed because it does not fit with the position taken by one of the parties to the negotiation.

If the focus is on the interests of the parties concerned, and not the positions taken by the opposing sides, the negotiation can proceed focusing on these interests. See Figure 8.1.

**FIGURE 8.1**    Mutual interests

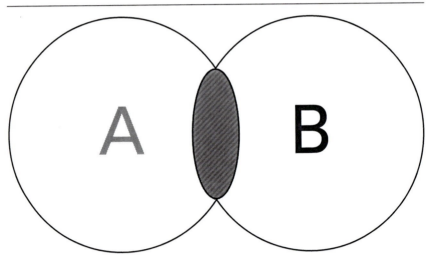

Both party A and party B have mutual interests in the issues relating to the shaded ellipse. Only party A has any interest in the issues in the unshaded area of the left-hand circle. Only party B has any interest in the issues in the unshaded area of the right-hand circle.

It is clearly less effective to raise an issue in the negotiation that is outside of the area of common interest – since this is of interest only to one party (the party raising it). It may be appropriate to recognize an issue which is only of interest to the other side and is not relevant to you. By doing so you can demonstrate empathy with their situation; the fact that you do this shows that you recognize that this is a real issue for them.

Where there are three parties to the negotiation the potential area of common interest is much smaller (see Figure 8.2):

**FIGURE 8.2** Mutual interests in a tripartite negotiation

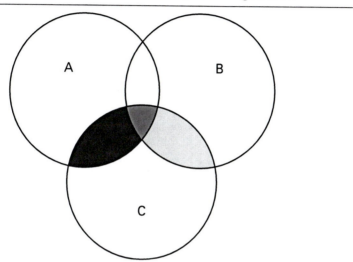

Parties A, B and C have mutual interests in the triangle where all three circles meet. This is the focal point for negotiation. A and C have mutual interests in the ellipse to the left and C and B have mutual interests in the ellipse to the right. A and B have mutual interests in the ellipse in the middle.

## Invent options for mutual gain

This means looking for new ways forward. If there are ways in which both parties to the negotiation could gain, which have not previously been considered, then look for them and table them for consideration.

## Insist on objective criteria

Be prepared only to negotiate on objective issues. This is in part an adjunct to 'separate the people from the problem' (above) but it also focuses attention on fact rather than subjective opinion, views or prejudice.

The subjective viewpoint of the negotiator or their client is irrelevant – that is, it is relevant only to them and not to anyone else involved in the negotiation. So, looked at objectively, after having removed the subjective viewpoints of the protagonists and their advisers, what are the issues to be negotiated?

'Trust' is a significant factor in any negotiation. Your client may not trust the other side's client; this may be because of a history of events, or a feeling of mistrust between them. However, a principled negotiator will only address 'facts' that are objectively verifiable, and will not consider subjective issues such as a lack of trust. What this means is that the principled negotiator will have to treat what the other side's negotiator says at 'face value' and seek to verify it objectively through further questioning, investigation or other legitimate means.

## Develop a 'best alternative to a negotiated agreement' (BATNA)

This is a fundamental aspect of principled negotiation and a key idea from Fisher and Ury's book *Getting To Yes*. It is a useful methodology and you should understand it and seek to use it when negotiating.

First you need to identify your BATNA – there may be more than one. Having identified your BATNA(s), how will you address it? It may well be that in certain situations there is no BATNA within your control.

---

### Example

ABC business needs a loan in order to continue to trade – it has significant liquidity problems. ABC applies to the Bank of Zorro for a loan to enable it to meet its short-term cash requirements.

What BATNAs are available (if any) to ABC if the Bank of Zorro refuses ABC a loan?

One BATNA for ABC is to apply for a loan at another bank. If ABC's business case for a loan was weak (the Bank of Zorro declined ABC a loan), what will their BATNA be if a second bank refuses to lend to them?

They still have a BATNA. They may not like it, but ultimately their only BATNA will be to accept the inevitable insolvency of their business.

---

## Important things to remember about BATNA

It is always very important when preparing for a negotiation to consider what you will do if no agreement is reached, ie what is your BATNA?

You always have a BATNA even if you do not like it. Develop your best possible BATNA to strengthen your negotiation position. Having identified your BATNA when preparing to negotiate, re-evaluate it at times through-out the negotiation – particularly when considering making a concession or responding to an offer from the other side.

Do not reveal your BATNA. Doing so will usually harm your position in the negotiation. If your BATNA is very strong, revealing it may appear threatening to the other side. If your BATNA is strong, the likelihood is that the other side (or at least the other side's adviser) will have identified it and will be aware of it – revealing it will therefore come as no surprise and will have little impact.

Always research your opponent's BATNA. Consider all possible BATNAs that the other side may have – that way you will not be surprised.

## Further thoughts on principled negotiation

William Ury wrote a second book, *Getting Past No* as a postscript to *Getting To Yes*. In this book, he puts forward a structure for the principled approach to negotiation. He bases this structure on what he calls the 'counter-intuitive approach' and 'breakthrough strategy', and goes on to explain the link between the two. The counter-intuitive approach is based on taking the initiative in a way that your opponent does not anticipate. Breakthrough strategy describes how by using a counter-intuitive approach you can 'gain ground' in a negotiation because no one had anticipated your idea – and your counter-intuitive approach has made the other side rethink theirs.[13]

This could be positive – it could lead to an agreement and resolution. It could lead to capitulation: the other side agreeing to your terms (unlikely though that may be). It might lead to the other side putting forward another new idea to get you thinking. In any event, the negotiation is moving forward and not getting entrenched – as so often happens with competitive negoti-ations or losing direction and impetus, which can happen with cooperative negotiations.

## Principled negotiation: the five-stage process

William Ury's five-stage process is fairly self-explanatory. Although he may use unconventional terminology, for example 'go to the balcony' to describe stage one, the process involves some straightforward ideas:

Stage 1 – go to the balcony:

- Identify your interests.
- Decide if you should negotiate.
- Recognize tactics.
- Buy time to think.

**Stage 2 – step to their side:**

- Use your listening skills effectively.
- Agree on points whenever possible.
- Build a working relationship.
- Acknowledge differences with optimism.

**Stage 3 – do not reject – reframe:**

- Ask problem-solving questions.
- Seek your opponent's advice.
- Make reasonable requests.

**Stage 4 – build them a 'golden bridge':**

- Make it easy for your opponent to say 'yes' and agree a deal.
- Expand the options for consideration.
- Help write your opponent's victory speech – make some concessions.
- Help your opponent save face.

**Stage 5 – make it hard for your opponent to say 'no':**

- Let your opponent know what will happen if agreement is not reached.
- Warn, do not threaten.
- Allow time for a final consideration of options for moving forward.
- Make lasting agreements.
- Obtain mutual satisfaction, not victory.

## *Expand the options for consideration*

This is also described as 'expanding the pie', ie increasing the options that are available to both parties and that they are prepared to consider.

Let's start with the idea that the focus of this negotiation is set within the boundaries of the inner circle, primarily in the bottom-right quartile. This means there is limited scope to move forward. If both parties to the negotiation are prepared to 'expand the pie' (see Figure 8.3) by considering further related options, then the scope for potential agreement is increased. The additional area in Figure 8.3 is that which is beyond the inner circle and bordered by the outer circle in the bottom-right quartile. The total area is now much greater than the initial area for negotiation. The new outer area is itself larger than the original inner area – this gives both parties further scope to reach agreement.

**FIGURE 8.3**   Expanding the pie

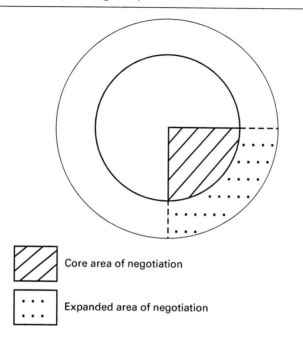

☐☐ Core area of negotiation

☐☐ Expanded area of negotiation

There are some basic foundations on which this approach is built:

- That there is more than one issue to be negotiated – indeed this approach works best where there are a number of related issues.
- Both parties to the negotiation share some goals, but there are areas of disagreement and conflict.
- Long-term, continuing relationships between the parties to the negotiation are important.
- Following a recognized process may assist in identifying and reaching agreement on the further options, eg a mediation process in a legal dispute.

# Preparing for a negotiation

This is not rocket science. If it is so easy, why do so many people fail to prepare adequately for a negotiation?

## Be ready to negotiate at any time

The key steps to take to enable you to be ready to negotiate are:

- Identify your interests and the interests of your client.
- Consider and talk through with your client all the relevant options.
- Plan your strategy and tactics.

## Identifying interests

The key steps are:

- Draw up a basic checklist to identify your party's interests and the issues that are likely to form the basis of the negotiation.
- Where there are multiple issues, assess and rank their relative importance.
- Identify your ideal position/your client's ideal position on each issue, together with alternative fall-back positions. Think of all realistic options.
- Look at the same questions from your opponent's point of view. Are you able to predict/understand their (or their client's) interests and positions?

## Consider all the relevant options

Understanding the available options if the negotiation does not succeed is a vital part of the preparation process. What is your client's BATNA? What is your opponent's BATNA?

## Planning your strategy and tactics

Use a structured approach to planning your negotiation. It is important to recognize the different phases in a negotiation and to plan for most (if not all) eventualities as the negotiation proceeds through each phase. Do not just plan for the first or early phases and hope that you have done enough (see Figure 8.4).

## Preparation plans

As an integral part of your preparation consider the following points:

- What are the three most significant facts in this negotiation?
- What are you seeking to achieve on behalf of your client?
- Be objective in your assessment. What are your client's expectations?

**FIGURE 8.4** Negotiation planning notes

| 1. Preparation & Planning (1) | | |
|---|---|---|
| **Item** | **Us** | **Them** |
| **Objectives**<br>Best deal (ideal)<br>Acceptable (realistic)<br>No go (unacceptable) | Our:<br>B<br>A<br>N | Our best guess of their:<br>B<br>A<br>N |
| **BATNA** | Ours: | Theirs: |
| **Information**<br><br>Identifying information gaps<br>– What areas do we want to explore<br>– What information don't we want to reveal<br><br>How can we use this information? | Information we can/wish to give:<br>•<br>•<br><br>Information to give carefully<br>•<br>•<br><br>Cannot/would not wish to give<br>•<br>• | Information we expect to get from them<br>•<br>•<br><br>Information we hope to get from them<br>•<br>•<br><br>We want but are unlikely to get from them<br>•<br>• |
| **Potential Concessions**<br><br>What could we concede of value to them to get something of value to us? | What can we offer them<br>•<br>•<br><br>What would we want from them<br>•<br>• | What will they want from us?<br>•<br>•<br><br>What might they be prepared to concede to us?<br>•<br>• |

**FIGURE 8.4** *continued*

| 1. Preparation & Planning (2) Issues for Discussion | Our Interests/Arguments/Case | Their Anticipated Responses and Our Counters |
|---|---|---|
| 1. | | |
| 2. | | |
| 3. | | |
| 4. | | |
| 5. | | |
| 6. | | |

| 2. Opening & Exploring | 3. Proposing | 4. Bargaining | 5. Agreeing & Closing |
|---|---|---|---|
| Opening position/statement | Making requests/offers | Trading – simple swaps/concession making | Specific statements of agreement sought |
| Agenda definition | Developing alternatives | Developing options | Implementation sought |
| Testing assumptions | Matching needs | Testing common ground | |
| Seeking/providing data | Stating limits | Repacking/trial closing | |
| Conditioning | Summarizing | | |
| Developing trust | | | |

- Are these negotiation style(s) and approach(es) best suited to the circumstances of the negotiation?
- What are the negotiation style(s) and approach(es) you expect your opponent to use?
- What are your client's areas of strength and weakness?
- What are your opponent's areas of strength and weakness?
- What are your client's optimum, desirable and essential positions?
- The anchor effect of your opening position – remember this is your choice, choose well; having considered your opponent's acceptability range for agreement (ie their zone of potential agreement).
- Is there likely to be 'trust' between the parties and reciprocity when a concession is made?
- What would be the best outcome for your client? (ie their aspiration point)
- What is your client's bottom line?
- What alternatives are available if the negotiation fails (BATNA)?
- What information would you like to have about your opponent's interests, position, BATNA?
- What are the possible lines of questioning open to you to obtain this information?
- What key questions will you ask of your opponent's adviser?
- What tactics (if any) will you use?
- How will you identify potential concessions that your client is prepared to make and when they might be made?
- What settlement options are available?

## Your negotiation toolkit

The purpose of this section is to help you consider the techniques that you can use to negotiate successfully. The tools, when used effectively, make a difference. They are simple to use and it is important to ensure that you use them effectively.

### Be flexible: (tool 1)

Use different techniques to suit each particular negotiation. Be prepared to use a negotiation plan: draw one up and use it effectively to identify the negotiation techniques that will produce the best result at each stage in the negotiation.

- Avoid defend/attack spirals and getting into situations where you have limited choice over the next step that you will take, ie you make a point that attacks the other side's earlier point, they respond by defending on that point and attacking you on your last point – and so the process spirals and repeats itself.

- Focus on interests, not positions, and try to find common ground so that you can identify and seek out mutual gain so that both parties get something out of the negotiation.

- Build trust, for example by using a 'feelings commentary', eg 'I am pleased to hear that you will agree to…'

- Use behaviour labelling to structure the negotiation, eg 'I'm going to make you an offer that you will not be able to refuse.'

- Ask appropriately framed questions – see tool 2 (below).

- Try to avoid directly answering your opponent's difficult questions; to answer them may not benefit you or your client's interests and it may hinder the negotiation.

- Break a deadlock in the negotiation by using well-directed 'What if' questions, eg 'What if I was able to get my client to…?'

- Break a deadlock in the negotiations by putting difficult issues on the 'back burner', ie saving them for later and not dealing with them at this point in time.

- Win concessions by 'onus transfer', ie by asking the other party to provide a solution: 'How can we (meaning you) solve this problem?' – without having committed to any solution.

- Use the 'salami technique' to break down complex issues. You can do this by serving up a difficult issue in thin slices, piece by piece. This aids ultimate acceptance of something that might otherwise be unpalatable.

## Listening skills: (tool 2)

Earlier in this book, in Chapter 2 'Communicating with clients, professionals and third parties', and in Chapter 5 'Presentation skills', we looked at listening and questioning skills. These skills are very important in the context of a negotiation.

Most negotiators make the fundamental error of not listening effectively to their opponent during the negotiation. The key message is that accomplished negotiators always listen – not just appearing to listen but to actively listen to what is said and, where appropriate, make an effective note of what they have heard.

Active listening should be applied not only to what is said by your opponent as part of the negotiation, but also to what is said by your own client when taking instructions and preparing to negotiate on their behalf.

Empathic listening enables you to 'dig deeper'; to understand the background and perspective of the person speaking – whether that is your client, the other side, or the person representing the other side in the negotiation.

Often it is what is said by the client that is missed by you (because you have not been listening actively to what the client has said) and you may fail to identify a gap in their 'story' about which you should ask further questions to obtain information or clarification.

Negotiations can go wrong not because of what the negotiator knows, but because of what they do not know or did not ask their client about. This is often caused by a failure on the negotiator's part to listen effectively to their client's explanation or version of the matters that form the subject of the negotiation.

## *Asking questions: (tool 3)*

When negotiating, obtaining more information about your opponent's interests and positions is vital. Effective questioning provides the means of obtaining this information. Most negotiators spend little time (perhaps as low as 10 per cent to 20 per cent of the time spent negotiating) sharing information. It is easy, therefore, to conclude that negotiators do not use enough questioning.

How do you use questioning techniques effectively in a negotiation?

As we already know, an open question enables the person to whom it is addressed to choose their response. A closed question invites a yes/no answer.

Consider how best to formulate and sequence your questions. Ask yourself:

- Why am I asking the question?
- What information am I seeking to extract?
- Will my opponent fully understand the question?
- What are the sensitivities?
- Would I answer this question myself?

Effective negotiators will pose questions that:

- Seek information about your opponent's underlying interests rather than their stated position or demands.
- Seek specific facts and minimize your opponent's incentive to misrepresent their position.
- Use direct questions so that your opponent has to confirm or refute, avoiding rhetorical questions that provide the answer in the question. It is much better to ask of your opponent: '*Do you accept that* (insert your proposition)*?*'

## Revealing information: (tool 4)

Why might you reveal information in a negotiation? The conventional wisdom of competitive/positional negotiation is that you should reveal as little information about your position and interests as possible. However, in the absence of information, entrenched positional negotiation can lead to 'lose–lose' situations.

Negotiators who provide information to their opponents usually improve the outcomes that they achieve in their negotiations. A further reason for revealing information is the reciprocity principle – revealing information about your interests is likely to increase the chances of your opponent revealing information about their interests. Encourage your opponent to reveal information, eg 'Which issue is more important to you, A or B?'

As well as deciding whether to reveal specific information in a negotiation you must also have a clear idea about the issues you would *prefer* not to address in the negotiation and those that you *will not* address. Identify issues and questions that you wish to avoid. For example, you would not want to answer a question or discuss an issue that would reveal your BATNA. Indeed, you may want to use blocking or diversionary techniques if your opponent asks such questions.

## Note taking and verification: (tool 5)

In Chapter 6 we considered the importance of taking a clear, accurate contemporaneous note of key points in meetings. The same importance is attached to note taking during negotiations – not just at more formal negotiation meetings or teleconference calls but also as an effective note of a one-to-one telephone discussion with the other side, a third party (eg counsel, an expert) or with your client.

It is not unknown for the other side in a negotiation (or their professional adviser) to inaccurately summarize the key points and decisions agreed during the negotiation. You will never do this – it is unprofessional. Watch out for others who may do it. The way in which it is done is by adding something that was not agreed, or missing out something that was agreed. The way to prevent this being effective is for you to always take a clear, contemporaneous written note of the key points agreed in the negotiation.

# Tactics in negotiation

People often talk about negotiation tactics as if they are the key to achieving a successful outcome. They can play a role, but the keys to a successful outcome rest with the points already discussed: planning and preparation, effective use of the negotiation toolkit and understanding the fundamental principles of negotiation skills. Set out below are some recognized 'tactics' commonly used by negotiators.

## Silence

People cannot handle silence, particularly on the telephone – it is a vacuum and it will usually be filled by one party making a concession or providing some information (often ill-advisedly).

## Back-burner or parking-up

Putting off an issue (or issues) to another meeting or later stage in the negotiation. This can be used as a way of avoiding early discussion of a matter on which the parties will not agree.

## One more thing

Often used to deal with a controversial point at the end of the negotiation (eg one that has been put 'on the back burner') when all the other points have been agreed. Consensus may now be possible and the difficult issue may be resolved, whereas it would have been a deal-breaker if confronted earlier on.

## Broken record

Repeating over and over again the point you are making. It may have a number of effects (eg irritating your opponent); it could also be the way to get a concession on the point that you keep repeating. It might also lead to entrenchment and your opponent deciding never to give in on that point – because you keep going on about it.

## Linking issues

It may be useful to link issues that had previously been dealt with separately by offering concessions when there is apparent deadlock. In order to get agreement on issue A you may concede that issues B and C, looked at together, can now be agreed.

## Armageddon

Suggesting that your opponent's failure to concede an issue or to agree a key point will have catastrophic consequences, which you then spell out in the negotiation. This is a risky card to play. Make sure you understand your opponent's BATNA(s) and hold an acceptable BATNA yourself. Your opponent may well not agree to your demand and bring the negotiation to an end.

## Messenger

Using the absence of an important third party at the end of a crucial stage in the negotiation, as the reason to say that you do not have the authority to make a final decision. You may buy time to consider the other party's case, which will probably have been fully argued when this tactic was used. This is a useful tactic for less experienced negotiators who need to get the approval of the partner or director they work for to the terms of the negotiation. You might say 'I need to speak to X, on this point.' The absent third party may also be the client, where the adviser wants to use them as the reason for not agreeing. You might use the classic phrase, 'I will have to take my client's instructions before I can give you an answer.'

## Break time
Take a break to reassess the situation.

## Deadlines
These can be imposed or agreed and can encourage parties to concentrate on creative solutions whilst at the same time making them realize that concessions are necessary.

## The hypothetical question – 'what if…' or 'suppose…'
Useful for introducing a new idea or to help break deadlock. Matters can be discussed without fear of commitment.

## Seeking justification
Never be afraid to seek justification from the other party, especially at the earlier stages when positions are being defined. You might ask 'Why do you say that?' Just asking 'Why?' may appear a little aggressive and may provoke the other side.

## Guilty party
Make the other party feel guilty by suggesting that they are breaking some code (possibly an issue of professional ethics) or going back on a point that was agreed earlier, or that they are refusing something that would be readily conceded by reasonable people. They may make a concession to convince you that they are reasonable.

## Salami
Taking a difficult and complex issue and 'cutting it up' into thin slices, dealing with each sub-issue piece by piece. This may increase the time taken but it aids ultimate acceptance of something that may otherwise be unpalatable.

## Full disclosure – openness
This depends very much on the atmosphere that has been created – each party needs to feel that it will not be exploited by the other if it makes a significant disclosure. This tactic can lead swiftly to an agreement that both parties consider satisfactory. It has little if any use where there is no trust between the parties to the negotiation.

### 'All I can afford'

This needs to be accompanied by persistence of the 'broken record' approach if the other party is to be convinced. And it must be true – you cannot go back on this.

### Onus transfer

Asking the other party to provide a solution: *'How can we* (meaning you) *resolve this issue?'* without having committed yourself or your client to any next step.

# Completing a negotiation

This is a simple checklist for the situation where the negotiation has been successful:

1 Check the points of detail of all terms to ensure that there can be no misunderstanding.
2 Check that the agreement covers every point that is of interest to you and the client, including who pays costs.
3 Who is to draft any written settlement?
4 How is the agreement to be enforced?
5 Is the agreement subject to client approval?

This is a simple checklist for the situation where the negotiation has been unsuccessful:

1 Are you sure that it is time to exit?
2 Is there any basis for future negotiation?
3 Try to define more clearly the issues between the parties.
4 Try to identify the key barriers to settlement.
5 Try to disengage with dignity.

# Telephone negotiations

Most professionals conduct the majority of their negotiations either by e-mail or telephone. Face-to-face meetings are time consuming and potentially very costly to the client in terms of professional fees.

This chapter has been written on the basis that negotiations involve both oral and written communication. Oral communication is usually by telephone, either one-to-one or through teleconferencing. With video conferencing and Skype being readily available, face-to-face meetings need not involve the physical presence of all of the parties to the negotiation in one place.

The following checklist is to help you with negotiations conducted by telephone at your desk (or using a mobile phone) or in the context of a tele-conference call. Before a telephone negotiation:

**1** Prepare thoroughly: go through all the information you need.

**2** Arrange to call about the issue so that the other person is expecting your call and is ready to discuss it and confirm available time for the duration of the call.

**3** Decide on your objectives for the telephone negotiation.

**4** Plan your approach to achieving the objectives, including how you are going to build rapport and thinking about how and at what stage you are going to raise the points you want to make.

**5** Consider the tone and the pace with which you speak.

**6** Consider what the other person might want to know and what questions s/he might ask.

**7** Plan what to do if the person you want to speak to is not there and you have to leave a message. For instance, do you want to phone back or ask them to phone you? How much information do you want to leave etc?

During the negotiation:

**1** If you have not done so beforehand, agree the available time for the duration of the call.

**2** Have all the paperwork you need to hand.

**3** Take an effective note of the negotiation.

**4** Listen carefully to the other person to check their understanding and acceptance of what you say, eg by summarizing.

**5** Adjust your tone and pace depending on how the negotiation is progressing, eg 'mirror' where appropriate.

**6** Be ready with follow-up questions and points as the negotiation progresses.

**7** Be ready to end the negotiation on a positive note even if you have not achieved your objective and will have to have another discussion. If possible, make arrangements for any necessary future discussion before ending the call.

**8** Summarize any agreement, decisions, action points and time frames for completion.

After the negotiation:

**1** Make sure your note covers all the points while they are still fresh in your mind; type them up, if appropriate. Make sure this note is retained on the master file.

**2** If appropriate, send off the e-mail(s) or letter(s) confirming the conversation.

**3** Follow up action points.

# Conclusion

It is always important to be both practical and realistic when negotiating. What may work in theory may not yield a practical result or a viable outcome in day-to-day professional life.

You will enhance your negotiation skills if you understand and consider practical ways to apply your knowledge of the theory of negotiation. However, understanding the theory does not necessarily make you a good negotiator. If you lack a sound understanding of how to apply the theory, you are unlikely to ever become a successful negotiator.

This chapter has demonstrated the importance of thorough and effective preparation prior to each negotiation. Don't 'wing it' and think it will be alright. It won't. Many negotiations have been lost through inadequate preparation because the adviser believed they had a 'cast iron case' and was bound to succeed.

Use the five tools in the negotiation toolkit wisely; they are: be flexible, listen, ask questions, reveal information, and note taking and verification.

It is important to remember that in our professional lives the objective is not always to 'win'. In certain instances it is to retain an effective long-term working relationship (eg with an established client who is not prepared to pay your bill). In this instance, you will need to adapt your approach to enable you to achieve a result that is in line with your goal(s) (eg to ensure that the client pays the bill, that they return when they want further advice, and preferably that they recommend you to other potential clients who may instruct you and the business you work for).

# Team working

## Introduction

Effective team working is vitally important to your success as a professional and to optimizing the performance of the professional services business that you work for. Professionals have classically seen themselves as 'individuals' rather than as team players – this is a mistake. It may well be that some professionals take this view based simply on building a reputation for themselves in the marketplace.

In a professional services business the ability to work effectively in a team is a key attribute that recruiters look for when recruiting at all levels. The cult of the individual – someone who works outside the team in their own way – is hugely disruptive and is seen as a negative.

Team working is also needed to ensure that the right tasks are undertaken by the right people, in order to deliver the business's services effectively to clients. Getting this right has a direct and positive impact on profitability; getting it wrong means that the business will never realize its full potential.

Where a professional services business is appropriately structured (with teams that have the skills and expertise to deliver the services to clients), then the key to success is how the people within each team work with one another and how the teams work together, including the interface between teams advising clients and business support teams (eg Business Development, HR, IT, L&D and Finance).

In this chapter we will look briefly at what motivates us as individuals. We will then look at groups and teams in order to consider their essential attributes. Having identified these, we will look at models for effective teams and identify individual roles within teams. You will need to consider the team(s) in which you work and reflect on how the models can assist you in understanding how they function.

## Individual performance and motivation

Let's think about the job that you do, the environment in which you work and the business that you work for: 1)What motivates you at work?; 2)What are the things that detract from your job role and sap your motivation?

Motivation is complex and comes from within each person; we all have different motivators and reasons for doing what we do. It can be described as a 'driving force' that causes a person to attempt to achieve a goal in order to fulfil an expectation or a need that they have.

If an individual's motivational driving force is blocked and they are unable to satisfy their needs and expectations, this can result in either a positive and constructive problem-solving approach or in negative frustration-induced behaviours (eg aggression, regression, fixation or withdrawal).

There are many competing theories that attempt to explain motivation at work. Not one of these is able to explain fully why people behave in different ways in similar situations. However, the theories do help us to focus on how people feel and think in these situations.

## Theory X and Y

This theory defines human behaviour in the work environment in two contrasting ways: theory X makes the assumption that people are lazy and uninterested in work or responsibility and therefore must be pushed and cajoled if they are to get anything done in a disciplined way, with reward assisting the process to some degree. Theory Y takes the opposite view. It assumes that people want to work. They enjoy achievement, derive satisfaction from responsibility, and are naturally inclined to seek ways of making work a positive experience.

Is it right to assume that all professionals fall into Y? No. It is important to recognize that there is truth in both positions and that we will all derive our motivation from somewhere between these two extremes.

We need to consider what motivates young professionals to succeed. It may be any one of a number of things: the quality of the work delegated to them; the development opportunities that a particular piece of work affords for them (eg to gain a new specialism, develop or strengthen an existing skill); the place or environment in which the work is to be done (eg a secondment to an overseas office or to a client's organization); the opportunity to have their views listened to and their contribution acknowledged. This simple list highlights a small number of the many things that motivate us. What you need to do is to recognize what your 'drivers' are and seek out opportunities that allow you to capitalize on them.

The next theory we will consider draws a sharp distinction between motivators and factors that limit or erode our motivation.

## Herzberg's 'hygiene' factors

Herzberg addressed workplace motivation rather than the whole human condition, looking at two factors: 'hygiene factors' and 'motivators'.

Poor business conditions create an 'un-hygienic' atmosphere (ie one that demoralizes staff and deflects their energies into moaning and complaining). Hygiene factors include:

**Team policies:** do the rules under which teams operate make sense or do they just irritate people?

**Supervision:** within clear guidelines, team members should be encouraged to be responsible for their own work with guidance available rather than imposed.

**Team management:** management of the team must be effective. If team members cannot work because of infrastructure issues (ie the IT network is down) motivation levels rapidly sink.

**Remuneration:** salary levels need to be right for the job and comparable to the rates paid for that job in other professional services businesses in the area.

**Working conditions:** these must be satisfactory. If the office is too hot in the summer and freezing cold in the winter, people will become demotivated and unwilling to give their best.

**Good working relationships:** turf wars and petty disputes must not get out of hand or people will become increasingly dissatisfied and efficiency levels will drop.

It is worth noting that not all hygiene factors relevant to a given job role relate to the place of work, the person you work for or the job itself. They include related issues such as the journey into work, the cost of the travel to and from work, traffic congestion on your journey etc. Even the weather or the short daylight hours in winter ('going to work in the dark and coming home in the dark') may impact on some people's motivation. However, the hygiene factors or conditions will not produce good 'working health' on their own. It is the motivators – such as recognition and advancement – that lead to satisfaction. Motivators include:

**A sense of achievement:** this is essential if you are to value what you do. By setting challenging but attainable targets and monitoring performance to let people see how well they are doing, management can motivate team members.

**Being recognized:** by everyone – eg as the 'employee of the month' – has a stronger and longer motivational effect than a one-off increase in your salary, which is usually known only to the employee.

**Responsibility:** allowing team members to use their own judgement on day-to-day issues makes people feel more involved. Otherwise, they will feel like a cog in a machine and abdicate responsibility, with the result that the quality of work falls.

**Advancement:** no one wants to get stuck in a rut. This does not mean that everyone expects to advance quickly, but we do want the opportunity to advance in our career. Where possible, promote from within the business, offer people the opportunity to develop and allow them to advance when they are ready and a vacancy occurs.

**The attractiveness of work:** this is a key motivator. Not all jobs are glamorous, but neither do they have to appear worse than they are.

## Placing motivation into the professional services environment

Research has shown that high achievers in professional services businesses are typically motivated by three factors:

1 Appropriate challenge and variety of work.
2 Appropriate autonomy to reflect increasing experience.
3 Regular and constructive feedback so they know what they have to do to develop further.

Everyone is different and people change. What motivates one person will not necessarily motivate another and we need to be aware of how our behaviour motivates others.

---

We spend a great deal of our waking lives at work; much more time is devoted to it than any other activity. It is therefore worth asking yourself on a regular basis:

- What motivates me?
- Am I still motivated by my work?
- If not, what can I do to enhance my motivation?

---

# Roles, relationships and groups

## Roles

Whether you are at the start of your professional career (eg a newly qualified teacher, a trainee accountant) or you have considerable experience (eg a partner or director of a professional services business), you will occupy a particular position within the structure of the business in which you work. Expectations of your behaviour are automatically associated with that position, whether they arise from the people that you interact with or are self-imposed.

The role that you play within any group is influenced by two primary factors: 1) **situational factors**: such as your role or task, the style of leadership of your group or team leader and your position within the hierarchal chain; 2) **personal factors**: such as your values, attitudes, motivation, ability and personality.

The concept of role is very important in the functioning of groups. Establishing clear roles for each member of the group helps establish the following areas for a work group:

- the group's structure;
- the relationship between its members;
- how effective the group is in achieving its objectives and getting tasks done.

The development of a work group helps identify distinct roles for each of its members. The concept of roles helps significantly to clarify that structure and to define the pattern of relationships within any group.

Each year, in the late summer, graduate trainees will join professional services businesses. Much time has been taken, considerable money spent (eg recruitment advertising, participation in university careers fairs etc) and substantial effort made (eg interviewing candidates) to recruit 'the best'. The graduate trainees fortunate enough to get a job will doubtless appreciate that it has been a very competitive process, that they have been selected from a very strong field of applicants, and they are now part of a high-quality professional services business. What they may not appreciate on their first day at the office is how others view graduate trainees – what that may mean for them (ie the work they will have delegated to them) and how they will 'fit in' to their work group and make an effective contribution.

## Relationships and interactions within the workplace

Each of us will interact with people within the business in which we work, (eg with our colleagues, supervisors, managers, directors and partners) but we will also have a number of role-related relationships with people outside our work group (eg other work groups within the business, clients, external specialists etc). Take time to identify all those people that you currently interact with at work – you may want to draw a 'spider diagram' on a piece of paper to illustrate the connections. Having identified the interactions, which ones will you approach differently as a result of identifying them and thinking about the nature and context of them?

## Role problems

Role problems arise from inadequate or inappropriate role definition and need to be distinguished from personality clashes or from issues in working groups that do not have defined roles or objectives.

Role incompatibility: arises where an individual faces a situation in which simultaneously different or contradictory expectations create inconsistency for them. Compliance with one set of expectations will make it difficult to comply with another. For example, when work is given to them by different people and they each have competing and demanding deadlines for completion of the tasks.

Role ambiguity: occurs when there is lack of clarity regarding the precise requirements of the role and the individual is unsure of what to do. Your perception may differ from the expectations of others, implying that insufficient information is available for the adequate performance of the role. For example, a lack of clear instructions regarding your role and how to perform it.

Role overload: occurs when you face too many separate roles or too great a variety of expectations, leading to an inability to satisfy all expectations or to some under-performance on your part. An example is where too many people are delegating work to you, because they recognize you to be efficient and effective.

Role underload: arises when prescribed role expectations fall short of your own perception of the role, leaving you with the feeling that you are not being stretched or that you have the capacity to undertake a larger or more varied role, or an increased number of roles, ie you feel undervalued and underutilized. An example is simply not being given enough work to do, either because there is insufficient work within the team or because it is allocated to other team members.

Any of these problem areas may lead to role stress, which will become a major influence on motivation, personal job satisfaction and ultimately work performance.

---

It is worth taking time to consider these role issues:

- Do any of the role issues outlined above relate to you in your role at work?
- Is any one of these issues a problem area for you?
- If so, what steps (if any) can you take to address that role issue?
- What steps can the person you work for take to address that issue?

# Groups

Groups are a characteristic of all social situations and almost everyone in a professional services business will be a member of one or more groups. Most of us work in groups at some stage and for some purposes, and our overall effectiveness is affected by their operation.

Groups take many different forms: from the small group charged with executing a very specific task, such as a project team, to the large, loose groupings of individuals who may share a common expertise or area of practice but do not necessarily work together on specific client matters. It is worth taking time to accurately identify all groups of which you are currently a member at work. You may be surprised by the number and range of your group memberships.

The essential feature of any group is that its members regard themselves as belonging to that group. A group is any number of people who: interact with one another; are psychologically aware of one another; perceive themselves to be a group.

Groups develop through a series of stages. These stages have been described as:

- forming;
- storming;
- norming;
- performing.

Each stage is unique and is characterized by certain types of individual behaviour and different issues faced by the team and the leader. For further details please see Table 9.1 below.

**TABLE 9.1**　The first four stages of group development

| Stage | Task | Major processes | Characteristics | Leadership |
|---|---|---|---|---|
| Forming (Orientation): Why are we here? | Introductions; group purpose; objectives. | Process is driven by the leader. Some people are reluctant to contribute openly. | Simple ideas; saying 'acceptable' things; avoiding serious topics; keeping feedback and shared feelings to a minimum; avoiding disclosure. | More directive approach, outlining how the process will develop and laying down a clear structure. |

**TABLE 9.1** *continued*

| Stage | Task | Major processes | Characteristics | Leadership |
|-------|------|-----------------|-----------------|------------|
| Storming (Conflict): Sorting out process – bidding for control and power | Operating rules; decision-making processes; communication processes; authority levels. | Process is likely to break down until conflict is resolved. | Strongly expressing views; poor listening; challenging leadership and authority; withdrawal by some; full expression of emotions; lack of collaboration; competing for control. | Leader needs to be supportive, actively listening to group members, managing the conflict, generating ideas, and explaining decisions. |
| Norming (Cohesion): Self-organization | Relationships; interfaces. | The core process should operate smoothly, although there is a danger of focusing on smaller process issues rather than the core work of the group. | Shared leadership; methodical way of working; preparedness to change; preconceived views; receptiveness to ideas; active participation by all; mutual problem-solving versus 'win–lose'; open exchange of ideas. | Leader acts as a group member as leadership is starting to be shared. Leader helps to develop consensus. |
| Performing (Performance): Maturity and mutual acceptance | Productivity. | The process functions well and is adjusted as necessary. Leadership is shared and tasks delegated. | High flexibility of contribution; high creativity; openness and trust; shared leadership; strong relationships; feelings of warmth; easy acceptance of differences in views. | Leader takes overview, but within the day-to-day running, the group is sharing leadership between members. |

Two more stages – dorming and mourning – have subsequently been added to the original model. These extra stages are very helpful in understanding the difficulties in maintaining a 'high performance team'.

## Dorming

The group has now been together for a length of time and has achieved a degree of success, which the members may start to take for granted. They then start to take their eyes off the ball, which causes their performance to become a little stale, and they stop achieving such good results.

## Mourning

Groups, like everything else, do not go on forever. Sooner or later they disband or individual members leave. So, as with every other life cycle, the group can go through a mourning phase when either the group as a whole ceases to exist or members leave to go off on other assignments. The effects on individuals can be very marked, often producing a feeling of loss, frustration and stress.

# Teams

So far we have looked at groups, and we now understand the group to be a well-proven way of getting people to work together. Why do we need to bother with teams?

The answer is simple: a team is a special sort of group. It has the potential to capitalize on individual efforts, bringing them together in a way that is greater than the sum of the individual parts, ie the whole is greater than the sum (whole > sum).

However, this is a feature of good teams. The 'whole > sum' equation shows that a group of people is working well together, but there are some teams whose collective performance falls short of what you might expect, given the quality of the individuals.

It is clear that team composition is important. People need to understand, and be able to perform, the role intended for them in the team, so that the team can achieve its objective(s) and maintain optimum performance.

A team is a small number of people with complementary skills who are committed to a common purpose, performance goals and approach for which they hold themselves mutually accountable.

Katzenbach, J and Smith, D, *The Wisdom of Teams*
(Harvard Business Review, 1993)[14]

The team has:

- a facilitator/coach rather than a leader;
- goals that are set by its members rather than from outside the team;
- communication patterns that flow both up and down the team.

Members take decisions together, work together cooperatively and are jointly responsible for the outcomes achieved.

A team is a tool that enables a professional services business to achieve its goals. It does this by tapping into and bringing together the talents of the team members. Clearly, to make a team 100 per cent effective you have to work at it – create it, maintain it and sustain it.

## Characteristics of effective teams

Successful teams share certain attributes such as team members being: loyal to each other and the team; able to identify and agree a collective outcome rather than have a collection of individual ones; keen to cooperate and collaborate in order to achieve the collective outcome; focused on creating team (rather than individual) outcomes, and able to define these outcomes in ways that are specific, tangible, measurable and meaningful to all team members.

The attributes of successful teams include:

**A clear unity of purpose:** there is free discussion of the objectives until team members can commit themselves to them and all of the objectives are meaningful to each team member.

**The team is self-conscious about its own operations:** the team has taken time to discuss how the team will function to achieve its objectives and it has clear, explicit and mutually agreed approaches, methodologies, norms, expectations etc. The team will stop to review how well it is doing.

**The team has clear and demanding performance goals and objectives:** these have been set by the team itself and have been translated into well-defined milestones against which the team measures itself. The team defines and achieves a continual series of 'small wins' along the way to larger goals.

**The atmosphere tends to be informal, comfortable and relaxed:** there are no obvious tensions and the team maintains a working atmosphere in which people are involved and interested.

**There is a lot of discussion in which virtually everyone participates:** however, all discussion remains pertinent to the purpose of the team. If discussion goes off track, then someone will bring it back in short order. The team members listen to each other. Every idea is given a hearing. People are not afraid of sounding foolish by putting forward a creative thought. People feel free to express their feelings as well as their ideas.

**If there is disagreement, this is viewed as a virtue:** disagreements are not suppressed or overridden by premature team action. The reasons behind disagreements are carefully examined and the team seeks to resolve them rather than dominate the dissenter. Dissenters are not trying to dominate the team; they have a genuine difference of opinion. If there are basic disagreements that cannot be resolved, the team figures out a way to live with them without letting them block its efforts.

**Most decisions are made at a point where there is general agreement:** however, those who disagree with the general agreement of the team do not keep their opposition private or let an apparent consensus mask their disagreement. The team does not accept a simple majority as a proper basis for action.

**Each individual carries his or her own weight:** in supporting and enabling the team to meet or exceed the expectations of other team members, each individual is respectful of the mechanics of the team: arriving on time, coming to meetings prepared, completing agreed-upon tasks on time etc. When action is taken, clear assignments are made (who–what–when) and willingly accepted and completed by each team member.

**Feedback is frequent, frank and relatively comfortable:** any feedback has a constructive flavour and is oriented towards removing any obstacle that faces the team.

**The leadership of the group shifts from time to time:** the issue is not who controls, but how to get the job done.

## Individual and team roles

Each individual member of a team will have a different personality and different talents. These need to be recognized and exploited in order to ensure that the team works effectively and efficiently.

Behavioural psychologists have developed different team models and classification systems. These can be helpful tools in recognizing and understanding an individual's needs and aspirations, not only to identify ways of motivating them, but to ensure the best results for the team of which they are a member.

Dr Meredith Belbin defines a team role as: '*A tendency to behave, contribute and interrelate with others in a particular way.*'

**TABLE 9.2** Belbin's model of team roles

| Overall | Belbin role | Contributions to the team | Allowable weaknesses |
|---|---|---|---|
| Doing/acting | Implementer | Disciplined, reliable, conservative and efficient. Takes basic ideas and makes them work in practice. | Can be slow to respond to new possibilities. Somewhat inflexible. |
| | Completer/ finisher | Painstaking, conscientious, anxious. Turns ideas into practical actions. | Inclined to worry unduly. Reluctant to delegate. |
| | Shaper | Challenging, dynamic, thrives on pressure. Has the drive and courage to overcome obstacles. | Prone to provocation. Can offend people's feelings. |
| People/feelings | Coordinator | Mature, confident, a good chairperson. Delegates well. Clarifies goals, promotes decision making. | Can be seen as excessively controlling. Offloads work. |
| | Team worker | Cooperative, mild, perceptive and diplomatic. Good listener and works to resolve social problems. | Can have problems making difficult decisions. Can be indecisive in crunch decisions. |
| | Resource investigator | Extrovert – exploring new ideas and possibilities energetically and with others. Good networker. | Can be over-optimistic. Loses interest once initial enthusiasm has passed. |

**TABLE 9.2**  *Continued*

| Overall | Belbin role | Contributions to the team | Allowable weaknesses |
|---|---|---|---|
| Thinking/ problem solving | Plant | Creative, imaginative and unorthodox. Solves difficult problems with original and creative ideas. | Too preoccupied to communicate effectively. Ignores details. |
| | Monitor/ evaluator | Sober, strategic and discerning. Thinks carefully and accurately about things. | Lacks drive and ability to inspire others. |
| | Specialist | Single-minded, self starting and dedicated. Provides knowledge and skills – often in rare supply. | Contributes only on a narrow front. Dwells on technicalities. |

Belbin's model describes a pattern that characterizes one individual's behaviour in relation to another in facilitating the progress of a team. Belbin maintains that accurately delineating team roles is crucial to understanding the dynamics of any team. To be successful, a team should have individuals fulfilling these roles.

The individual profile is unique to a particular person. The two roles with the highest scores for each individual are their primary and secondary roles. It is not desirable for a member of a team to take on a team role that is not their primary or secondary role. Individuals will try to hide their weaknesses, but Belbin maintains that it is dangerous to try to correct those weaknesses.[15]

# The life cycle of a team

You have now spent some time reading about the theory of groups, teams and team roles. It is important to consider how this theory relates to reality, ie the environment in which you work. Please reflect on what you have read, your job role and the environment in which you work, then, thinking about the people you work with, consider the following questions:

- Do you work in a 'group' or a 'team'? What, if anything, is the significance of this difference to the way the people you work with function?
- At what stage of development is the group or team in which you work?
  - Forming? (the key issues are dependency and inclusion)
  - Storming? (the issues are 'counter-dependency' and conflict)
  - Norming? (the issues are trust, goal setting and structure)
  - Performing? (the focus is on maximizing work and productivity)
- What is the significance of this stage of development, both for you and for the group/team as a whole?

Having identified the group/team and its stage of development, let's now focus on its structure and consider the group/team in which you work.

- Can the structure of the group/team in which you work be readily and accurately identified by you and other team members?
- Could a more effective structure be introduced?
- What benefits could be derived from a change in team structure?

## Your role in the team

It is important that we reflect on the role that we play in the team(s) in which we work. You may have an established role in a team that is 'permanent' or 'semi-permanent'. You may also be called on from time to time to work in project teams that are more fluid in the short or medium term. Project teams can involve intensive activity set against a tight timetable. It is often these project teams that test us as individuals, the team as a unit and the leadership skills of the team leader.

You may be a member of a number of different project teams as well as a departmental or practice area team. Your role may be different (to some degree) for each project or there may be a difference between the role that you undertake in the department to that which you play in a specific project team(s). In answering the two questions set out below, try to be as objective as possible – inevitably your answers will include elements of subjectivity based on your perceptions: recognize these and be as objective as possible.

Thinking about you and the team in which you work, using Belbin's team roles: 1) identify your role within the team in which you work; 2) identify the roles of other team members.

## How do other team members perceive your role?

You need to consider the subjectivity with which other people view your role in the team. For example: if you are a graduate trainee joining the business following your academic studies, this is your first step on the ladder to a professional career and you and those close to you are proud of what you are achieving. In reality your role at work is to learn and to develop the skills that the business needs from you to meet the demands of its clients. This may entail a considerable amount of dull, repetitive and basic tasks that need to be completed (eg document bundling and copying) in order to deliver the service effectively to clients.

In this context there is likely to be a 'disconnect' between your perception, the perception of other team members and of the team leader regarding your role in the team. There is also an essential core that you and others recognize as your role, ie that you are there to learn and become an effective team member. However, the pathway that you thought you might take to that destination and the route that client work demands – and other team members need you to take – may be very different indeed.

The team leader and the other team members expect that you will be given the tasks needed to deliver the projects on time for the client, regardless of what you may learn from them, the time it takes, or your work–life balance. It can be exhilarating to be a member of a project team that is in demand and enjoying recognition and success – it can also be mind-numbingly dull and exhausting if your role is to do the 'grunt-level' tasks in that team, time and again as each project dictates.

## How does the team leader perceive your role?

A further thought is that many time-served partners and managers went through the same process when they were 'trainees'. It may well be that a generation (or more) ago they joined after leaving school rather than completing a university degree and/or postgraduate qualification. Therefore, they see the role of 'trainee' as a 'rite of passage' – 'I got through it. I don't see the problem. If they can't hack it they should get out.' These sorts of attitudes infect how some people view the role of trainees in the workplace. Hopefully this approach is not common.

If the team leader is more enlightened, they will have taken the time to consider what the business needs from both 'trainees' and 'qualified' entrants to the profession. It may well be that the business you work for has designed a set of competencies (skills sets) for trainees. Typically these will set out the 'outcomes' that are expected of a trainee at the point of qualification, ie the point of entry into the profession. These outcomes are a target that need to be achieved by each person in order to qualify into the profession.

The role of both the team leader and team members supervising trainees is to ensure that trainees receive the experiences and work needed so that they can demonstrate that they have the competencies of a newly qualified entrant to the profession at the time when they complete the period of training.

Using this approach, the period of training is structured to achieving clear outcomes and team leaders, supervisors and trainees are focused on their roles in ensuring that trainees achieve those outcomes and qualify.

# Effective team members

We are often asked by young professionals: 'What should I do to be the most effective team member?' There is no simple answer to the question. There are, however, a number of points that should be borne in mind:

Competencies and skills sets: to be fully effective, and in certain situations to progress and qualify into the profession, you may have to demonstrate that you have certain competencies or skills. These may be objectively assessed by a third party reviewing your work or observing you demonstrating the skill, eg by delivering a presentation.

You need to understand the expectations set out in the competencies, develop your skills to the required standard (seek assistance if needed to help you develop the skills) and be able to demonstrate that you have the skills.

Be prepared to learn: you may not always get things right first time – we rarely do. You must be prepared to learn from your mistakes and try not to repeat them. An effective team member develops and learns from experience and endeavours not to make the same mistake again.

Seek supervision and support: if you do not understand what you have been asked to do, or need further guidance in order to complete a task effectively. Seek out the person who supervises, explain the situation, seek guidance and progress with the task. Ineffective team members have a go, get it wrong and make excuses as to why they did not seek support.

Endurance and tenacity: when there is a lot of work on and you are having to 'work all the hours', where an emergency occurs or the project/task turns out to be far larger than originally scoped – stick with it. Be tenacious, be prepared to stay late, work the hours and treat the task/project as your key priority. Endurance and tenacity can be exploited in an inappropriate way by some employers. Good employers recognize these attributes and call on you to use them only when necessary.

Be a team player: unaligned behaviour is when an individual chooses to behave in a way that may benefit them but is to the detriment of others in the team, the team itself or the business as a whole. This sort of behaviour is negative and hugely disruptive. To be the most effective team member, your behaviour will always be aligned with the team's needs and objectives.

Empathy and understanding: a truly effective team member will be empathic to the needs of other team members and the team leader. Understanding the situations in which other team members find themselves and being prepared to assist them for the benefit of the team is an important attribute of the best team members. When team members support and help one another – because they understand the need to do so, empathize with the situation in which the other team member or team leader finds themselves and do so willingly – they are behaving in the most effective way.

An adjunct to all of this is a degree of selflessness, ie putting the team's needs ahead of one's own. This is a positive attribute of the best team members.

**Personal organization and effectiveness:** the best team members are those who are well organized and effective at all times. They understand what is needed in their team role and are able to undertake the tasks delegated to them effectively and in a timely manner. They meet agreed deadlines and will manage expectations if this is not possible.

**Quality output:** the work product of the best team members is of a consistently high quality. Consistency of output is a key attribute of an effective team member, because they can be relied upon to do a good job each and every time. This means that good work will be delegated to them and they will be entrusted to deliver the normal high-quality service.

**Profitability:** the team as a whole should meet the budgets set for financial performance. The best team members will make a strong contribution to the team's profitability. This should not be at the expense of other team members (to do so is unaligned behaviour) or at the expense of other teams within the business. Some team members place their own 'financials' ahead of the team's. They wrongly believe that their individual financial performance will mark them out as a 'star' even if it is at the expense of other team members – they are wrong. Astute team leaders recognize that the overall financial performance of the team is more important. An individual team member's performance is outstanding if it meets (or exceeds the budget set) and supports the overall 'financials' for the team. The former without the latter is not the way in which the best team members conduct themselves.

# The team leader

What do you expect from your team leader?

Most people want their team leader to ensure that they have a regular flow of interesting and challenging work from which they can learn and develop their skills. This is a good starting point, as it introduces the need for effective delegation of tasks by the team leader.

You will also want support, in the form of supervision and constructive feedback. On a day-to-day basis this will be evidenced by clear instructions when tasks are delegated to you, their being approachable and your being able to ask questions when you are not sure what to do. When you have completed the task, you expect them to review the work, give guidance and suggest amendments, and at some point provide constructive feedback on how you could improve the quality of work delivered on that task.

You will also want the team leader to be calm and effective under pressure and at times of crisis, eg when mistakes occur, you want them to assist you in resolving them and to provide support if difficult issues need to be dealt with. You do not want a leader who panics, becomes rude and aggressive, or who withdraws and provides no support.

It is not always easy to find the perfect team leader – though you may be lucky and work for someone who has most, if not all, of the attributes of an effective leader.

# Conclusion

In this chapter we have sought to get you thinking about your own motivations, how groups and teams function, and team roles, specifically *your* team role and how that relates to other team members. We have also looked at the attributes of an effective team member and the legitimate expectations you may have of a team leader.

You have learned that your motivation and what motivates others may vary. It is important to be aware of your own motivation, how it affects you, your work and your role within the team. Equally, it is important to understand the motivation of other team members (including the team leader), what motivates them and the likely impact of this. You need also to be aware of the motivation of clients and third parties for whom and with whom you work.

In order to make a contribution as an effective (and profitable) team member you need to understand your role within the team, the roles of others (including the team leader) and know when to involve other people in the tasks that have been delegated to you. You also need to understand and implement the behaviours that will make you an effective team member in the team in which you work.

You now appreciate that effective teams are vital structures within professional services businesses. They are the means through which the business delivers a high-quality service to its clients; they generate profitability and are of logistical importance to developing the business. Effective teamwork enables the business to get the right things done by the right people in a timely and efficient way, which enhances the profitability of the business and helps secure its success and long-term viability.

# Managing performance, setting objectives, maintaining momentum and responding to feedback

## Introduction

Your role as a professional is to give clear, knowledgeable, relevant and useful advice, as well as to play your part within your own organization. Professionals who perform their role well never stop learning. They continue developing their knowledge and skills to keep up with a changing world, a changing profession, and a changing regulatory environment. They set themselves goals, they seek and act on feedback, and they maintain their own momentum at work.

We are all used to having, and achieving, goals. To progress to the next stage we must perform and meet particular standards. The world of work requires us to use those same skills (setting goals and meeting standards), making sure that we define our goals in the context of our organization's needs and our own career development.

It is never too early to look at your own performance at work and to see how you can maintain and improve it. From your first day onwards, you have the opportunity to show that you are self-motivated, want to develop your knowledge and skills and have the foresight to manage your career.

In today's environment, these attributes are what separate really good professionals from the rest. The people who focus on where their career is heading, and who look for ways to develop the knowledge and skills they need, using feedback from others and reflecting on their own performance, are the ones who will get to where they want to go. Of course, it is still possible to do this by sheer luck alone, but it is a risk to leave your entire career to chance. It is far better to be a good manager of your own performance and the agent of your own destiny.

By the end of this chapter you will understand how to:

- gauge the standards you need to achieve;
- set your own objectives;
- give and receive feedback;
- approach performance reviews;
- maintain your own momentum in your job.

Practise all of these things and you will grow in confidence in managing your own performance.

# The benchmark for good performance

You will need to know what the benchmark of good performance is for professionals at your level in your organization.

## *Available information*

Some performance standards are clear and readily available. You might already know about, and should have access to:

- written competency frameworks;
- written codes of ethics and standards for your profession;
- targets for hours worked, or billings, for your level;
- other development targets that you need to achieve (for example, particular training that you have to undertake at a certain point in your career).

Make sure you familiarize yourself with these, and with the professional skills we outline in this book.

## Information you will need to uncover

Other performance standards are not as clear. For instance:

- What are the unspoken rules of your organization?
- What is your manager expecting of you, both now and in the next 12 months?
- What does being professional mean in your profession?

The best way to find out these things is to talk to other people. Talk to them as much as you can about your organization and how it works. Have frequent conversations with your manager (which you may need to initiate) into what his or her expectations are for you. Your human resources team will also be able to give you a great deal of guidance. They might even be able to help you to find a mentor – someone with a lot of experience who can act as a confidential sounding board and source of guidance and support for you, and who is not managing you.

## Build up your own picture

Use all these sources of information to build a picture for yourself, showing you what you need to achieve over the next year and over the medium term. Be as clear as you can about what will constitute success, so that you can aim for that and show what you have done at the end of the year. Be confident about asking questions so that you can form this picture.

Perhaps in your organization you have a formal review with one or two managers at the end of every year. You want this to be a positive experience during which your achievements are recognized and praised, and areas to work on are discussed. You do not want this to be the first time that performance standards are mentioned that you did not previously know about or understand. There are countless people who have gone into their formal performance review only to find out that there is a gap in their performance that is being mentioned for the first time.

### An example

Your role often requires you to speak to clients on the telephone. When you started work, you had an hour of telephone training and, following that, you have been speaking to clients very confidently.

However, in your review, your manager says that she has overheard you a few times in the last week on the telephone. She has noticed that you have been abrupt with one or two clients, who have not provided you with the information that they had promised they would supply. She says that, from your tone when you responded, it was clear that you were cross with the clients and felt they had let you down. In one case, she happened to know that one of the clients in question had a huge amount of urgent work to do and was feeling rather under pressure. In the other case, the client had been on holiday and therefore had not been able to supply the information to you. She adds that being professional is inextricably linked to understanding your clients, and that in the cases she mentions, you had got the tone wrong because it would have left the clients feeling more pressurized, or told off, rather than helped. Even though your work has been held up by the clients, your manager adds that your role is to make the clients feel they have a trusted and helpful adviser. She asks how you would feel if you were either of those two clients – and you agree that your manner would not have been helpful. Here is an expectation that you had failed to understand and which is affecting the view your manager has of your overall performance.

You discuss this with your manager, and you agree that you need to think more about your client-care skills. You have never been challenged like this on these skills before and you have always felt that you are 'good with people'. But you do agree that, if this situation happens again, you will need to see things from your client's point of view and make allowances, since otherwise you are destroying the rapport you have built up with that client. You agree to do more to understand each of your clients and the pressures on them, which will help you to respond to them appropriately.

# Objectives

## *Setting your own objectives*

For much of our early lives, our objectives are set for us. We have years of school and university to go through, we have examinations, and we have certain things we need to show we have done in order to secure our jobs. We know what we need to do and we do it. However, at an early point in your career as a professional, you will need to take over the goal-setting process for yourself – if you have done a few years of training at the start of your professional life, this point comes once the training is over and you have qualified. Or it may come on the day you start work. From this point on, how you achieve, and at what rate, is largely up to you. Yes, there will still be support available for you, but you will need to seek it out, and the motivation to achieve goals must come largely from within yourself. As a professional, there are many different areas in which to set goals: you need to develop your subject area skills, but also all of the other aspects of practice concerned with giving advice and help to others, many of which we deal with in this book.

When you understand the benchmark for good performance, based on your knowledge of the readily available information, and the information you have obtained by observing your organization and talking to others, you are ready to set yourself some goals, or objectives.

## SMART objectives

You may already know about making your objectives SMART. To remind you, this acronym stands for:

| | | |
|---|---|---|
| **S** | Specific | Choose a specific result that you can reasonably expect to achieve within a defined time frame. |
| **M** | Measurable | Make sure you will be able to measure what you achieved. Think about how you will actually know and prove that you have achieved what you set yourself. |
| **A** | Agreed | Agree the objective with your manager or a mentor, so you know that it is appropriate for your role and level and so you can expect that person's support. |
| **R** | Realistic | Make the objective realistic. If the task is too daunting, or it is impossible to achieve, then you will be demotivated. |
| **T** | Timed | Set the right timescale. If it is too short then the objective will be unachievable; if it is too long then you might lose interest. |

Remember that your objectives are there to help you to achieve and to improve your own performance as a professional, and to help you plan and develop your career. Make them challenging but achievable, and set yourself a conservative number to start with. As you tick off objectives achieved, you can set yourself some more.

## An example

Let's say you want to improve your presentation skills, because you are slightly daunted by presenting. You also know that most professions demand more and more presenting ability from those working within them, as they move higher up the ladder – therefore this is an important skill to master. How can you set yourself a SMART objective? Your first attempt to write your objective says: *Do two presentations by the end of the year.* But you are not sure whether this is SMART, so you discuss it with your manager. He suggests that you start by doing some presentation skills training, and then you focus on raising the profile of your team's work within your organization. So you rewrite it as:

- *Go on a presentation skills course by April.*
- *Develop a half-hour presentation on the work of our team by May.*
- *Deliver the presentation to two other teams by the end of July and get feedback by mid-August.*
- *Review feedback by end of August and find two things I do well and two ways to improve skills.*

You check this with your manager. He agrees that it is SMART. It is specific and measurable: you will be able to tick off each of the four aspects of the objective. Your manager has also suggested ways to improve it and you feel confident that it is realistic. And you have set yourself a definite timetable.

At the end of the process you will have practised your presenting, and will also have some evidence for what you already do well and what you can improve. You can see that setting a SMART objective needs you to pay attention to all the five aspects of the acronym, and sometimes to break down an objective into small chunks.

## Stretching and challenging yourself through your objectives

Although many of your objectives are set within the context of your day-to-day work, they should still stretch and challenge you in ways you will enjoy. You will probably have some goals in your area of technical expertise, and some goals around other necessary work you are doing. But don't forget to set yourself some other personal development goals as well. This might be the year in which you would like to write your first article, or you would like to work towards your first promotion with a mentor, or you would like to get better at networking. All of these are suitable subjects for your objectives and will help you show at the end of the year that you are motivated to learn and to develop your skills, which (as we have noted earlier) is a vital part of being a professional.

# Maintaining momentum

Professionals who enjoy their work and who succeed in their aims are self-motivated and seek out opportunities. They understand that seeking out and taking opportunities requires both strategic thinking, and effort.

## Self-review

A good habit to get into is putting aside some time, regularly, to:

- review your objectives to see what progress you have made;
- check on what you still need to do;
- assure yourself that your objectives are still relevant and stretching;
- set more objectives if some have already been achieved, or are no longer relevant.

This does not have to take a lot of time. You could do this review once a month, perhaps during a lunchtime or at the start of a quiet day.

## Use others to help you achieve

If you have regular meetings with your manager or a mentor, you could use one of those meetings to discuss particular objectives, for example if you have completed an objective and have something to report, or if you need particular help with another objective. Talking to someone else about our objectives and goals can often help to increase motivation and can also generate new thinking and ideas to add to our own. At the same time, if you are getting stuck with a particular objective, talking it through with someone else can often be a spur to moving on. Use others within your organization to help yourself maintain momentum throughout the year. Remember that part of being a professional is to teach and mentor the next generation of professionals, and this means that people who are more experienced will often be pleased to help you if you ask them.

## Prioritize career objectives

We showed you in Chapter 3 how you can use the urgent/important grid to bring into focus the things that are strategically important for you and your long-term career. Set yourself objectives around things that you position in the grid as important – as we noted, it is often the hard things that we put off, and things that may not have particular deadlines – but these are also often the things that can really raise our own profile and propel our careers forward. Seek out the opportunities for learning knowledge and skills within your profession and organization, and use them. You will generally find that there are many seminars and workshops that you can go to, if you search them out. See below for a short checklist on maintaining momentum.

> ### Maintaining momentum at work
>
> - Set yourself SMART objectives at the start of the year – some short term and some medium term.
>
> - Anything important but not urgent should be the subject of a SMART objective.
>
> - Put aside some regular time to review your objectives.
>
> - Find a mentor to discuss your objectives with (or your manager).
>
> - Put aside some regular time (perhaps twice a year) to think about your own career and how you want to develop it.
>
> - Balance your on-the-job learning with courses and other development opportunities.
>
> - Find your own role models within your profession and organization, and reflect on how they maintain momentum and motivation.
>
> - Be open to new ideas.
>
> - Keep a note of your achievements throughout the year and what you have learnt from fulfilling your objectives – it is easy to forget these things over time.

## An example

You have just started a new job and so you are keen to show that you are motivated and focused. You do not yet know many people outside your immediate team. What can you do?

You start by asking your manager if you could talk to her over coffee about what she would like you to achieve over the next year. In preparation for this you make a short, bullet-pointed list of the technical areas you would like to work on, the types of work you would like to experience, and the skills you would like to develop.

To your surprise, the first thing your manager talks to you about is the strategy of your organization for the coming year. She wants to put your objectives into a wider context and to make sure you understand what your department is aiming to achieve. You have a vague understanding of the organizational strategy but this discussion is much more detailed. It is enlightening: you realize that you should change some of the objectives you had been thinking about.

Your manager suggests that you use one of the more experienced members of the team as a mentor for the first six months – she knows that the other team member would be happy to do this, and you are also keen. You meet your mentor, who offers to take you to a talk he is going to one evening on a technical area that your department is trying to break into. You go along, and afterwards you decide that this could be an area where you could focus and really help the team – but you hadn't known about it before.

You go back to talk to your manager about your revised list of objectives, which are now tilted more towards the organization's strategy and the department strategy. You feel you have shown early on that you are motivated by taking the initiative, using the resources that you have been offered, and tailoring your objectives to fit into the bigger picture. You set up the next coffee with your mentor and decide on the topics you would like to discuss with him/her.

This example shows the value of talking to people openly about what you would like to do, and what they would like you to do, of setting yourself objectives that show you are contributing, and of taking the help and support that is offered. All of these will help you to set the right goals and maintain momentum.

# Receiving feedback

Many professionals find receiving feedback hard. They are used to giving advice to others, and being right. But they themselves may not be practised in giving good feedback to others and they may interpret feedback given to them as criticism. In fact, seeking out feedback is the best way to understand how your own performance is being viewed by others, and of finding out what you are really good at and what you can improve on. Few of us know ourselves well enough to have all this information without being given any clues. As a professional, you need to keep learning and improving your performance – and an easy way to help yourself with this is to practise the art of asking for – and being open to – feedback.

## When might you be given feedback?

You should be given feedback in your regular performance reviews, and ideally should be given feedback regularly so that nothing in your performance review is a surprise. You may be given some feedback after a particular piece of work has been finished, or if you are part of a team that is reviewing its group performance in order to learn lessons for the future. If your manager is diligent, you may be given feedback often on how you are doing. This is the ideal situation.

For many professionals, though, the reality is that they will be given little useful feedback unless they ask for it. There is still a view that feedback only needs to be given if something goes wrong, and that no news is good news. However, a lack of feedback (at best) means you don't improve as quickly as you could, and (at worst) can leave you feeling unsure of how well you are performing. So if you are not being given enough feedback, then ensure that you ask people, and make it easy for them to give you their views.

## *How to make it easy for others to give you feedback*

There are a few simple things you can do to make it easy for others to give you feedback. Here are some points to help you:

1 Think about an area of skill or a piece of work on which you would like feedback to be given.

2 Choose someone who has seen you using that skill, or has first-hand knowledge of your contribution to the piece of work, to give you feedback.

3 Fix a time and a forum that suits you both – this could be a formal setting in a meeting room, or informally over a coffee.

4 Tell the other person what you would like their feedback on, and that you are seeking feedback to help you understand what you do well and what you could improve.

5 Assess for yourself how good you think you are at that skill area, or how well you did the piece of work. Be as objective as you can.

6 When you are receiving the feedback, listen carefully and do not interrupt.

7 Keep in mind that you are trying to get insight and information about yourself, so ask questions to help you to understand.

8 Even if the feedback is not what you had hoped for, maintain your composure and do not get defensive or argue.

9 If you do not agree with the feedback, discuss your reasons – be objective.

10 End the discussion on a positive note, and an action point, which will show the other person that you value what they have said.

11 Thank the other person for their feedback and for helping you.

At times, every professional has been given constructive feedback that he or she was not expecting to get, and which has initially been demotivating. If this happens to you, remember that it is not uncommon, and what will set you apart as a high performer is what you choose to do with that feedback. Let the dust settle and then think about it carefully. Discuss it with someone else you trust, and who knows you well. Work out what parts of the feedback are correct, and what parts may not be quite right – there is usually a kernel of truth, and this is what you are trying to get to. When you understand that, you will be able to act on it and enhance your performance by making some changes.

### An example

You have been in your job for three months. You have asked your manager for some feedback on how you are getting on, and the meeting has generally gone well, but you have been given one piece of constructive feedback that you were not expecting. Your manager has found some examples of your written work and suggested that you improve your grammar, showing you how she would have rewritten particular sentences of yours. Your manager mentions that professionals really need to have the best written skills possible, as so much of their advice and help gets put into written form, and it needs to be clear, properly written, easy to understand and well structured. You have never been given this feedback before – you have always felt confident about your written skills. You have agreed with your manager that you will look at ways of improving but secretly you are slightly annoyed.

You mull things over for a few days and then decide to talk to a friend, who you know has a very good writing style, about your feedback. You say to your friend that you would appreciate his honest opinion and you take extracts from the pieces of work with you.

Your friend thinks that, in some instances, your manager's comments were a matter purely of personal style. But he also agrees with your manager that you could improve your grammar in certain respects, particularly when writing more formally. He suggests a good website and a short book on grammar, which he himself sometimes refers to, and you decide that you will use these resources and also ask your manager more regularly for feedback on your writing.

In this example, despite initial disappointment with the feedback, you have used the information to motivate you to improve – and when your manager sees this, she will be encouraged to see that you have acted upon her feedback and that you have maintained your own momentum.

# Giving feedback

Accurate and honest feedback is a vital element in strengthening the performance of team members. Professionals today often work in environments where, even at entry level, they are asked to give feedback on other people – so it is worth learning early on how to give effective feedback.

It is usually easy to give good feedback, because both the giver and the receiver can feel pleased about a job well done. It is not always easy to provide constructive feedback, because emotion and subjectivity can take over. It may also be difficult for the individual to accept the feedback that he or she is being given about performance, as we have seen from the example above.

Feedback is more readily acceptable when it is given promptly and when it is objective and supported by details and examples (rather than generalizations). If it is expressed as a direct criticism or is made personal, then it will have a negative impact and will not assist the person to improve.

## *What are the components of constructive feedback?*

Constructive feedback has the following key components:

E = **Example** – a clear example of the issue.

E = **Effect** – an explanation of the effect of the issue on you, or others who have been affected.

C = **Change** –the performance that you would like to see and the benefits of this change for the person concerned.

C can also mean **Continue**. See Positive Feedback (below).

This model is a way to ensure that you always provide effective and useful feedback that will be helpful to the other person.

### An example

Let's say that you need to give some feedback to a trainee about a meeting you have just been to. The trainee was meant to be taking notes of the meeting but a couple of times you caught her staring into the middle distance when something important was being discussed, and although you did remind her in the meeting about taking notes, you are unsure about whether she got everything down. The same thing happened in a meeting you went to yesterday. As we mentioned in Chapter 6, taking good notes when in a meeting is a professional skill (and the time spent in training is the best time to get into good habits in this skill area).

It is important that you give this feedback promptly so that you give the trainee a chance to improve straight away. You always have a regular 15-minute meeting every Friday, which is the next day. You use the EEC formula and start with an example: that in two meetings you had asked the trainee to take notes but that you had noticed that she appeared not to be concentrating fully and had missed writing down some important points. You had also nudged her a couple of times. You then talk about the effect by explaining that the trainee's notes are important as a record of what was discussed and agreed, and that you might need to refer to them later, and therefore it is really important that she keeps full notes. You add that with so many different things to do, it is very easy to forget the details of what happened in any one meeting, and that good, reliable notes are often vital reference points, enabling the best standard of service to be given to clients. This is an important aspect of being professional.

At this point, you ask the trainee for her response. She agrees with you that her concentration did lapse in those meetings because she did not really understand what was being discussed and it was difficult to follow. She was also tired after working late every night this week. However, she agrees that her performance needs to improve and she understands why. You have a discussion about what being professional actually means and the trainee is quite surprised by some of the aspects you mention. She had not seen her own note-taking as part of being professional – to her it was a trainee 'chore'. You point out that you yourself still take careful notes in every meeting and have often needed to look back at them.

You discuss how things could change and you agree that you will talk to her briefly before meetings to explain the key elements of the meeting and give her some context. She also says that if she does not understand something in the meeting, or is not following the discussion, she will ask a question. She will also review her notes after each meeting to check that they are a full record. You agree that you will both discuss progress again in a month. The trainee leaves feeling positive about the conversation and does make the changes.

## Positive feedback

Professionals have high expectations of themselves and are driven to achieve. But however self-motivated a professional is, it is always a pleasure to receive positive feedback. To give effective feedback on something positive, you can still use the EEC model. Here **C = Continue**. Start with a specific example of what was done well, and remember to talk about the effect. So instead of saying to someone: *'well done, the client says you did a good job'*, you might say: *'the advice you wrote for the client was concise, commercial and easy to follow, and the client has contacted me to say that it was a very helpful piece of work as a result – well done'*.

In the second example you can see that there is a lot more information than in the first – it is easy to see exactly what made the job good (writing in a concise, commercial and easy-to-follow way) and this will reinforce the positive for the future.

## Give regular feedback

If you are responsible for managing others, then part of your role is to give them regular informal feedback throughout the year, so that they always have a clear idea of how they are performing and what your current expectations are. Remember to balance out constructive feedback with positive feedback – so you need to notice what people are doing well, not just what they could improve upon. If you give regular feedback, nothing which comes up in a formal performance review will be a surprise.

# Performance reviews

Most professionals now have at least one formal performance review a year and many approach them with some dread. However, like feedback, reviews are a key component of evaluating performance and of being open about strengths and weaknesses. Therefore, whether you are reviewing someone or being reviewed, it is important to prepare for the review and approach it in a positive way. In this section we give some practical tips on how to do so.

## *If you are the reviewer*

If you are the reviewer, put aside enough time to prepare carefully for the meeting in advance. You should have readily to hand the criteria against which you are reviewing (which may be the relevant role description, or set of competencies or skills) and any other information that you will need to refer to.

If possible you should also try to collect feedback from others on the person being reviewed, and should question them about their feedback, if not given in the EEC format. You will need specific examples and an understanding of effect, and if you or others cannot think of an example to use as the basis of a piece of feedback, the feedback should not be given until you do have an example. So, rather than make a generalization such as: *you are spending too much time chatting to friends at your desk*, you will need a specific example and a reason why this is not appropriate. If you cannot think of one, do not give the feedback. In particular, beware of passing on this kind of generalization from someone else, because it destroys trust and may well lead to passive resistance and demotivation.

In preparing for the meeting think about the following:

- How will I open the meeting so that it feels relaxed, open and positive?
- What will I say and do?
- What are the key things to cover?
  - Two-way discussion of performance over the previous year.
  - Two-way discussion of specific positive and constructive feedback.
  - The future: what I would like to see being achieved.
  - The future: what the person being reviewed would like to achieve in the short and medium term.
  - Help with objective setting.
  - Asking for feedback for myself from the person being reviewed.
- How will I show that I value the work that has been done and the commitment made to the team and organization?
- How will I end the meeting and what are the follow-up actions?

A good way to think about the meeting is that about 30 per cent should be focused on the past (past performance and feedback) and about 70 per cent should be focused on the future (the aims and objectives for the following year). If you have been giving regular feedback, then the first section can be short because it is only a summary of what has already been discussed. This leaves the rest of the meeting being future focused – it is a two-way planning process based on the plans of the person being reviewed, and the plans of the wider team, department and organization.

Write some notes for yourself so that you cover all the key points you have prepared: try to anticipate how the person being reviewed might feel and how you can make the review experience as positive as possible, even if you have some hard messages to give.

Do find time in the meeting to ask for feedback about yourself, or ways in which the two of you can work better together. If the discussion has been genuinely two-way and open then you may find that some good ideas are generated.

## If you are the person being reviewed

Again, put aside enough time to prepare for the meeting in advance. Have to hand all the performance benchmark information you have collected, and use it to review objectively your performance over the last year. Think about the following:

- What have I achieved over the last year and how can I evidence what I have done, and the impact?
- What skills and knowledge have I developed?
- Where could I have done better?
- How do I want my career to develop over the short and medium term?
- What would I like to achieve over the coming year?
- How can I make the best contribution to the organization?
- What feedback do I have for my manager (using the EEC format)?
- What do I need to do following my review?

Make some notes of your key points and take them with you to the meeting so that you can be sure you have covered everything that you want to. If you have an objective sense of your performance over the last year, backed with examples, then you are unlikely to be surprised by your manager's view – and if you do not agree with his or her view, you will be able to draw on specifics to make your own case. Remember that a review is a two-way process – it is your opportunity to have an open discussion with your manager and to give him or her some feedback as well as to receive feedback. If you do not understand any of the feedback that is given to you, ask for examples and make sure that you are clear about the effect, so that you can use the feedback to make changes.

Even if you receive some difficult messages in your review, keep listening carefully and ask questions so that you are really clear about why those messages have been given. If you feel you need some time to think, request a follow-up meeting with your manager and resume the discussion then.

Finally, once the review process is finished, complete any paperwork needed, and start work on your objectives for the next year.

## An example

Your performance review is in two weeks and you put aside sufficient time to prepare for it. You have got your skills framework to hand and also a list of the objectives you set yourself last year.

- You start by reviewing your objectives. For those that have been achieved you make a note of what the impact was and what you learnt from them. For those that have not been achieved, you make a note of what has stopped you.
- You then think about your achievements as a whole this year. You have been involved in a number of things in the organization that fall outside your written objectives and have received good feedback. You are aware that your manager may not know about all of this feedback so you make a note of it.
- You consider the constructive feedback you have received, what changes you have made and how you have developed as a result.
- You think about the development and training (both on and off the job) you have received this year and what it has helped you to achieve.
- You think about what skills and knowledge you would like to develop next year and the following one in order to help you with your next promotion.
- You think about the organization's strategy and realize you do not completely understand how your team's strategy fits into it, so this is something to discuss with your manager.
- You think about the impression you want to make in your review.
- You decide how you will react if there are any surprises in your review – the most important thing is to listen very carefully and ask questions to make sure you have understood clearly.
- You think about feedback for your manager and decide to ask for a regular monthly meeting to discuss progress. Your manager has preferred ad hoc meetings up to now, which have tended to happen once every few months, but you would prefer to have them in the calendar so that they happen each month.

You then set up the meeting with your manager and feel ready to have a positive review.

# Conclusion

We began the chapter with the thought that the good professional never stops learning. All of the things that have been described – understanding the benchmark, setting objectives, maintaining momentum, seeking feedback and having formal reviews – are there to help with your development as a professional. In order to progress, you not only have to be experienced in the technical aspects of your job, but you have to acquire all the other knowledge and skills expected of your profession and in your organization. You can only do this if you are open to new ideas, to making changes, and to learning about yourself through reflection and feedback.

# Financial and commercial awareness

## Introduction

There are many different interpretations of financial and commercial awareness, but ultimately it is about understanding that the key driver for almost every business is money. So an understanding of the factors that can impact on the ability of a business to make money or effectively manage its assets is crucial. Commercial awareness, therefore, involves understanding business concepts and how businesses work but to do this you do not need a corporate or financial background nor an accountancy qualification.

In this chapter we will look at what we mean by financial information and how it is used within businesses both internally and externally. We will then look at how to interpret the main financial statements of a typical company. The purpose of the chapter is to raise your awareness and understanding of financial and commercial issues.

Professionals do, however, need to be able to drill down into an industry, a sector or into a specific business and understand what is happening. Ultimately, the best professionals – the ones that clients want to work with and are happy to pay – are not those who can demonstrate that they know all the intricacies of their specialism, but rather, those who can demonstrate an in-depth knowledge of the client's business, strategy, industry and personality and then apply that knowledge to formulating the best professional and practical solution in the circumstances.

A starting point would be to keep up to date with the business sections on websites such as **www.ft.com**, **www.timesonline.co.uk**, **www.economist.com**, **www.telegraph.co.uk**.

## Types of trading entities

We looked briefly at and explained the trading options for professional services businesses in Chapter 1. In this chapter, we set out the various trading options for the clients of those businesses: sole traders, partnerships and companies.

## Sole trader

This is the simplest way to run a business. However, the sole trader is personally liable for any debts that the business runs up, which can carry a high level of risk.

## Types of partnerships

- **Partnership:** a partnership is an association of two or more persons who co-own a business for profit. Each partner carries joint and several liabilities for the partnership liabilities.
- **Limited liability partnership (LLP):** a limited liability partnership is a legal entity in its own right and enables its partners (known as 'members') as well as the LLP itself, to limit their liabilities. An LLP must submit its accounts to Companies House, just like limited companies.

## Charities, social enterprises and not-for-profit organizations

These may trade as unincorporated associations or as charitable incorporated organizations and as limited companies with a social purpose.

## Types of company

- **Private company limited by shares:** most private limited companies are owned by their shareholders and are limited by shares. This means that the liability of each member is limited to the amount unpaid on shares held by them.
- **Private company limited by guarantee:** companies limited by guarantee do not have shares, and its members are guarantors rather than shareholders. The members' liability is limited to the amount they have agreed to contribute to the company's assets if it is wound up. This structure is often used by charities, right-to-manage and commonhold companies and social enterprises to limit the personal liability of their directors and trustees.
- **Private unlimited company:** this type of company may or may not have a share capital but there is no limit to the members' liability. There are relatively few unlimited companies.
- **Public limited companies (plc):** this type of company has a share capital and limits the liability of each member to the amount unpaid on their shares. PLCs can raise money by selling shares on the stock market but must have share capital of at least £50,000 or the

prescribed equivalent in euros and must have at least two directors and a qualified company secretary.

No matter what entity is selected (organizations can and do change status subject to the appropriate compliance and regulatory rules), all have a profit motive and so must account for all of their financial dealings.

# The role of financial information within a business

In this chapter we are going to review financial information primarily in the context of a public limited company, but the principles and acquired knowledge are equally applicable to all trading entities.

The owners of a public limited company are the shareholders. Although they do not normally take part in the day-to-day running of the company (unless they are also directors or managers), they are entitled to know about and to be informed about key areas of the strategy and performance of the company, including its financial results.

## Role of the directors

Directors of a company are always going to be judged on their performance and they have wide-ranging responsibilities under the Companies Act 2006. Figure 11.1 illustrates the roles and responsibilities of the Board and is taken from the Department of Trade and Industry (DTI) Publication *Better Board* (2004).

That same publication, *Better Board*, set out seven key issues for directors to consider:

- **The purpose of the organization:** why it exists and what it wants to be.
- **Its strategy:** how it proposes to achieve success.
- **Performance management:** implementation and monitoring of the company's financial and non-financial indicators, and assessing the Board's own performance and that of the executive team.
- **Accountability and communication:** the processes of dialogue and reporting by which it informs its shareholders and wider stakeholders, and takes account of – and learns from – the feedback received.
- **Added value:** generated by constructively questioning and challenging the thinking of the executive management team and ensuring that appropriate controls are in place and operate effectively.
- **The company's values:** what it stands for and what it will not stand for.
- **Its key relationships:** who and what it depends on for success, the delivery of its values and the development and/or protection of its corporate reputation.

**FIGURE 11.1**    Responsibilities of the Board of Directors

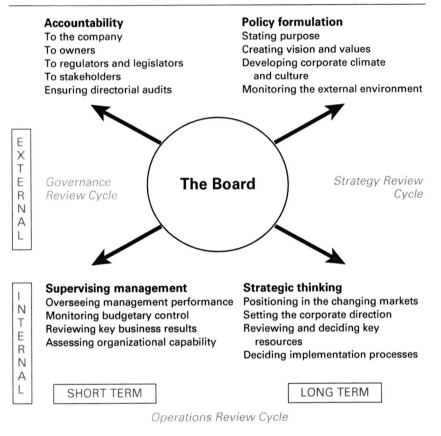

These key issues are relevant to the running of any of the types of business already discussed and represent best practice if a business is able to answer them. They also highlight the need for directors to be asking the right (but often difficult) questions about their companies and themselves, such as: 'Are we the right people?', 'Do we ask the right questions?', 'Do we provide the right sort of leadership?', 'Do we challenge management in the most productive ways?'

## Financial information

The accountancy or finance functions of a company are concerned with collecting, analysing and communicating financial information so that the directors can, as a result of that information, make more informed and better decisions for the benefit of the company.

Examples of these decisions might be:

- developing new products or services;
- the pricing structure for a product (or service) and the quantities to be produced or provided;
- whether funds need to be borrowed to fund any expansion or new product ranges;
- increasing or decreasing the operating capacity of a business;
- changing the methods of purchasing, production or distribution.

In addition, there will be many external users or observers of the company who will need that financial information to help them make decisions in regard to the business, whether to:

- invest in the business (whether in shares or a lump sum investment);
- lend money to the business (for example, the banks, venture capitalists or private investors);
- offer credit facilities (a supplier offering deferred payment terms).

Financial information is also concerned with the ways in which funds for a business are raised and invested. This is the central hub of any business, as a business owes its existence to the money that is raised by those who invest in it (eg the owners, investors and lenders), and it will then use those funds to make investments (whether in premises, equipment, stock etc) in order to make the business (and its owners and investors) wealthier by providing them with a healthy return on investment. So it is important to have an understanding of:

- what forms of finance are available at any one time;
- the cost and benefits of each form of finance;
- the risks associated with each form of finance;
- the role of financial markets in supplying available sources of finance.

The funds having been raised, they must then be invested to give a worthwhile return on investment. So it is also important to understand and evaluate the returns from those investments and the risks associated with those investments.

The financial information that a company produces is for both internal and external users and for both internal and external accountability purposes. External observers will make value judgements on the performance of the company from the financial information supplied.

Figure 11.2 illustrates some of the many observers who will be looking at and appraising the performance of a company.

**FIGURE 11.2**    Main users of financial information

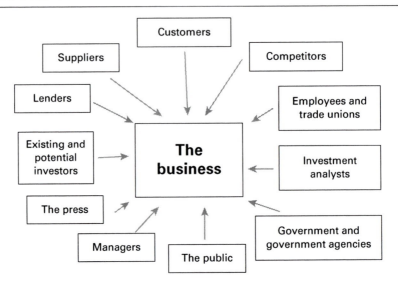

# Internal application of financial information: management accounts

It is very important that the financial performance of any company is measured against its strategic plans and objectives. These plans need to be dynamic and the information provided needs to be clear and accurate.

Any business having completed its strategic planning process should have completed a **business plan**. This is a roadmap for the future development of the business. It describes the business, its objectives, financial forecasts and the market for its products. The business plan supports attempts to secure external finance, provides a measure of success and provides a plan and the stimulus to grow the business.

For internal management purposes, budgeting against the business plan will usually be the most effective way to control the cash flow of a business and allow it to invest in new opportunities at the appropriate time.

A **budget** is a plan to:

- control the finances of the business;
- ensure that the business can continue to fund its current commitments;
- enable the business to make confident financial decisions and meet its objectives;
- ensure that the business has enough money for its future projects.

A budget outlines what a business will spend money on and how that spending will be financed. However, it is not a forecast (a forecast is a prediction of the future, whereas a budget is a planned outcome that the business wants to achieve).

**Management accounts** analyse recent historical performance as well as forward-looking elements such as sales, cash flow and profit forecasts. This analysis is usually performed against the forecasts and budgets produced at the start of the year. These help directors to make timely and meaningful management decisions about their business.

There is no legal requirement to prepare management accounts, but it is difficult to run a business effectively without them. Most companies produce them regularly (eg monthly or quarterly). The format of management accounts is not prescribed, so the amount of information that they will show will vary from company to company.

For businesses selling more than one product, it is advisable to provide a financial breakdown for each product category. This will ensure that profitable products are not subsidizing those that are selling poorly (although some companies intentionally promote loss leaders to attract further custom).

# External application of financial information: financial statements

The directors of any company have to file yearly statutory accounts with Companies House; the directors of a public limited company also have to report to their shareholders yearly within the Annual Report and Accounts. The directors of every company must prepare accounts for each financial year. It is the personal responsibility of each director to ensure that the appropriate accounts are prepared, signed and delivered to Companies House within the time allowed: six months from the end of the trading or accounting year (called the accounting reference date) for a public company; nine months from the accounting reference date for a private company.

At the end of the accounting year, three main financial statements are produced and used by limited companies, which take into account the ongoing receipts and financial obligations of the company and place that information into an understandable format to record as fully as possible the financial position of the company at the accounting date. The financial statements are:

- **An income statement (or profit and loss statement):** this measures the financial performance of the company for a particular period of time. Think of this as a filmed record of the financial performance of the business for a specific period.
- **A statement of financial position (or balance sheet):** this provides a statement of the financial position of the company at a particular date (normally the end of each trading period). Think of this statement as a photographic record of the financial position on that date.
- **A cash flow statement:** this links profit with changes in assets and liabilities and the consequent effect on the cash held by the company. This is akin to a film and shows the cash position of the business over time.

**FIGURE 11.3**    The main accounting statements

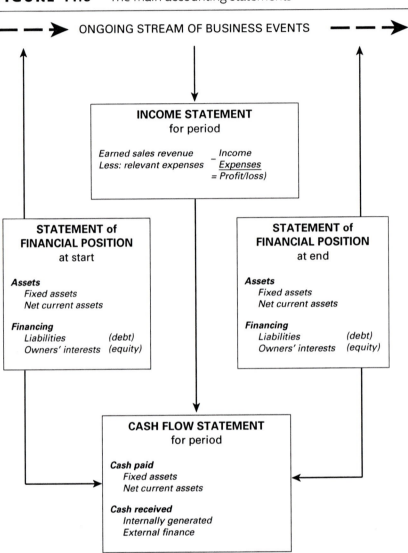

SOURCE: Adapted from Reid, W and Myddelton, DR (2005) *The Meaning of Company Accounts*, Gower Publishing Ltd, UK

The balance sheet gives a static picture of a company's financial position at a single point in time, while the profit and loss account and cash flow statements summarize flows through the year.

What is the difference between profit and cash? Profit is a measurement of economic activity that considers a number of factors that can be assigned a value or a cost. Cash is immediate – it simply is money (see Figure 11.3).

**FIGURE 11.4**  Consolidated income statement: Xtra Special plc

|  | Year 2 £m | Year 1 £m |
|---|---|---|
| **Revenue** | **2,145** | 1,870 |
| Cost of Sales | (1,785) | (1,430) |
| **Gross Profit** | **360** | 440 |
| Operating Expenses | (315) | (245) |
| **Operating Profit** | **45** | 205 |
| Interest Payable | (35) | (10) |
| **Profit before Taxation** | **10** | 195 |
| Taxation | (15) | (50) |
| **Profit/Loss for the Year** | **(5)** | 145 |

To prepare these statements, accountants must analyse the continuous stream of transactions at regular intervals in order to measure and identify the relevant sales revenues, the expenses, the company's assets and its borrowings.

## The income statement (profit and loss account)

The income statement (see Figure 11.4) summarizes the turnover (sales or revenue) and operating expenses of the business for the financial year in order to reveal the operating profit. The interest expense (finance cost) and tax are then deducted from the operating profit to produce the profit after tax or net profit for the accounting period.

The two key parts of the statement are profit and expenses. Each is divided into four headings (or levels) and the performance of a company is assessed in line with these four headings. Profit may be defined as turnover (sales or revenue) less the total expenses incurred by the company during the accounting period.

The four headings or levels of profit and expenses are:

Level 1 – gross profit: the account starts with turnover (sales or revenue) for the accounting period, from which is deducted the cost of sales (the cost of bringing the goods to a saleable condition). *Turnover less cost of sales = gross profit.*

Level 2 – selling and administrative expenses: selling and administrative expenses are the costs incurred by the business in selling the goods and running the business. These expenses are deducted from the gross profit to produce the operating profit. *Gross profit less selling and administrative expenses = operating profit.*

Operating profit is also referred to as 'profit before interest and tax' (PBIT) or as 'earnings before interest and tax' (EBIT). Operating profit is a key figure in analysing performance as it represents the return (before tax) earned on the assets employed in a business.

Level 3 – interest expenses: the net interest expenses (the interest earned deducted from the costs of borrowing) are then usually deducted from the operating profit to give the profit before tax. *Operating profit less interest expenses = profit before tax (PBT or EBT).*

Level 4 – tax on profits: the final level deducts the tax on profits to reach the bottom line, which is the profit after tax for the accounting period. *Profit before tax less tax = profit for the year/profit after tax/net profit.*

All companies listed on a recognized stock exchange must show, as part of the income statement, the earnings per share (EPS) for the current and previous reporting periods. This is the profit for the year (profit after taxation) attributable to the average number of ordinary shares issued (not authorized) during the period and shows the net profits per share. This can be useful in the comparison of different companies' earnings and year-on-year earnings, and the trend in earnings per share over time is used to help assess the investment potential of a business's shares.

## Statement of financial position (balance sheet)

The statement of financial position or balance sheet is a classified summary at the end of the financial year showing: 1) how much the business has invested in fixed assets and in working capital; 2) how these amounts (total assets less current liabilities) have been financed by long-term borrowing (debt) and by shareholders' funds (equity).

In total, net assets must always equal capital employed, and that is why the balance sheet always balances (see Figure 11.5).

The categories within the statement of financial position are:

Fixed assets (or non-current assets): fixed assets are intended for use on a long-term basis in the company's business. They include tangible assets such as land, buildings, plant and equipment, and intangible assets such as purchased goodwill or brands as well as long-term investments.

Current assets: current assets will be expected to turn into cash within 12 months of the statement of financial position date (or within the operating cycle of the business if that is longer). The items usually appear in reverse order of liquidity (ie inventory (or stocks), receivables (or trade debtors) and finally cash (which is the most liquid asset).

Current liabilities (creditors due within one year): current liabilities are due for payment within one year from the statement of financial position date and often much sooner. They include any short-term borrowings such as overdrafts, amounts due to suppliers (payables or trade creditors) and current tax payable.

**FIGURE 11.5**    Statement of financial position: Xtra Special plc

|  | Year 2 £m | Year 1 £m |
|---|---|---|
| **Assets** | | |
| **Non-current assets** | | |
| Land and buildings | 356 | 325 |
| Fixtures and fittings | 245 | 165 |
|  | 601 | 490 |
| **Current assets** | | |
| Inventories at cost | 420 | 300 |
| Trade receivables | 225 | 190 |
| Cash at bank | 2 | 10 |
|  | 647 | 500 |
| **Total assets** | 1,248 | 990 |
| **Liabilities and equity** | | |
| **Current liabilities** | | |
| Bank loans and overdrafts | (129) | (3) |
| Trade and other payables | (277) | (180) |
| Current tax liabilities | (15) | (50) |
|  | (421) | (233) |
| **Non-current liabilities** | | |
| Borrowings | (250) | (175) |
| **Total liabilities** | (671) | (408) |
| **Equity** | | |
| Issued share capital | 250 | 250 |
| Retained earnings | 327 | 332 |
| **Total equity** | 577 | 582 |
| **Total equity and liabilities** | 1,248 | 990 |

Creditors due after one year (or non-current liabilities): the creditors due after one year mostly represent long-term borrowings such as loans, mortgages or debentures that amount to semi-permanent capital for a company. They are often for fairly long periods (say, 5 to 15 years) and when repayment becomes due, the company may seek to refinance them by more long-term borrowing.

Equity (capital and reserves or shareholders' funds): the capital and reserves represent the called-up share capital – usually in the form of ordinary shares – and this is the permanent capital of the business. Within this classification is a subcategory called the retained earnings or revenue reserves account, which represents the cumulative retained profits for each year that are legally available to pay dividends to shareholders (although these are usually paid out of the current year's profits).

Two key practical concepts derive from these classifications:

Working capital (net current assets): this is the difference between current assets and current liabilities. Although the various items are all short term, the net balance of working capital requires long-term capital to finance it.

Capital employed: this is made up of the creditors due after one year added to the equity.

## Cash flow statement

The income statement shows profitability and the statement of financial position shows asset strength. While these financial statements give a great deal of information on the progress and performance of a company during an accounting period, profit does not equal cash, and strength in assets does not necessarily mean a large bank balance.

The key roles of the cash flow statements are to:

1 **Provide an overall view of money in and out:** by showing the sources and amounts of cash receipts in the year from operations, the sales of fixed assets, borrowing, the issue of shares and other sources, and then how the cash has been used in paying tax and dividends, investing in fixed assets, repaying borrowing etc. So, the cash flow statement links profit (the surplus of income over expense) with changes in assets and liabilities and the effect on the cash of the company. It provides an overall view of money flowing in and out of a company during an accounting period.

2 **To provide a view on the liquidity of the business:** the cash flow statement helps to explain to shareholders and observers why, for instance, after a year of good profits there is a lower bank balance than at the start of the year. Liquidity is a measure of a company's ability to pay its debts as and when they fall due.

3 **To help with cash flow planning:** there is no requirement for limited companies to file a cash flow statement at Companies House as part of the annual statutory accounts, but it is a requirement for public limited companies. However, prudent management principles dictate that careful cash flow planning is a necessity for any successful business.

Fundamentally, the cash flow statement (see Figure 11.6) looks at three main areas in building up the overall cash flow picture:

Operating activities: these are the main revenue-producing activities of the business, together with the payments of interest and tax.

Investing activities: these are the acquisition and disposal of long-term assets and other investments.

**FIGURE 11.6**    Cash flow statement: Xtra Special plc

|  | Year 2 | Year 1 |
|---|---|---|
|  | £m | £m |
| *Cash flows from operating activities* |  |  |
| Operating profit – continuing operations | 45 | 205 |
| Depreciation and amortization | 35 | 32 |
| Increase in inventories | (120) | (18) |
| Increase in trade and other receivables | (35) | (21) |
| Increase in trade and other payables | 97 | 18 |
| Cash generated from operations | 22 | 216 |
| Corporation taxes paid | (50) | (50) |
| **Net cash flow from operating activities** | **(28)** | **166** |
| *Cash flows from investing activities* |  |  |
| Net proceeds from disposal of subsidiary |  |  |
| Proceeds from sale of property, plant and equipment |  |  |
| Additions to land and buildings | (66) | (100) |
| Additions to fixtures and fittings | (80) |  |
| Payment of deferred consideration |  |  |
| **Net cash flow from investing activities** | **(146)** | **(100)** |
| *Cash flows from financing activities* |  |  |
| (Repayment)/proceeds of unsecured bank loans and overdrafts | 201 | (50) |
| Interest paid | (35) | (10) |
| Dividends paid |  |  |
| **Net cash flow from financing activities** | **166** | **(60)** |
| Net increase/(decrease) in cash and cash equivalents | (8) | 6 |
| **Closing cash and cash equivalents** | **2** | **10** |

**Financing activities:** these are receipts from the issue of new shares, payments to repay shares and changes in long-term borrowing.

An important aspect of financial planning is trying to forecast future cash receipts and payments in order to ensure that enough cash is on hand to make payments when needed. Failure to pay creditors on the due date may, in extreme circumstances, lead to the winding-up of a business, even if it is making a profit.

These final comments on the cash flow statement highlight a rather old accountancy 'saying' that *'turnover is vanity, profit sanity and cash reality'*, but this statement is just as relevant now as ever. Businesses go bust in the long term through lack of profit, but they fail in the short term because they do not have enough cash to pay their bills. Cash flow is the blood supply of any business.

# The regulatory framework for statutory accounts

The regulatory framework forms the rules of accounting. Accountants follow these rules when drafting financial statements, allowing broad comparisons to be made between the financial results of different companies.

The regulatory framework for accounting consists of three elements:

- Generally Accepted Accounting Practices;
- Accounting Standards (both UK and international standards);
- Company Law (contained within the Companies Act 2006).

## *Generally accepted accounting concepts and practices (GAAP)*

Over time, accountants have developed accounting policies and concepts known as the generally accepted accounting practices (GAAP). The application of GAAP not only means complying with accounting standards (see below), but also includes elements derived from accumulated professional judgement.

Accountants have developed fundamental accounting concepts that form the bedrock of the preparation of financial statements. A short review of some of these concepts follows:

**Materiality:** some items are of such a low level of importance that it is not worth recording them separately as they are not material. These include:

- small expense items that are grouped together as sundry expenses;
- small end-of-year items of office stationery;
- low-cost non-current assets.

**The going concern concept:** the organization is assumed to be an enterprise that will continue to be in business for the foreseeable future, and there is no need or intention to close it down or reduce its size. In practical terms, this means valuing assets at cost on the assumption that they are worth at least that amount. If a business were planning to close, the value would be the realizable value (value if sold) of the assets, which might be more or less than cost.

**FIGURE 11.7**    Accounting concepts

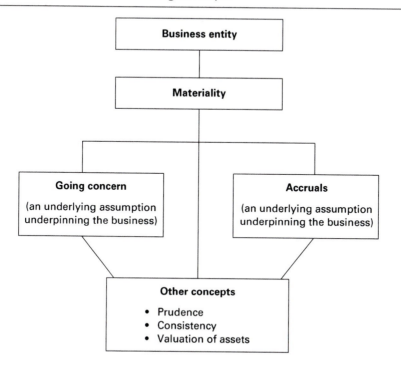

The **accruals or matching concept:** this concept recognizes revenues and costs as they are earned or incurred and not as money is received and paid.

The **prudence or conservatism concept:** accounts must be prepared on the basis that caution is exercised when dealing with uncertainty and that financial statements are neutral in nature. Profits should not be recognized until there is a reasonable certainty of their being paid, whilst all expenses and losses should be accounted for immediately.

The **consistency concept:** this means adopting the same procedure every time for recording and measuring transactions. If this were not followed, the comparison between one period and another would be meaningless.

**Valuation of assets:** the historic cost convention is the traditional way of valuing assets in a balance sheet, as well as costs in the profit and loss account or income statement. The criterion for valuation is the cost of a particular item at the time of purchase, while liabilities are recorded as the amount expected to be paid. Some financial statements are prepared under the historic cost convention modified by the revaluation of certain assets, usually property, to their current value. Such a revaluation will need to be explained in the accounting policies.

Other measurement bases for valuation include:

- **Current (or replacement) cost:** what it would cost to replace assets and liabilities at today's prices.
- **Net realizable value:** what the assets could be sold for and the amount required to settle the liabilities as at that time.
- **Present (or economic) value:** assets and liabilities are valued at the present discounted values of their future cash inflows and outflows.

## Accounting standards

### UK accounting standards

Accounting standards were first introduced in 1969 to provide a framework for accounting and more consistency in the ways the items are treated in accounts. These standards apply to all limited companies apart from publicly listed companies (plcs) and Aim (Alternative Investment Market) listed companies.

The current standards are the Financial Reporting Standards (FRSs), which have been issued since 1990, a task now undertaken by the Financial Reporting Council.

### International accounting standards or the International Financial Reporting Standards (IASs or IFRSs)

All EU listed companies, all plcs and Aim listed companies registered in England and Wales now have to comply with the International Accounting Standards (IASs) and the International Financial Reporting Standards (IFRSs) published by the International Accounting Standards Board (IASB).

The IASB is an independent, privately funded accounting standard setter based in London. It is committed to developing, in the public interest, a single set of high quality, understandable and enforceable global accounting standards. More than 130 countries worldwide are now using IFRSs, either directly or indirectly or through local accounting rules linked to them.

## Company law

All limited companies in England and Wales are regulated by the Companies Act 2006 and various other statutory instruments.

## Other Protections

**Audit:** an audit is the annual inspection of a company's financial records and its financial statements conducted by an independent firm of auditors. The auditors produce an audit report, which is a report on the truth and fairness of financial statements. It is addressed to the shareholders.

An audit is automatically required on any company that has a turnover in excess of £6.5 million and balance sheet totals in excess of £3.26 million. If the accounts have been audited, it will give shareholders greater assurance about the figures, as a firm of registered auditors will have subjected them to a detailed review.

True and fair: both the auditors and the directors should ensure that the accounts give a 'true and fair view' and comply with the appropriate legal and statutory requirements. This is a matter of judgement for them. However, this term is not actually defined or explained within the Companies Acts or the Accounting Standards, although in accounting terms it is a technical phrase that means:

- appropriate measurement, classification and disclosure of items;
- the consistent application of generally accepted accounting practices;
- compliance with official accounting standards.

However, the term 'true and fair' can often be misleading. For instance, current assets are conventionally required to appear within the balance sheet at cost unless the net realizable value is lower or interests in land and buildings have been revalued. So the actual figure displayed in the balance sheet representing those assets may be below the current market value and, accordingly, the phrase 'a true and fair view' does not disclose the market value or true worth of a company.

# Interpreting the financial statements: assessing the financial health of a business

Having the correct financial information displayed in the correct financial statements is what enables the users of the financial statements to place reliance upon and make decisions from that information.

Non-accountancy professionals do not have to know how to produce those statements but what they should be able to do is interpret that information, just like other users. We interpret the financial statements using financial ratios. They can be used as a relatively quick and relatively simple means of assessing the financial performance and position of a company. A ratio simply relates one figure to another within the financial statements.

Ratios are useful because they can be used to:

- summarize briefly relationships and results that are significant to an appreciation of critical business indicators of performance;
- compare the performance of a company from year to year;
- compare the performance of different companies (subject to the proviso that aggregate figures are always of differing magnitudes).

Companies differ from one another in many ways and may also change from year to year in terms of strategy. Since the future is uncertain, the analyst has to rely substantially on past behaviour for predicting future changes. In this respect, the trends indicated by ratios are very useful for making predictions.

However, unless ratios are collected in a systematic and uniform manner, comparisons can be very misleading, and ratios on their own will not be sufficient providers of information about a company. Information of a non-financial nature will also be required to provide a more meaningful, complete and holistic picture by researching, for instance:

- The history of the business (this may be available from, for instance, the company website, trade magazines etc).
- Staff turnover levels and whether key members of staff have been lost or recruited recently.
- The reliance (or over-reliance) of the business on a small number of suppliers or customers.
- Information about the sector in which the company operates (analysts' reports).
- Recent press articles about the company or its sector.
- The general economic and competitive situation in the industry as a whole (ie is the market depressed and what is the short- or medium-term future?).

In this chapter we shall be looking at some key ratios that will help illustrate four key areas of financial performance (out of over 100 possible ratios). The interpretative areas we are going to look at are:

- **Profitability:** is the business sufficiently profitable and how effective is the Board's cost and asset management?
- **Financial gearing strength:** how is the business funded?
- **Liquidity:** are there sufficient resources available to meet financial obligations?
- **Efficiency:** these measure which resources are used in the business.

## *Profitability*

Profit is the difference between sales, revenue or turnover and the different levels of costs and expenses incurred in sourcing or making and then selling products for a specific accounting period.

We have already seen that businesses generally exist with the primary purpose of creating wealth for their owners. So profitability levels are one of the first areas that are looked at. They should be used to obtain a greater understanding of how profit (or loss) has arisen, giving an indication of the health of the trading operations of the company and whether the business has achieved its profitability targets.

## Gross profit margin – how profitable are the products or services of the company?

Gross profit relates the gross profit of the business to the sales revenue generated for the same period, representing the difference between sales revenue and the cost of sales before any other costs of the business are taken into account. It is calculated as sales (revenue or turnover) minus all costs directly related to those sales. These costs can include:

- the cost of raw materials or in sourcing and then purchasing products for re-sale;
- the manufacturing expenses incurred in turning raw materials into the end product;
- the costs of employing people.

The gross profit ratio is calculated as follows:

$$\frac{\text{Gross profit (sales less cost of sales)}}{\text{Sales (revenue or turnover)}} \times 100\%$$

Generally, all businesses in the same sector should have a similar gross profit margin. If the margin is higher, then this may indicate one or a combination of the following:

- Better management of the cost of producing the goods or service.
- Obtaining a higher sale price for the same goods – pricing policy.
- Purchasing raw materials/stocks/products for a lower price – purchasing policy.

Retailers usually have very high cost of sales, and profit levels tend to be lower, whereas professional services firms have much higher gross margins as their costs of sale are relatively low.

## Operating profit margin – how effective is the cost management?

Operating profit is a natural progression from the gross profit margin. It shows the profit earned from the core business operations when all other administrative and marketing costs have been taken into account but before interest charges and tax have been accounted for. This ratio is often regarded as the most appropriate measure of operational performance, especially when comparing different companies, as the different ways in which a business is financed will not influence this measure. Operating profit is also known as PBIT (profit before interest and tax) – and EBIT (earnings before interest and tax).

The operating profit ratio is calculated as follows:

$$\frac{\text{Operating profit (PBIT or EBIT)}}{\text{Sales (revenue or turnover)}} \times 100\%$$

Exceptional items can distort the operating profit figure. These can include one-off expenses for a trading period, which do not reflect the true operating expenditure of the business, eg financial penalties, reorganization costs, closure costs of an office etc. Therefore, when looking at the expenses, it is best to strip out any that would give an unrealistic comparison with previous years.

A business may have the same gross profit margin year on year, whilst the operating profit margin is slowly decreasing. This would indicate that the general expenses of the business are slipping out of control, which then raises issues about the competency of the leadership and the management of the directors.

## Return on capital employed (ROCE) – is the business sufficiently profitable?

ROCE is one of the key measures of business performance. It is calculated by comparing the operating profit of the business against the average long-term capital invested in the business and does so before any deductions have been made for borrowing costs, or before dividends have been paid to shareholders.

The ROCE ratio is calculated as follows:

$$\frac{\text{Operating profit (profit before interest and tax)}}{\text{Equity (capital and reserves) + non-current liabilities}} \times 100\%$$

For example:

Company H makes a profit of £100 on sales of £1,000, so its profit margin is 10 per cent. Company J makes a profit of £150 on sales of £1,000, so its profit margin is 15 per cent.

Now factor in the amount of capital employed in each case. Company H employs £500 of capital and Company J £1,000 of capital. Company H therefore has a ROCE of 20 per cent, while Company J has only 15 per cent.

Despite being less profitable in terms of margin, Company H is making better use of its capital, squeezing more earnings out of every pound of capital:

- A high ROCE means that a larger proportion of profits can be reinvested into the company for the benefit of the shareholders.

- ROCE should always be compared to the current cost of borrowing. An investor will want to see a return significantly above prevailing interest rates to justify his risk.

- ROCE is especially important for capital-intensive companies, eg those in telecommunications, power utilities and heavy industries.

There is, however, no definitive definition of the terms used. For instance, the definition of capital employed that we have used includes both equity (the same figure as net assets) and non-current liabilities. This can lead to one potential limitation with the ratio as, if the balance sheet includes significant assets (for example property) at lower historic cost levels rather than potentially higher current market values, the ROCE will look higher than the real return the management are achieving. It is best to use market values wherever possible.

## Financial gearing: how is the business funded?

Gearing ratios measure how much a company is funded by debt, relative to the amount contributed by the owners or shareholders and, as such, indicates the level of financial risk that faces both the company and the shareholders. Net debt and equity effectively represent the types of financing available to a business.

In terms of risk, the directors must decide first on the business risk (ie the types of activities/business carried on by the company) and then, second, on the financial risk (ie how the company is funded and the proportions between debt and equity).

A business that is mainly financed by long-term loans is said to be highly geared (higher risk), whereas a business that has secured most of its finance from its shareholders is said to be a low-geared business (low risk). Generally, if a company has low business risk it will generally be able to absorb more financial risk.

The financial markets accept that there will always be a need for businesses to borrow. In assessing the financial strength of a company, observers look at its total borrowing and relate this to its trading cash flow. In the post-2007/8 economic climate, the credit ratings of businesses must be monitored carefully, especially if they are clients of professional firms.

Although no explicit rules of thumb exist regarding desirable shareholders' equity ratios, the less variable a company's underlying business activities and profits, the more safely it can use long-term debt. It is generally felt that the larger the proportion of the shareholders' equity, the stronger the financial position of the company. By increasing long-term borrowing, a company may increase its current assets, thereby creating a more favourable ratio, but at the same time this may reduce the shareholders' equity, signalling a possible over-dependence on outside sources for long-term financial needs.

## Debt/equity ratio – are the borrowings too high (or too low)?

The debt/equity ratio is one of the most fundamental measures in corporate finance. The purpose of the ratio is to measure the mix of funds in the balance sheet and to make a comparison between: 1) debt – interest-bearing liabilities or borrowings, including lease obligations; 2) equity – the funds provided by the owners of the business, ie share capital and reserves.

The debt/equity ratio is calculated as follows:

$$\frac{\text{Debt}}{\text{Equity}} \times 100\%$$

Financial gearing can be measured in various ways including non-current liabilities expressed as a percentage of equity and non-current liabilities.

## Implications of borrowing

If we look in more detail at the implications of having a loan, as an example of debt, then we will note the following:

- The loan must always be repaid at some point (normally agreed at the start of the loan).
- Interest payments (and capital repayments) will be made on a regular basis.
- The lender will have different requirements from a shareholder.
- Interest is always going to reduce the amount of profit available to the shareholders.
- The lender will normally have the right to impose conditions in order to protect itself and this will allow the lender to wind up the company if it defaults on the repayments.

It can be seen from the above that if a business is highly geared then the risk to the equity holders (being shareholders or proprietors) of not being able to remove any profits for themselves is increased, as interest and capital repayments will have to be paid out of the profits first. This will, in turn, magnify the variations in earnings attributable to shareholders and ultimately affect the share price. This is one reason why the most highly geared businesses are normally regarded as the riskier businesses.

## Interest cover ratio – can the business afford the interest charges?

This ratio illustrates the ability of the firm to service or pay interest on its borrowings by relating operating profit to before-tax interest on all borrowings. The ability of a company to keep up with interest payment obligations is critical if the company is to be a 'going concern'.

The term 'financial leverage' is used to reflect the relationship between profit and the fixed interest charge. If financial leverage is high (ie if interest is a high part of pre-interest profits) then a small change in operating profit will be greatly magnified in its effect on the return to shareholders. Generally, a highly leveraged company does well in boom times but quickly falls into difficulty in recession.

The interest cover ratio is calculated as follows:

$$\frac{\text{Operating profit (PBIT or EBIT)}}{\text{Interest payable}}$$

A ratio figure of 10 or above will usually illustrate that the company has debt capacity. So, this ratio shows the relative safety of loan interest from the income statement, whereas the debt/equity ratio aims to measure the loan capital cover from the statement of financial position.

## Liquidity and solvency

Although many people will look at a business and make a judgement according to its apparent profitability, it is very important not to forget the saying 'cash is king'. The most successful businesses, in terms of profit, can also become victims of insolvency because, due to a lack of available cash, they are unable to pay their debts as they fall due (as discussed earlier).

Liquidity ratios are, therefore, concerned with the ability of the business to meet its short-term financial obligations. However, given the nature of financial reports, it follows that ratio analysis may make only a limited contribution to assessing solvency because:

- The firm's current liabilities and total current assets are historic figures for the end of the last accounting period. Solvency happens in the present and not in the past and so does not reflect, for instance, the sudden withdrawal of a credit facility.
- The balance sheet does not reveal sources of credit or the willingness of creditors and investors to see the company through a difficult period.
- The accounts do not reveal the complete nature of a company, eg what is the receipt and payments pattern and how quickly can assets be liquidated?

At any one time, a business should be able to pay its short-term debts, ie its trade creditors and any other current liabilities, including loans, due to be paid in the short term.

There are two ratios that are primarily used to assess the liquidity of a business: current ratio and acid test ratio. These are outlined below.

## Current ratio

This is simply an indication of whether the current liabilities of the business can be paid off in the short term from the 'liquid' assets (cash and those assets that can soon be turned into cash) and whether the company will be able to pay its bills over the next trading period.

The current ratio is calculated as follows:

$$\frac{\text{Current assets}}{\text{Current liabilities}}$$

The higher the ratio, the more liquid the business is considered to be, but this will not always be the case. A manufacturing company will often have a relatively high current ratio because it has to hold inventories or stocks, raw materials and work in progress, whereas a supermarket chain will have a relatively low ratio as it will be selling fast-moving products and the majority of its sales will be for cash (no long-term credit sales).

## Acid test ratio

This ratio is calculated in the same way as the current ratio but takes inventories (stock) out of the equation as some of these, such as finished items or raw materials still requiring conversion, may not easily be convertible in the short term.

The minimum level for this ratio is normally stated as being 1 or 1:1, ie the current assets (excluding inventories) equal current liabilities. However, it is not unusual for successful businesses to have adequate liquidity levels below 1, particularly retail businesses and supermarkets.

The Acid test ratio is calculated as follows:

$$\frac{\text{Current assets less inventories (stock)}}{\text{Current liabilities}}$$

## Efficiency – managing the operating cycle

The liquidity ratios highlight the importance of managing the operating cycle, which was discussed in Chapter 1 (see Figure 1.2 on page 15). The effective and efficient working of this cycle is a must for any business.

Given that current assets normally consist of cash, debtors and inventories, the company's ability to meet current liabilities depends on the rate at which cash flows into the business from current operations. Sales are the critical event in this respect, as the rate at which stocks are sold is clearly crucial, but the main flow of cash into the 'cash reservoir' comes from receivables (trade debtors). Where a substantial proportion of sales is on credit terms, the rate at which debtors settle their accounts may be delayed, and these time periods are crucial to managing the cash cycle within a company. Three ratios are used to help work out the key timing of the operating cycle. They are usually worked out in days.

## *Average inventory turnover – how well does the business manage its inventories?*

This will show the average amount of time it takes to turn an inventory item (stock) into a sale and, therefore, into a debtor. Inventories can represent a significant investment for businesses, as already discussed above.

$$\frac{\text{Year end or average inventory}}{\text{Cost of sales}} \times 365$$

## *Average receivables – how long, on average, does it take customers/clients to pay?*

This will determine how quickly receivables (trade debtors) – and which mainly consists of customers/clients – are taking to pay. Selling on credit is the norm for most businesses, although not so much for retailers. A business will rightly be concerned with having too much money tied up in trade receivables, as it could be used for more profitable purposes. Information about credit terms is not included within the company's accounts.

$$\frac{\text{Trade receivables/trade debtors}}{\text{Turnover}} \times 365$$

Each industry sector will have a standard payment period. If the average 'debtor days' period is greater than the sector norm then this may be due to the inability or reluctance of customers/clients to pay, or it may signify poor credit-control processes being implemented by the business.

## *Average payables – how long, on average, does the business take to pay its suppliers?*

Essentially, this is worked out in the same way as the average 'debtor days' period above, but this time from the amount of money that the company owes to its creditors. As trade payables provide a free source of finance for the business, it is perhaps tempting to delay payments to the company's suppliers but this may result in a loss of goodwill.

$$\frac{\text{Trade payables/trade creditors}}{\text{Cost of sales}} \times 365$$

# Conclusion

On the basis of the information supplied through the accountancy function, directors and managers make key business decisions about the strategy of their organizations and the allocation of resources to support that strategy. If that information is incorrect or is wrongly interpreted, then both of those situations could have real consequences for the business and the many different people connected to it.

In the same way, professional advisers cannot just give a technically accurate answer, as that advice has to be placed into the commercial and trading position and context of that particular client. Providing correct but commercially orientated advice is what clients want. This requires, of the professional, a deep understanding of the strategy and the financial performance of each client's business.

Commercial and financial awareness is a continuous process and is something that you cannot simply pick up overnight. Like most of the skills discussed in this book, it involves an ongoing learning process. It means that you should have:

- awareness of events occurring in the business world and in current affairs;
- understanding of the implications of these events for your clients;
- knowledge of business concepts relevant to your clients' business;
- understanding of how your clients work and make decisions;
- ability to view things from your clients' perspective;
- strong financial awareness.

## CASE STUDY   Xtra Special plc

This case study enables you to put into practice the financial interpretation covered within this chapter. By studying the information within both the income statement and the statement of financial position of Xtra Special plc (pages 213 and 215), and then using the example ratios, you should be able to draw out some key financial performance trends for the company, then compare those trends to the company's cash flow statement (page 217).

*Xtra Special plc is a hypothetical company. It is a fast expanding electronics and computer company with a large number of out of town stores across the country. To meet a high level of demand for its products, the company has embarked on an energetic expansion of its store network as well as investing heavily into a new computerized distribution system at the same time as moving into a new purpose-built warehouse-centre complex.*

Identify the key financial performance trends for the company by:

1 **Stage 1:** reviewing the Year 1 and Year 2 income statements and the statements of financial position (pages 213 and 215). Try to identify any key changes in the financial performance of the company or its resources from Year 1 to Year 2.

2  **Stage 2:** completing the ratios, as set out in the table below, and then identifying key trends or differences between Years 1 and 2.

3  **Stage 3:** hypothesizing as to what may have happened within that trading period to cause those differences.

### Stage 1: review of the financial statements

*Set out below your understanding of the key changes.*

### Stage 2: Ratio analysis

Set out on the next pages are the ratios contained within Chapter 11, which have been calculated for Year 1 within the categories of profitability, debt capacity, liquidity and efficiency. Your task is to complete the Year 2 ratios.

### Ratio analysis

Profitability

#### Gross profit

$$\frac{\text{Gross profit (sales less cost of sales)}}{\text{Sales (revenue or turnover)}} \times 100\%$$

| Year 1 | Year 2 |
|---|---|
| $\frac{440}{1{,}870} \times 100\% = 23.5\%$ | $\times 100\% = \quad \%$ |

#### Operating profit

$$\frac{\text{Operating profit}}{\text{Sales (revenue or turnover)}} \times 100\%$$

| Year 1 | Year 2 |
|---|---|
| $\frac{205}{1{,}870} \times 100\% = 11.0\%$ | $\times 100\% = \quad \%$ |

### Return on capital employed (ROCE)

$$\frac{\text{Operating profit}}{\text{Equity (capital and reserves) + non-current liabilities}} \times 100\%$$

| Year 1 | Year 2 |
|---|---|
| $\dfrac{205}{582 + 175} \times 100\% = 27.1\%$ | $\times 100\% = \quad \%$ |

## Debt capacity

### Debt equity ratio or gearing ratio

$$\frac{\text{Debt (non-current liabilities)}}{\text{Equity (capital and reserves) + non-current liabilities}} \times 100\%$$

| Year 1 | Year 2 |
|---|---|
| $\dfrac{175}{582 + 175} \times 100\% = 23.1\%$ | $\times 100\% = \quad \%$ |

### Interest cover ratio

$$\frac{\text{Operating profit}}{\text{Interest payable}}$$

| Year 1 | Year 2 |
|---|---|
| $\dfrac{205}{10} = 20.5$ | $=$ |

## Liquidity

### Current ratio

$$\frac{\text{Current assets}}{\text{Current liabilities}}$$

| Year 1 | Year 2 |
|---|---|
| $\dfrac{500}{233} = 2.1$ | $=$ |

### *Acid test ratio*

$$\frac{\text{Current assets less inventories (stock)}}{\text{Current liabilities}}$$

| Year 1 | Year 2 |
|---|---|
| $\dfrac{500 - 300}{233} = 0.9$ | $=$ |

## Efficiency

### *Average inventory turnover*

$$\frac{\text{Year end or average inventory}}{\text{Cost of sales}} \times 365$$

| Year 1 | Year 2 |
|---|---|
| $\dfrac{300 \times 365}{1,430} = 77\ \text{days}$ | $\times\ 365 = \quad \text{days}$ |

### *Average receivables*

$$\frac{\text{Trade receivables/trade debtors}}{\text{Turnover}} \times 365$$

| Year 1 | Year 2 |
|---|---|
| $\dfrac{190 \times 365}{1,870} = 37\ \text{days}$ | $\times\ 365 = \quad \text{days}$ |

### *Average payables*

$$\frac{\text{Trade payables/trade creditors}}{\text{Cost of sales}} \times 365$$

| Year 1 | Year 2 |
|---|---|
| $\dfrac{180 \times 365}{1,430} = 46\ \text{days}$ | $\times\ 365 = \quad \text{days}$ |

*Stage 3: Interpretation*

The answers to both the Year 1 and Year 2 ratios have been inserted into Table 11.1 in the four categories of profitability, debt capacity, liquidity and efficiency.

Your task is now to work out what these answers tell you about the trading position of the company.

**TABLE 11.1**   Year 1 and Year 2 ratios

| Ratio | Year 1 | Year 2 |
|---|---|---|
| **Profitability** | | |
| Gross profit ratio | 23.5% | 16.8% |
| Operating profit ratio | 11.0% | 2.1% |
| ROCE ratio | 27.1% | 5.4% |
| **Debt Capacity** | | |
| Debt/equity ratio | 23.1% | 30.2% |
| Interest cover ratio | 20.5 | 1.3 |
| **Liquidity** | | |
| Current ratio | 2.1 | 1.5 |
| Acid ratio | 0.9 | 0.5 |
| **Efficiency** | | |
| Average inventory turnover ratio | 77 days | 85 days |
| Average receivables ratio | 37 days | 38 days |
| Average payables ratio | 46 days | 57 days |

**What do the ratios mean?**

**Profitability:**

- The gross profit has reduced by just over 16 per cent. This could mean that the purchase costs of the goods were higher, the sale prices were lower or the sales mix has changed.

- There has been a 78 per cent drop in operating profit. This can primarily be attributed to a big increase in higher operating costs (£70 million) together with the drop in gross profit. Operating expenses were substantially higher against the Year 2 turnover rising by nearly 30 per cent against only a 15 per cent rise in turnover.

- ROCE has reduced by 80 per cent due to the large reduction in operating profit and because of the increase in non-current liabilities.

## Debt capacity:

- There has been an increase in the gearing ratio due to the increase in long-term borrowing. This level would not necessarily be considered to be very high for a company that is trading effectively but this ratio does not take into account short-term borrowings.

- The large increase in short-term borrowings from £5 million to £129 million potentially causes more immediate concern.

- The increase in both short- and long-term borrowing is, however, reflected within the large decrease in the interest cover ratio (amplified by the large reduction in operating profit). Looking ahead, only a small reduction in profitability during Year 3 would leave the company with insufficient operating profit to cover interest payments and, therefore, with less room for negotiating further borrowing with the company's banks.

- For more detailed analysis, it would be necessary to know what the business planned these ratios to be in Year 3, but the lenders would be viewing this situation with concern unless the reduction in the interest cover ratio had been planned. This appears to be a short-term problem, but a longer-term solution could be to raise equity by a share issue, although the firm's current profitability levels might affect the willingness of investors to take up any future share offer.

## Liquidity:

- Both ratios show a decline in liquidity, which will be of concern. This could be linked to a planned short-term expansion of the business, which would almost certainly have needed increased staff and an increase in non-current assets.

- We know that there has been a drive for short-term expansion and we must assume that when the expected expansion brings its expected returns, then liquidity levels should improve. The danger for the company is whether its short-term debtors will be prepared to wait until those benefits start to accrue or whether they will require early repayment and/or require higher returns (eg higher interest rates or lower borrowing levels) to enable creditors to manage their risks.

## Efficiency:

- The inventories turnover ratio figure has increased quite considerably in Year 2 due to the higher levels of inventory. To find out whether this increase is part of the firm's planned expansion will involve looking at the firm's planned and projected inventories period as well as comparing the figures against those for other leading competitors.

- The receivables figure has stayed roughly the same, although the payables figure has lengthened by 20 per cent. This may not help the goodwill of the suppliers to the business, who may be on notice that the company has potential liquidity problems.

*Overview*

The trends that have been identified show a large increase in borrowings and in inventory. These trends are indicative of the expansion of the company. Short-term and aggressive expansion needs short-term funding and higher levels of inventory, and needs to be carefully planned.

However, the trends may also be indicative of resupply problems from the new distribution system, which could also then account for the loss of profit as goods are not delivered on time or available for purchase when clients want them. It is potentially a high-risk strategy to bring on line new distribution systems at the same time as expanding the business.

There must be worries about the company's ability to access future lending, as the large increase in funding in Year 2 might have taken the company close to its lending facilities.

If you would like to take an online assessment in financial interpretation, please go to **www.freshpd.com** and follow the links you find there.

# Behaving professionally

## Introduction

This is not a skills-based chapter; it does not provide you with the skills to be a professional. It focuses on another aspect of professionalism – the ethical behaviour and standards of professionals. Every professional needs to ensure they act at all times in accordance with these broad general principles. The guidance for them is to be found in the relevant regulations and the code of conduct for their profession.

If you are embarking on a professional career, or contemplating training for one, a key reason for reading and taking this chapter on board is that the ethical issues considered here are not always made explicit to you on becoming a professional but you will be expected to behave ethically and professionally at all times. Severe sanctions can result if you do not abide by the applicable regulations and code of conduct – these include criminal sanctions (eg fines) and being 'struck off', ie being prevented from practising your profession.

In this chapter we will consider the component parts of professional behaviour that are common to a number of professions and look at what distinguishes professionals from others. We will consider the key tenets of the client relationship, which is fundamental to the professional and separates this relationship from what would otherwise be a simple and straightforward customer relationship. Effective communication skills, well-managed client relationships and professional behaviour are the essence of what it is to be a professional.

How an individual professional behaves demonstrates their professionalism. Whilst membership of a particular professional body, professional qualifications and the exercise of professional skills are also important elements of what it means to be a professional, they are not the full picture.

In this chapter we will not look at regulatory issues, for example the issuing of 'practising certificates' or regulating entry into a profession. Nor will we look at the ways in which professional bodies and regulatory authorities exercise their disciplinary role. Nor is it possible in this chapter to outline the ways in which the various entities represent and regulate members of their professions.

Certain professional bodies (eg RICS, RIBA and BMA) are still wholly self-regulating. However, one of the consequences of the Legal Services Act 2007 is that both the solicitors' and barristers' professions have to separate out the role of representing the profession from the function of regulating it. The representational role is usually that of the professional body; the latter is that of the regulator, eg The Law Society of England and Wales is the professional body that represents solicitors (in those jurisdictions), the Solicitors Regulation Authority regulates them.

By the end of this chapter you will have considered:

- professional behaviour – what it is to be a professional;
- client confidentiality;
- conflicts of interest;
- client care and complaints handling;
- managing risk.

# Professional behaviour

What is professional behaviour? It is easier to pose the question than to answer it. You could, for instance, define professional behaviour by reference to what is unprofessional.

Let us take for an example the Royal Institution of Chartered Surveyors' (RICS) (**www.rics.org**). The RICS Rules of Conduct are mandatory for all members, students and trainees as well as all firms regulated by RICS. They are short, simple and principles-based, covering those matters for which individual members are responsible and accountable in their professional lives. They are designed so that RICS members can follow them regardless of where in the world they practise and whatever their sphere of work.

RICS defines ethical behaviour in the following way: 'RICS members shall at all times act with integrity and avoid conflicts of interest and avoid any actions or situations which are inconsistent with their professional obligations'.

RICS require that their members abide by five ethical principles:

- act with integrity;
- always provide a high standard of service;
- act in a way that promotes trust in the profession;
- treat others with respect;
- take responsibility.

These principles underpin and are applied throughout the RICS's Rules of Conduct.

Turning to the teaching profession, there are new statutory regulations for teacher appraisal and capability. The Teachers' Standards 2011 set out the benchmarks for teachers:

- high expectations;
- good secure knowledge of the curriculum (including English);
- accurate and productive use of assessment;
- plan and teach well-structured lessons;
- manage behaviour effectively.

They also embody five principles for teachers: fairness, consistency, balance, enablement and confidentiality.

Implicit in all professional relationships with clients are certain key behaviours that underpin those relationships.

## Honesty and trust

Stealing money or assets entrusted to you by the client is clearly unprofessional – it is the crime of theft and should result in prosecution before the criminal courts. If you are found guilty, appropriate punishment, eg a prison sentence, will be administered.

Recently, there have been a number of criminal prosecutions brought against solicitors who have stolen clients' money or money from their firms. In May 2012, Christopher Grierson was jailed for three years for stealing £1.7 million from the global law firm where he had been a senior litigation partner. He began falsifying his travel expenses in 2008, when he made false claims totalling £167,000. A year later this escalated to £526,785 and in 2010 he took £516,785 before the theft was discovered in 2011.

In February 2012 Kevin Steele, a senior partner in a respected London law firm, was jailed for five and a half years for his part in a £18.4 million fraud. Steele had provided fake paperwork to enable his client to obtain a multi-million pound loan to build a luxury spa and holiday complex in Turkey.

There have also been criminal prosecutions of secretaries and support staff working in professional offices who have stolen from both clients and/or their employer. Leanne Harris, a secretary at a solicitors' firm in Hove, was jailed for four years and nine months for stealing almost £500,000 of client money, some from the savings accounts of elderly and infirm clients. Her actions contributed to the closure of her employer, a long-standing and respected law firm, and the loss of 30 jobs.

Breach of trust is the significant aggravating factor where theft, fraud, etc is committed by a professional or an employee of a professional services business. Professionals and their employees are trusted by their clients because they are professionals. Where that trust is betrayed by a person in whom it has been placed, the judges must take this into account when sentencing.

Society expects professionals to be honest and to behave with integrity, especially when they are holding on trust client money or assets. This will include not only safely looking after any money on behalf of a client but also accounting to the client for any interest earned by that money which is in the professional's care.

## Integrity

Acting with integrity is a fundamental behaviour that we expect of all professionals and it covers a wide range of issues. Transparency and openness is one aspect, which includes ensuring that any conflicts of interest are resolved appropriately. For example, professionals should not make a 'secret profit' from their clients, such as an introduction fee for introducing the client to another adviser.

Integrity is at the core of professional behaviour, particularly for doctors, who will have to exercise their judgement in various difficult circumstances. For instance, is it right for a doctor to divulge a poor prognosis to a terminally ill patient, when the family feel it may not be in their best interests? This is a rare situation, as in the majority of cases it is the right and usually the wishes of the patient to receive all the information about their condition. Acting with integrity (and in the best interests of the patient) should guide the doctor into making the right decision.

## Acting in the client's best interests

We expect professionals to 'act in our best interests'. We instruct a professional to act on our behalf, expecting them to 'fight our corner' and do the best that they can for us. Acting in the best interests of the client is a fundamental behaviour that is expected of all professionals. As a consequence, professionals may have to make difficult choices, and certainly their own interests must not conflict with the best interests of their clients. They may also have to make decisions where the best interests of their client conflict with their professional duties. A solicitor is under a duty to 'uphold the rule of law and the proper administration of justice' and could not act in a way that would benefit their client yet deceive the court.

Doctors swear 'The Hippocratic Oath', which includes the following words: 'And I will use treatments for the benefit of the ill in accordance with my ability and my judgment, but from what is to their harm and injustice I will keep them.'

This entreats doctors to act in the best interests of their patients, and when unjust circumstances arise – for instance, a certain life-prolonging drug may not be available on the NHS – they should strive to correct the injustice harming their patients. The next part of the Oath seemingly concerns euthanasia or doctor-assisted suicide, saying: 'And I will not give a drug that is deadly to anyone if asked, nor will I suggest the way to such a counsel.' To many people, this is highly controversial. There have been cases before the English courts, including those on behalf of patients suffering from incurable illnesses seeking immunity from prosecution for the medical practitioners and the patient's family if they were to facilitate the assisted suicide of the patient.

Doctors have to act in the best interests of each of their patients. However, GPs work within a huge organization, the National Health Service (NHS), which has finite financial resources. There may be times when a GP is unable to fulfil the wishes of their patients (eg to make a referral to a consultant) even though it could be in the patient's best interests to do so. An example is with regard to 'low priority' procedures that are no longer funded by the NHS. If a patient requests a referral for a low priority procedure their GP may decline to make the referral, which would not necessarily be in the best interests of that particular patient; but it is in the greater good of managing the finite financial resources of the NHS.

## Independence

Independence is another professional behaviour – a professional is not 'in the pay' of any person, authority or entity. Professionals should not allow their independence to be compromised. Professionals should be free to take instructions from any person or entity. For example, everyone is entitled to representation before the courts, therefore solicitors and barristers are expected to be independent and prepared to take instructions from any person or entity that needs their services.

## Providing a proper standard of service

Providing a proper standard of service is fundamental to professional behaviour. Regulators may set standards of service expected of members of their profession. They may enshrine these standards in a code of conduct applicable to that profession and the regulator may monitor compliance and be responsible for enforcing standards. It will be a matter for each regulator to determine the extent to which they set out detailed service standards.

In 2008 the General Medical Council (GMC) issued a paper entitled 'Good Medical Practice for GPs'. This document is a guide as to the expectations of how a GP should be acting and caring for their patients. This document sets out the standards to be expected of GPs providing an 'excellent service' and the attributes of 'a poor quality service'. If there is a complaint against a GP, this document is used as guidance of what is the proper standard of service to help resolve the complaint.

## Encouraging equality and diversity

Professional behaviour includes encouraging equality of opportunity and respecting diversity. Equality of opportunity should ensure access to professional services for everyone – without fear or favour, prejudice or discrimination. Many professionals will work with charities (eg advice centres, medical charities) and offer their services free of charge to that charity's users / clients as part of their own pro-bono / social responsibility activities.

Respecting diversity is important to enabling access to professional services. All individuals regardless of their gender (male / female / transgender), disability (physical or mental) beliefs (political, religious or other beliefs), sexual orientation or any other distinguishing factor should have access to the services that professionals provide. Behaving professionally includes enabling this to happen.

Doctors have to deal with patients who may be distressed due to their illness (either physical or psychological). Whilst GPs will have a 'zero tolerance' policy to abusive behaviour, they have to remain impartial and professional when dealing with these patients, even if the patient's behaviour means that the doctor's human instinct is to ask them to leave the consulting room because of their behaviour.

Doctors may also have to deal with patients who have been found guilty of serious crimes (eg child abuse). It remains the duty of the doctor to treat these patients professionally at all times, putting the patient's medical needs ahead of any personal feelings that the doctor may have.

# Confidentiality

Confidentiality is a fundamental aspect of the doctor/patient relationship; the same is true of the solicitor/client relationship. If confidentiality is breached, the relationship is broken (possibly beyond repair). A breach of confidentiality can occur in any one of a number of different ways. For example, through a deliberate act by providing information to a third party, or inadvertent disclosure, eg a lost patient record or an incorrectly addressed e-mail.

When is a breach of client confidentiality unprofessional behaviour? One answer is, each and every time it occurs. Alternatively, you might draw a distinction between when a professional is personally involved in the breach of confidentiality and other situations, eg when the breach is attributable to another member of staff.

On each occasion, we must consider the applicable rules of professional conduct; these will set out the responsibilities of the professional for maintaining client confidentiality, and determine whether or not there has been a breach. If the rule imposes 'strict liability' then each and every disclosure will breach the rule, unless such disclosure is specifically authorized by statute, by regulations or by the rules themselves. The rule may only impose responsibility where there is some fault-based act (or failure to act) attributable to the member of the profession. The rule may only impose liability on individual members of the profession and not on their employees / staff. The professional may be held personally to account for the actions of the staff, but not the staff themselves, as they are not members of that profession.

The reality is that a regulator's role is to protect the client; therefore the likely response would be to ensure that all professionals are accountable to their clients for their actions and the actions of those who work for them. This means that a 'strict' approach to breaches of the applicable rules on confidentiality is the one taken by most professions.

The vast majority of professional services businesses will write into the employment contracts of their professional and support staff a confidentiality clause. For example, a GPs' practice will have a practice protocol regarding patient confidentiality, which every member of staff (clinical and non-clinical) will have to abide by. Schools will ensure that all staff sign a confidentiality clause as part of their contract of employment and all staff will be CRB checked before commencing employment.

For GPs a common issue of patient confidentiality is when another person (eg a family member or friend) asks for information about the patient or for the patient's test results. If there is no documented power of attorney then the GP will have to decline the request and not provide the information. The GP may ask for a signed letter from the patient agreeing to a specific individual or individuals being allowed to discuss their case with the GP, following receipt of which they can then discuss the patient's case with those named individuals.

We all need to be mindful that client confidentiality can be breached by simple acts or omissions (eg the incorrectly addressed e-mail, or the document wrongly attached to an e-mail), the consequences of which can be far reaching for all concerned, including the client, the professional and people working with the professional.

# Conflicts of interest

Professionals are expected to be impartial. Trust is necessary to underpin impartiality and it is trust that is at the heart of conflicts of interest. There are three kinds of conflicts of interest: own interest conflict, client conflict and commercial conflict.

## Own interest conflict

Own interest conflict is where the duty of the professional to act in the best interests of any client in relation to a particular matter conflicts with (or there is a significant risk that it may conflict with) the professional's own interests in relation to that matter. In simple terms, the client's best interests conflict with the professional's own interests in relation to the same matter. If faced with this situation, the professional should not act for the client in relation to this matter. If the professional had already started working for the client, before the conflict became apparent, then they should cease working for the client on that matter and follow the procedures required of them by the code of conduct, which applies to their profession. Example: a client wishes to lease a shop; she asks her solicitor to act for her in relation to this transaction. The solicitor, unknown to the client, is a shareholder in the company that owns the shop and will be granting a lease. The solicitor has an own interest conflict – and cannot act in the best interests of their client (ie negotiate the best possible terms for a lease) if they have an interest in the transaction as a shareholder of the property company granting a lease to the client. In this situation they should decline to act for the client.

Another example is where a patient proposes to make a gift of significant value (eg through a will) to their GP or to a member of the GP's family – this situation creates an own interest conflict. If a doctor was aware that a patient had bequeathed them a significant gift, it would be difficult for the doctor to continue to treat that patient. The doctor may feel some obligation or pressure may be put on them to treat the patient differently, possibly visiting them more frequently or prescribing treatments that are requested by the patient. The doctor may also have concerns that if the patient died, another party (eg a relative of the patient) might suggest that the doctor didn't do everything they could have done to treat the patient as the doctor knew that they would benefit when the patient died.

## Client conflict

Client conflict is a conflict between two or more clients. Where a professional owes separate duties to act in the best interests of two or more clients in relation to the same matter, and those duties conflict (or there is a substantial risk that they may conflict), there is a client conflict of interests.

The underlying issue here is that the professional is not able to give independent advice to each client. Because the interests of each client are different, if the professional were to advise both clients this would inevitably create a conflict between the duty to act in each client's best interests.

A classic example of client conflict is where a solicitor acts not only for the purchaser of a residential property (who is borrowing money by way of mortgage from a bank or building society to buy the property – the borrower) but also for the bank or building society from which the money is being borrowed (the lender). This situation is covered by the SRA Code of Conduct 2011. Acting for the lender and the borrower in this situation is permitted provided certain conditions are met; these include that the mortgage is a standard mortgage, and that the solicitor is satisfied that it is reasonable to act for both parties and it is in the client's best interests for the solicitor to act.

Doctors face similar conflicts of interest issues where a GP is treating two people who are in a relationship. If there is a conflict within that relationship and both patients see the same GP there can be issues in assessing the needs of each patient individually, as the GP may be told information by the other patient that could influence their assessment.

## Commercial conflict

These conflicts take many forms, because they relate to the commercial interests of both clients and professionals and are not a matter of professional conduct or ethics.

Professional advisers will often not want to act for a new client against the interests of an established client or of a potential client that the adviser would particularly like to advise. The reason is that this may reflect badly on an existing or burgeoning business relationship – even if there is neither an own interest or client conflict involved. Large commercial clients may not want their professional advisers acting for any of their competitors – eg supermarkets, retailers and airlines.

# Client care

Client care covers a number of aspects of the relationship between the professional adviser and their client. One major aspect is the proper standard of service, another relates to fees (eg providing clear information about the likely overall cost of the work at the outset and updating the client about cost as the work progresses). Further aspects of client care include informing the client about what you will do (eg scoping the work to be done), billing (eg detailing the costs to be charged to the client – including expenses incurred), and complaints handling (eg the firm's complaints procedure and how the client should make a complaint and to whom).

## *The client relationship*

First and most importantly, there are compliance issues imposed by statute; these relate to anti-money laundering, client identification/client due diligence. It is crucial that there is full compliance with these important provisions, which are backed by criminal penalties.

At the start of a professional relationship, terms need to be agreed between the professional services business and the client. These need to be clearly documented by the professional and evidence of the client's acceptance placed on the file/client record. Different professions will regulate the process of 'client engagement' in various ways; common to all will be agreement on key terms including:

- identifying who is the client (a person, a business entity, an organization);
- the work to be carried out for the client (and timescale for completion);
- the cost of the work to be done for the client (a fixed fee, an estimate or some formula for calculating the likely overall cost);
- who is responsible for the work being carried out for the client (the client's principal contact);
- who will do the work for the client (the client service team).

There will be other issues that are addressed in the client engagement letter or terms of business and set out there in detail. For example, these will include who the client should contact if they wish to complain.

It is important that the client engagement process records all of this information and that it does so in a way that is clear and understandable to the client. Some professions draw a distinction between 'sophisticated clients' (eg commercial organizations, businesses or individuals with previous experience of using the services of the profession) and 'vulnerable clients' who need further protection and issues explained in different ways (eg those clients who have little or no experience of using the services of the profession, or who have specific vulnerabilities, such as mental capacity, or may be under duress from another person).

## Proper standard of service

The information provided by the professional adviser at the outset of the work to be undertaken for the client – the scope of the work – must clearly set out: 1) what work is to be done; 2) what is not covered and will not be done for the client; 3) any assumptions made when scoping the work. For example, an accountant advising a client on a joint venture involving the client's business will set out clearly in their client engagement documentation the scope of the work to be done; they may specifically exclude advising on the tax structures for the joint venture entity, so as to limit the scope of the work on this matter, even if the client will inevitably need this advice. This may be because the accountant has assumed that the client will be taking separate advice on effective tax structures for the joint venture entity. Equally, the tax advice may have been 'scoped out' so that if the client needs this advice it will be a separate item and will be added at extra cost. Any agreement to limit the scope of the work must be clear and unambiguous if it is to be effective.

## An appropriate level of service

An appropriate level of service is what clients should be entitled to expect from their professional advisers. This can be agreed between the client and the adviser where the client has specific needs (eg a higher level of service) or where the client wishes to pay less for a lower level of service. A professional must never compromise the level of service beneath 'an appropriate level' in order to meet the price that the client wishes to pay for the work to be done. In other words, a professional cannot deliver a poor level of service on the grounds that the client asked for a lower level of service in order to meet their budget. For example, a professional can agree with the client on the type and frequency of communications so as to limit the cost of communication (eg communication will only be by e-mail and not by telephone). However, they would still have to offer a proper level of service – if circumstances dictated that they must call the client, they must do so and not rely on the agreement only to communicate by e-mail to absolve them from responsibility for not doing so.

## Errors, mistakes and claims

It is important to remember that professionals do not always get things right. Mistakes are made and this may cause anything from financial loss to physical harm, distress, inconvenience or other detriment. Professional services businesses take out professional indemnity insurance to cover them against claims brought by clients where the professional adviser may have made a mistake. The cost of professional indemnity insurance has increased markedly in recent years – it is a substantial cost of running a professional services business.

Clients should be informed of how to complain and the procedures that will be followed, if they believe that a mistake has been made or that they have or will suffer loss as a result of the actions or omissions of the professional adviser.

If a professional adviser identifies that a mistake has been made, they should not keep this information from the client – they are duty bound to inform the client. They must also ensure that they comply with the claims notification process set out in their professional indemnity insurance policy, otherwise 'cover' may be lost. They need to inform their professional indemnity insurer of the client's potential claim and then, in accordance with their duty to the client, inform the client of the circumstances that may give rise to a claim on their part.

## The cost of the work

Inadequate, inaccurate or poor-quality information about the cost of the work is a major source of complaints from clients; it is one of the biggest themes for complaints to the Legal Ombudsman. This covers not only an initial estimate of costs but also the failure to update clients about cost as the work progresses. The issues at the heart of cost complaints are fairness and clarity: have I been charged a fair amount for the service that I have received? I don't understand the costs information that I have been given – or I haven't been given any/adequate information about the cost, so I am not confident that the cost is fair.

Clients should be provided with the best possible information about the likely overall cost of the work to be done, both at the outset and as the work progresses. If this is not possible, clear reasons should be provided as to why it is not possible at that time, together with an indication of when and in what circumstances it will be possible to provide that information.

## Complaints about the bill

Clients should be informed that they have the right to challenge or complain about the cost of the work. If this is made clear by the professional adviser at the outset (ie the client is informed about the complaints process) then this is likely to reduce the number of clients who complain unjustly after the bill has been submitted. This is another example of the need to be open and transparent about fees with clients.

In order to minimize complaints, the expectations of each client need to be managed with regard to the likely overall cost of the work, both at the time of the engagement process and throughout the life cycle of the project.

## Expenses and disbursements

Professional advisers may charge for items consumed as part of the delivery of the service. Just as vets will charge the client for disposable items used in veterinary procedure(s), for drugs and for other consumable items, so similarly solicitors will charge 'disbursements' such as court fees, land registry fee etc. It is important that clients understand from the outset what will be charged as additional expenses and what is included in the fixed fee for the work in the fee estimate. GPs' surgeries will have a list of services that are charged for (eg verifying the identity of the applicant for a passport) and the fee will be collected before the specific service is provided.

It is not unknown for professionals to seek to charge a client for items that the client had assumed were included in the fees for the work. Examples include photocopying, telephone calls, courier fees and postage. These expenses can mount up, and it is understandable that professional advisers seek to pass on these expenses to their clients. However, they can do so only where they have made this clear in the terms of business or letter of engagement with their client. Clients feel that some of these expenses are simply the cost of providing the service (eg photocopying), and object to being asked to pay twice, first through the fees for the work, second by way of an invoice for expenses/disbursements.

Clients are entitled to a clear explanation of how the professional adviser has calculated the fees for the work. Equally, the professional adviser should be entitled to ask the client to pay an amount 'on account' at the outset, ie before they commence work for the client. Advisers are also keen to know how the client will pay, and will agree terms if necessary for monthly or quarterly billing and settlement of invoices on presentation or within 30 days.

Where the work done for the client exceeds the original scoped work, the professional adviser should have updated the client about the need for further work and the additional cost of that work. Where they have failed to do so, the client may challenge the additional cost, claiming they believed that all of the work was within the original specification. It is therefore very important to have clarity in terms of both the scope and the cost of work at the outset, and throughout the life cycle of the project.

All bills presented by the professional adviser should be clear, accurate and the information accessible to the client. Transparency is crucial so that the client knows what they are being charged, what it covers and how the total amount of the bill has been calculated.

## Complaints handling

What is a complaint? It can be defined broadly as an oral or written expression of dissatisfaction, which alleges that the person making the complaint has suffered (or may suffer) financial loss, distress, inconvenience or other detriment. If complaints have such a broad definition, it will be inevitable that some clients will 'complain' about the services provided, therefore all professional services businesses should have an effective, transparent and objective complaints handling procedure.

When a complaint is received, the professional services business should follow their complaints procedure and seek to resolve the complaint in an honest, open and fair manner. The complaints procedure should be in writing and sent to each client at the time when the client engagement process is undertaken, ie at the start of the client/adviser relationship. Any complaints procedure should ensure that complaints are dealt with promptly and fairly, with decisions based on a sufficient investigation about the circumstances that have led to the complaint being made.

Ultimately if a complaint cannot be resolved between the professional services business and the client, then processes are in place within professional bodies for the resolution of complaints and there are also quasi-judicial ways of resolving these issues, eg the Legal Ombudsman (**www.legalombudsman.org.uk**) whose job it is to resolve legal complaints in a fair, open, effective, shrewd and independent way.

# Risk management

Risk management describes the process conducted by management to understand and deal with uncertainties that could affect the business's ability to achieve its objectives. Professional services businesses should monitor and manage the probability and/or impact of adverse events happening.

## Roles and responsibilities

In line with this approach, all professional services businesses should clearly define roles and responsibilities so that every individual within the business knows and understands their role(s) and responsibilities, the extent of their authority and the circumstances under which consultation with others is required.

## Supervision and monitoring

There should also be a system of supervision and monitoring that provides oversight and periodic reviews of the work carried out by all professional advisers and members of staff working within the business. There should be written policies and procedures, with clear expectations regarding sign off and supervision of client work, backed up by a comprehensive and effective learning and development programme to ensure that all advisers and employees have the skills necessary to fulfil their role(s) and responsibilities.

## Recording and reporting

There should be mechanisms for recording and reporting mistakes, errors and circumstances that could give rise to complaints or claims against the business. This process should be open and transparent in order to encourage rapid 'no fault' reporting of such circumstances. There should be clear and effective enforcement procedures to ensure compliance with the business's risk management procedures and policies.

## Individual responsibility

Each and every employee of the business is individually responsible for ensuring compliance with the regulations and rules of conduct applicable to them as individuals, the business as an entity, and the profession as a whole. They are also responsible for ensuring compliance with the business's risk management processes and procedures.

Management of risk is an everyday occurrence – you do not set out to 'manage risk', you do it as a component part of your everyday work – at all times and in a variety of circumstances. A clear example is the taking of effective 'attendance note' when dealing with clients. This may be a written file note, an electronic note placed on the client's records or an 'e-mail to self' filed electronically on the client's file. For GPs it is vitally important for the doctor to keep full and clear notes of consultations, be they over the telephone or face to face. A significant proportion of the complaints against doctors relate to the keeping of patient records – the outcome of the complaint can be determined by the quality of the notes taken.

The important point with any note is that it is clear and accurate. It should be a contemporaneous record of what was said/agreed/decided etc. It also needs to be readily accessible to anyone dealing with the matter – ie it should be filed appropriately, where it can be found when needed. By making such a note you are protecting yourself and the business for which you work. You are also ensuring that there is an accurate record – which is of benefit to you, your employer and the client.

There have been cases brought by clients against former advisers where the client alleges that something was said/agreed or acted upon, which they now state they did not say/agree to, or authorize to be done. In the case of Tamlura N.V. v. CMS Cameron McKenna, it was the handwritten note drafted by a trainee, of a discussion late at night at a completion meeting, between the client and the solicitor acting for the client regarding the client's agreement to a certain financial formula to value shares the client was selling. That handwritten note enabled CMS Cameron McKenna to successfully defend a claim of professional negligence brought against the firm by its former client, who disputed that they had ever agreed to the financial formula being applied to value shares they were selling. The handwritten note was the best evidence of what had been agreed as the valuation formula for the shares. The fact that at the time the note was made it was just a simple record of the discussion, illustrates neatly the importance of good risk management processes and how these may be used in ways that are not anticipated.

## Conclusion

There is much more that can be said about behaving professionally. This is best done in relation to the profession of which you are a member and the regulatory regime that applies to it.

There are four things that GPs should take into consideration when dealing with patients: beneficence, non-maleficence, justice and autonomy. We are sure that whilst doctors do not actively think of these principles during each patient consultation, they do guide doctors in all that they do.

Suffice it to say, that in this chapter we have sought to set out the fundamental importance of behaving professionally – to enable you to understand that this is at the very core of all that we do.

# Where do you go from here?

**13**

When we set out to write this book our purpose was to challenge you to think about the professional skills that you already have, the level of skills that you need to be the best that you can be in your chosen profession and the 'gap' that you will need to bridge to attain that skills level (see Figure 13.1).

**FIGURE 13.1**   The skills gap

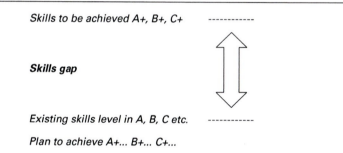

Skills to be achieved A+, B+, C+    - - - - - - - - - - -

Skills gap

Existing skills level in A, B, C etc.    - - - - - - - - - - -

Plan to achieve A+... B+... C+...

Three things are crucial: first that you audit and acknowledge your current level of skills; second, that you understand why there is a gap between your current level and the skills level you aspire to; third, that you design and implement a strategy to ensure that you continuously enhance your skills so that you reach the level you aspire to. The methodologies that you decide to use in order to achieve this result are up to you.

You understand that you have a unique combination of a number of professional skills – a 'cocktail of skills'. No two professionals are the same, we all bring something quite unique to the organizations we work for and manage. Your 'cocktail' should always be regarded as 'work in progress' and should be added to, supplemented and enhanced so that it is being constantly refined and nurtured.

It is the essence of your uniqueness that you need to understand and build on. If you are able to capitalize on your strengths, this will be a very effective way for you to stand out in your professional career and be the professional that you aspire to be. We all want to be recognized for the right reasons by our fellow professionals, clients and colleagues. Being recognized as behaving professionally and to be trusted by the people with whom you come into contact is very important for success.

Your objective should be to have complete confidence in the professional decisions and actions that you take – whether these are in relation to advising clients, managing people or leading a professional services business. The reason for your confidence should be that you have developed and fine-tuned your professional skills to ensure you rightly build your confidence through putting those skills fully and effectively into practice.

So, where do you go from here?

Our suggested first step is for you to ensure that you understand the 'benchmarks' for outstanding performance in your profession. These will differ according to the stage that you have reached and the journey that you intend to take from here.

Having benchmarked what 'outstanding performance' looks like, begin to assess your current skills levels against that benchmark. Examine the 'skills gap' and think about the practicalities of your bridging the gap and moving towards the benchmark.

Do not be too hard on yourself: be realistic, you cannot achieve 'Olympic Gold' in every professional skill. Start by reviewing the skills that you excel in, then set goals for maintaining and strengthening those skills. Then review your weaker skills areas. Why are you not attaining the level of skill that you aspire to in these skills? Consider what practical steps you can take to enhance these skills. Be sure to focus your activities on making improvements in one or two key areas – this will enable you to build your confidence so that you will achieve success. In other words, our prime focus should always be on developing our strengths whilst always being aware of where we are not so good. That helps set the right mindset.

You will need a plan. Set yourself SMART objectives regarding the professional skills that you wish to enhance. Do not set the bar too high – be realistic, but challenging. Do not set the bar too low – if you set the bar at a level you know you will be able to attain, there is little if any 'stretch' to achieve your objectives and little if anything is gained from the process.

You will need to stick to your plan. Maintaining momentum and motivation is not always easy. Make sure that you have both short- and medium-term objectives. Ensure that yours is a 'rolling plan' (eg for the next six months), which you review: tick off the successes that you have achieved, revise the goals that remain and add new goals for the next six months.

There is nothing wrong in ambition – set 'stretching' but realistic long-term career goals. Your 'rolling' plan must also enable you to achieve your longer-term career goals. Do not overlook these – your shorter- or medium-term objectives should be orientated to supporting the achievement of your longer-term goals.

Each of the skills that we have discussed in this book are important skills. We would not have discussed them otherwise. But looked at all together they do seem daunting. That is why we have re-emphasized the need for setting goals. Equally important is the need to regularly reflect on how you are doing, measured against those goals. The development of your ability to reflect, as discussed in Chapter 3, is a very important process and a skill in itself. Part of that process is also making the most effective use that you can of the constructive feedback that you receive from those you work for, clients and colleagues. We can all learn from our mistakes, but as importantly we can also learn from the things that we do well. If you are not getting the feedback that you need to develop your skills, take time to think about a strategy for obtaining the feedback that will enable you to thrive. To achieve this you will need the support of your team leader/manager.

Make effective use of the performance review process within your organization. It should not be a 'tick box' exercise; it should contribute to your 'rolling plan' by enabling you to objectively evaluate your current performance and identify areas for you to work on in order to develop your professional skills.

Two skills areas where it will be more difficult to get feedback, and which many professionals overlook, are commercial awareness and financial skills. The recession that commenced in 2007 – and the period of austerity that has followed it with limited growth (if any) – has provided a very challenging time for professionals.

Developing commercial awareness is not achieved overnight. It is an osmotic process – it slowly sinks in. You need to work at it and view what you do in your day-to-day work as a business activity (with all the issues that inevitably accompany that). Clients expect a level of understanding so that the professional advice that you give them is firmly anchored into the economic and financial realities for the client at that time.

Understanding the levers of profitability and the financial metrics of the professional services business in which you work is essential if you are ultimately to reach your goals within that organization, or if you are to succeed as a leader – either within the business in which you currently work or if you set up a business of your own. Soaking up these skills at an early stage in your career is really important, even if those skills are not part of your current job role.

And finally...

By using your professional skills – developing and enhancing them in a planned and goal-orientated way throughout your career – you should be able to achieve real success and become the professional that you aspire to be.

# REFERENCES

**1** Drucker, P (1954) *The Practice of Management*, Harper & Brothers, New York

**2** Koletar, J (2011) *Rethinking Risk*, AMACOM, USA

**3** Maister, D (1996) *True Professionalism*, Simon & Schuster, New York

**4** Larkin, P (2001) *Collected Poems*, Farrar Straus and Giroux, USA

**5** Mehrabian, A (1981) *Silent Messages: Implicit communication of emotions and attitudes* (2nd ed). Wadsworth, Belmont, California

**6** Senge, P (1990) *The Fifth Discipline: The art and practice of the learning organization*, Doubleday, New York

**7** Covey, S (1989) *The 7 Habits of Highly Effective People*, Free Press, USA

**8** Goleman, D (1995) *Emotional Intelligence: Why it can matter more than IQ*, Bantam Books, New York

**9** *Financial Times* (2011) A New Dawn: Lessons for law firm management, [Online] www.ft.com

**10** Schön, D (1984) *The Reflective Practitioner: How professionals think in action*, Basic Books, USA

**11** Tullier, L M (1998) *Networking for Everyone! Connecting with people for career and job success*, JIST Works Inc, USA

**12** Fisher, R and Ury, W (1991) *Getting to Yes: Negotiating agreement without giving in*, Penguin Group, London

**13** Ury, W (1993) *Getting Past No: Negotiating in difficult situations*, Random House, New York

**14** Katzenbach, J and Smith, D (1993) *The Wisdom of Teams: Creating the high performance organization*, Harvard Business School Press, USA

**15** Belbin, RM (2010) *Management Teams: Why they succeed or fail (3rd edition)*, Butterworth Heinemann, London

# INDEX

(*italics* indicate a figure or table in the text)

accounting concepts   *219*
accounting standards   220
audit   220–21

bank loans   14
behaviour   3, 4, 237–51
   'acting in client's best interests'
      240–41
   client care   245–49
   confidentiality   242–43
   conflicts of interest   243–45
   diversity   241–42
   equality   241
   ethics   237
   honesty   239
   independence   241
   integrity   240
   risk management   249–51
   trust   239
Belbin, Dr Meredith   179
   model of team roles   *180–81*
   *see also* team working
'best alternative to a negotiated agreement'
      (BATNA)   145, 152–53, 156
body language   31–38, 45, 101, 115
budget   210–11
business plan   5, 210
business structures   7–8
business writing   73–90
   accuracy   86–87
   choice of words   79–80
   common mistakes   77
   example   77–80
   grammar   87–88
   paragraphs   85
   punctuation   88–89
   purpose   75–80
   sentences   84–85
   spelling   86
   strategy   75
   structure   81–83
   tone   79–80
   what to avoid   73–75
   words   83

cash flow statement   211, 216, *217*, *218*
charities   206

client care   245–49
   claims   247
   complaints   247–48, 249
   cost of work   247
   expenses/disbursements   248
   level of service   246
   mistakes   247
   standard of service   246
   *see also* client relationships
client confidentiality   4
client relationships   2, 27, 127, 245–46
   *see also* networking
communication   2, 13, 29–48
   clients and   45–47
   decoding   35
   definition   30–31
   e-mails   67–68
   encoding   34–35
   feedback   35, 187, 195–99
   iceberg model   47
   intuition   31
   jargon   47
   listening skills   36–39
   mirroring   45
   mobile phone   68
   model   33, *34*, 35–36
   non-verbal   31–33
   paralanguage   31
   questions   40–42
   rapport   44–45
   verbal   31
   written   47
companies   206–07
Companies Act 2006   220
competitive advantage   8–9, 46
   cost   8–9
   differentiation   9
   focus   9
complaints   247–48
   handling   249
confidentiality   242–43
conflicts of interest   243–45
   client conflict   244
   commercial conflict   244–45
   own interest conflict   243–44
conscious competence model *see* four states
      of mind model

Covey, Stephen   39
culture of business   7, 8, 11, 30

delegation   69–72
   definition   69
   four stages   70, 71
   lateral/upward   71
difficult people   118, 119–21, 122, 140–41
Drucker, Peter F   6, 72

e-mails   67–68
emotional intelligence (EQ)   32, 42–44
   four dimensions   43
   relationship management   43
   self-awareness   43
   self-management   43
   social awareness   43
empathy   39, 45, 148, 184–85

feedback   35, 187, 195–97
   EEC model   198, 199
   example   196–97, 198–99
   giving   197–99
   performance reviews   201
   positive   199
financial/commercial awareness   205–36,
      255
   assessing financial health of a business
      221–29
   case study   230–36
   directors' role and responsibilities   207,
      208
   trading entities   205–07
   see also financial information, financial
      ratios
financial control   16–21
   charge rates   16
   costs   20
   credit control   19
   fees   18–19
   gearing   17
   information   20–21
financial information   208–36, 255
   accounting statements   212
   Annual Report and Accounts   211
   balance sheet   211, 212, 214, 215, 216
   capital employed   216
   cash   212
   cash flow statement   211, 216, 217,
      218
   equity   215
   financial statements   211–18
   income statement   211, 213, 214
   main users   210
   management accounts   210–11

profit   212, 255
   statutory accounts   218–21
   working capital   216
   see also financial ratios
financial management   13–16
   billing   13, 16, 18–19
   borrowing   226
   case study   21–26
   cash flow   15, 28
   fees   13, 16, 18–19
   funding   14–16
   investment   14
   operating cycle   15, 28, 228
   realization   13, 19, 28
   utilization   13, 19, 28
   work in progress (WIP)   13, 15, 18
   working capital   14, 216
   see also financial ratios
financial ratios   221–29
   acid test   228
   average inventory turnover   229
   average payables   229
   average receivables   229
   current   227
   debt/equity ratio   225–26
   efficiency measures   228
   gearing   225
   gross profit margin   223
   interest cover   226–27
   liquidity   227–28
   operating profit margin   223–24
   profitability   222
   return on capital employed (ROCE)
      224–25
   uses   221
Fisher, Roger   149, 152
four states of mind model   56
franchise   7

gearing   17, 225
General Medical Council (GMC)   241
generally accepted accounting practices
      (GAAP)   218–20
   accruals   219
   consistency   219
   current cost   220
   going concern   218
   materiality   218
   net realizable value   220
   present value   220
   prudence concept   219
   valuation of assets   219
Goleman, Daniel   42
groups   175–77
   stages of development   175–76

habits 55–57
Herzberg, Frederick 170
Holmes, Oliver Wendell 39
hygiene factors 170–72
    see also motivation

interruptions 65–66

Koletar, Joseph W 12

Larkin, Philip 30
Law Society of England and Wales 238
leadership 2
Legal Ombudsman 247, 249
Legal Services Act 2007 238
'learning by doing' 3
learning cycle 52
leverage see gearing
limited liability partnership (LLP) 7, 206
listening skills 36–39
    active 37, 38, 161
    empathic 37, 162
    generative 35
    guide 38–39
    layers 37
    negotiations 161–62

Maister, David 29
management
    accounts 211
    client-centred 6–7
    key roles 6
    structure 8
    see also performance management
marketing 27
medical profession 240–41, 242
    complaints 250
    conflict of interest 244
    guiding principles 251
    patient confidentiality 243
meetings 2, 107–26
    assertive behaviour 121–22
    case study 110, 112, 114, 116–17, 122, 123
    chairing 113
    checklist 111
    difficult people 118, 119–21, 122
    dos and don'ts 115
    dynamics 113–14
    efficiency 111–12
    follow-up 122–23
    messages 115–16
    notes 117–18
    participants 109
    participating effectively 114–18

preparation 110–12
process 112–13
purpose 108
telephone 123–25
types 108–09, 123–25
video 123–25, 166
Mehrabian, Professor Albert 32
motivation 169–72, 186
    'hygiene' factors 171–72
    professional services 172
    Theory X and Y 170

National Health Service (NHS) 240–41
negotiation skills 2, 145–68
    'best alternative to a negotiated agreement' (BATNA) 145, 152–53, 156
    breakthrough strategy 153
    checklist 160, 166
    competitive 146–47, 150
    completing 166
    cooperative 147–48
    counter-intuitive 153
    expand options 154, 155
    five stage approach 153–54
    flexibility 160–61
    listening skills 161–62
    mutual interests 150, 151
    note taking 163
    objective criteria 151–52
    planning notes 157–59
    positional approach 148
    preparation 156–60
    principled negotiation 149–60
    problem-solving approach 149
    questions 162
    revealing information 163
    'separate the people from the problem' 149–50
    styles 145–49
    tactics 163–66
    telephone 166–68
    toolkit 160–63
    'zone of potential agreement' (ZOPA) 145, 149
network 128–29
    diagram 130
networking 2, 127–44
    bad experiences 138–39
    benefits 128
    business development tool 143
    checklist 131–32, 137
    contact management system 141–42
    definition 128

difficult people/situations  140–41
generating conversation  136
goal setting  132–33
personal pitch  135–36
places to meet  133–34
plan  133
record-of-contact log  142–43
self-introduction  135
shyness  138–39
social media  127
strategy  132–33, 143
structured events  134
time management  143
unstructured events  134
not-for-profit organizations  206

overdrafts  14

Parkinson's Law  64–65
partnership  7, 206
performance management  2, 187–203
benchmarking  188–90, 254
example  189–90, 191–92, 194–95
feedback  195–99, 201
information  188–90
maintaining momentum  194
objective setting  191–92, 254
prioritization  193
self-review  193
SMART objectives  191, 194, 254
performance reviews  199–203, 255
example  202
personal organization  49–72
'body clock'  64
daily diary  62
deadlines  64–65
delegation  69–72
efficient working  63–64, 66
e-mails  67–68
energy  64
food/drink  64
forward planning  52–53, 54, 55
goal setting  52–53
habits  55–57
managing interruptions  65
prioritization  57–59
reflective practice  50–52
relationships  68–72
self-organization  55–68
three circles  50–72, 51
time management  49
'to do' list  61
tools  62–68
planning  53–55
short-term  60–62

presentation skills  91–106
checklist  94, 97, 101
content  95–96, 105
controlling nerves  101
delivery  101–02
example  98
first impressions  102
homework  92–94, 105
interaction with audience  96
key message  95–96
preparation  98–101
questions  100–01, 103–04
rehearsal  100
structure  97–98
unexpected events  102–03
vocal technique  102
prioritization  57–59
grid  58
performance management  193
procrastination  62–63
professional behaviour see behaviour
professional indemnity  13, 20, 247
profitability see financial ratios

questioning  40–42
closed  40–41
funnelling  41, 42
negotiations  162
open  40
probing  41

realization  6, 13, 19
reflective practice  50–52
relationships see networking
return on capital employed (ROCE)
224–25
risk  12–13
operational  12
regulatory  12
strategic  12
risk management  249–51
Robbins, Tony  30
roles  172–74, 182
perceptions of  182–84
problems  173–74
see also team working
Royal Institution of Chartered Surveyors
(RICS)  238
Rules of Conduct  238

Schön, Donald  50
Senge, Peter  36
skills  253
acquiring  3
gap  253

oral 2
  presentation 2
  written 2
SMART objectives 191
  *see also* performance management
social enterprises 206
sole principal/trader 7, 206
Solicitors Regulation Authority 238
spider diagram 97, 105
strategic planning 8–13
  alignment 10–11
  cycle *11*, 12
  implementation 11–12
  PESTL 10
  risk management 12–13

Tamlura N.V. v CMS Cameron McKenna
    250–51
Teachers' Standards 2011 238–39
team working 2, 169–86
  characteristics 178–79, 184–85
  composition 178
  effectiveness 184–85
  financial performance 185

group development stages *175–76*,
    177, 182
  leader 183, 185–86
  life cycle 181–85
  motivation 169–72
  personal factors 173, 185
  relationships 173
  roles 172–74, 179–81, 182–83
  selflessness 185
  situational factors 17
telephone negotiations 166–68
tendering 27
time management 49–72, 143
trading entities 205–07
Tullier, L Michelle 128

Ury, William 149, 152, 153
utilization 6, 13, 19

work-life balance 3
writing *see* business writing

'zone of potential agreement' (ZOPA) 145,
    149